When Every Road Whispers My Name

When Every Road Whispers My Name

A Wanderer's Tale

MARIA VANO

Copyright © 2021 by Maria Vano

All rights reserved. No part of this publication may be reproduced, distributed, or transmitted in any form or by any means, including photocopying, recording, or other electronic or mechanical methods, without the prior written permission of the publisher, except in the case of brief quotations embodied in critical reviews and certain other non-commercial uses permitted by copyright law. For permission requests, write to the author, addressed "Attention: Permissions" at everyroadwhispers@gmail.com.

Ordering Information:
For details, contact everyroadwhispers@gmail.com.

Print ISBN: 978-1-0879-6040-1
ebook ISBN: 978-1-0879-6041-8

Editor: Ross Dickinson
Cover design: Gina Marie Balog-Sartorio, GMB Creative Designs
Cover and back cover photos: Copyright © 2021 Aziz El Mehdi, Cité Portugaise

The compass or wind rose (seen on pages 1, 71, 183) is a replica of a wind rose from the chart of Jorge de Aguiar, 1492 (I, Alvesgaspar, CC BY-SA 3.0 <http://creativecommons.org/licenses/by-sa/3.0/>, via Wikimedia Commons)

Printed in the United States of America

Contents

Preface		xi
Part One		1
Chapter 1:	The Summer of Discovery—1971	3
Chapter 2	Life's 25-year Interlude aka Life in the US—1977–2000	12
Chapter 3	Ten Days That Forever Changed My Life	18
Chapter 4	Am I Going to Become an Expat?	60
Chapter 5	Making a Decision	63
Part Two		71
Chapter 6	The Dream Happens	73
Chapter 7	A Comedy of Errors: the Non-Shakespearean Version	77
Chapter 8	Back to the Hills and Life in a Small Umbrian Village	90
Chapter 9	And the Plans They Keep on a'Changin'!	105
Chapter 10	Greetings from Florence!	107
Chapter 11	Never Say "I'll Do Anything" to a Sicilian	111
Chapter 12	Little Snippets as Life Begins in a New Home	119
Chapter 13	Citizenship Happens and My World Opens	179

PART THREE		**183**
Chapter 14	Preamble to a New Life—The Final Goodbye: Tears, Fears, Love, and Most of All, Hope	185
Chapter 15	Stories From a Truly New Life—In All Ways	189
Chapter 16	Buddy Hugs, Kitty Kisses, and Fear	220
Chapter 17	My World Falls Apart As Death Pounds on My Door: A Not-So-Whirlwind Tour of Italy	228
Chapter 18	Answers Come and a New Passion is Born	238
Chapter 19	Can You Say Jamón? How About Flamenco, Baby!	246
Chapter 20	I Thought It Might Be Glue, But Velcro Reigns Again	253
Chapter 21	Is It Possible I've Learned to be Still?	268
Chapter 22	Of Pandemics, Lockdowns, and Animal Rescue	272
EPILOGUE		**279**

Dedication

This book is dedicated to all those
who believed they could fly.

To those who didn't—I hope you now soar free.

Acknowledgements

Every word on these pages is for ... Mom, without whom I'd never have had dreams. I wish you were here to hold this in your hands, and see what became of your efforts to instill in me your own passion for travel. Thank you for making me strong, for giving me wings, and making me believe I can do anything. I love and miss you more than any words could ever possibly convey.

Kim, the bestest bud ever, my tesoro—words are never necessary.

Messrs. Brophy and Fox, thank you for telling me to never stop writing.

Everyone from Slow Trav, thank you for starting this and insisting I tell my story.

Ross Dickinson, super-editor, thank you for your patience. The encouragement in your comments made this possible. You're amazing.

Thanks galore to Gina, graphic designer extraordinaire; my beta readers, Anna and Sarah; Maggie McLaughlin, the world's greatest book designer; and Martha Bullen, publishing consultant— without all of you, this book would never have come to light!

Everyone in my life who stood by me and believed in me. I thank you with everything in me.

And above all, to everyone who didn't.

Preface

Years ago, I had a dream. I wanted to return to the land of my glorious youthful days—Rome, Italy. Time had not tainted my memories although, as we know all too well, it does indeed march on and things must change.

When I lived in Rome during my formative teen years from age 12, I essentially became Italian, and began to think like a European. I spent my teens roaming (sorry!) among thousand-year-old ruins, the Colosseo and Forum were my playgrounds. Our school was international and at any one given time I was surrounded by at least 30 different nationalities.

When I went back to the States at 19, to say I was in culture shock is an understatement! I found it increasingly hard to adjust to life back in the States. My teachers in business school said don't use your hands to talk, stop speaking Italian; employers would suggest giving up my Italian citizenship. I just wasn't used to all that.

Anyway, over the years I moved around every few years, seeing new things, always seemingly trying to find what was missing, always trying to find a place I fit. Got married, got divorced, etc. Life happened; time went by.

Then, after a high school reunion 25 years later, I made up my mind that I would do whatever was necessary to return to Italy.

In August 2002 I sold pretty much everything I owned, packed three suitcases, gave two boxes of miscellaneous stuff to a friend who travels to Italy each year, bought a one-way plane ticket, and left the States on September 1st. I felt like it was where I needed to be, and where I belonged. I hadn't felt that "belonging" since I was 19. I was suddenly surrounded by the attitudes, thoughts and ways of living that I was used to.

What follows is a story that truly began when, at age 43, I decided to leave everyone and everything I knew, and with only a mere few thousand dollars to my name, a short-term rental lined up, and no job in sight, buy a one-way ticket back to the land of my memories.

The tale continues on to the life of travel and discovery that naturally followed such a huge decision. The roads that whispered my name with each lesson learned.

Come, join me in my journey and walk beside me through the laughter, the tears, the joys and sorrows, the love and loss . . .

I wouldn't change a minute of it. It is my honor to share this with you.

Part One

CHAPTER 1

THE SUMMER OF DISCOVERY—1971

In the early part of 1971, when I was twelve years old and living in Atlanta, Georgia, my three older brothers and I were called to the table for a "family meeting". The announcement that followed filled me with incredulity; in just a couple months we would be moving to Rome, Italy.

We would travel to London and Paris first, then Sicily to visit my paternal ancestors' home, and finally to Rome where we would find an apartment and live. While it was exciting to be going to Europe to see the sights, the realization that we would be living there for an undetermined amount of time was incredibly scary for a little girl who was just about to become a teenager.

A foreign country.

With a language I didn't speak or understand.

My parents were business people; Dad was a mortgage consultant and Mom, before marrying and becoming a housewife/stay-at-home mom, had studied "secretarial skills," worked a bit in this area, and helped my Dad in office management. Dad had a dream of going back to his family roots and had some foreign business ideas—with his knowledge of Italian (actually the Sicilian dialect), he and mom decided to try it for a year in Italy. As we were neither military nor embassy-affiliated, we would have no access to commissaries or the like, and would live as Italians.

I had moved many times before and saying goodbye to friends was becoming old hat; if you were to ask me why my family moved so often, I would have no answer because I was just a kid, and wasn't exactly involved in the decisions. Interestingly, it never occurred to me to ask as I grew up; it was just a natural part of my life. But this time was different: my head was filled with thoughts of going to an Italian school where nobody spoke English, in a land where everything was so "old," and having heard stories of the schools being year-round; this coupled with hormones raging. I wouldn't even get to attend the sock-hop dance on the last day of my seventh grade as it began at 5:00 p.m. and our plane would be leaving from Hartsfield at 7:00 p.m. for New York, where we would stay for a night with friends of my parents and get on a late morning flight bound for London.

In the span of a few weeks, I watched as our entire household was packed up; I said goodbye to my friends, who wrote their best wishes in a small book filled with references to a then-popular television show called *To Rome With Love*. But that was a fictional show, and this—this was reality.

Four months shy of my 13th birthday, I was left to wonder what was going to happen to my life.

◈ ◈ ◈

Such a wondrous time that one summer would turn out to be. What began as dread and fear would prove to be the beginning of a life filled with journeys, an intense desire to see everything, and find someplace new as often as possible.

London—getting lost in the hedge maze, staring in amazement in the wax museum, the pomp and circumstance of Buckingham Palace and the changing of the guards. A weekend was spent with friends of my parents at their house by the sea; me posing in front of their fire-engine-red Rolls Royce, pretending it was mine; attending a festival and having my first European crush (if only I could remember his name!).

Crossing the English Channel sparked the beginning of a love of travel on water.

Paris—what an incredibly beautiful city when viewed at night from so high up the Eiffel Tower, the lights sparkling like a sea of diamonds. Everywhere you looked, magic was in the air, reflected in the glow of lovers' eyes strolling along the Champs-Élysées. One day I would return and feel this magic again but through eyes of an appreciative adult; perhaps my own eyes would have a reflecting glow.

Florence and Venice—my mind was becoming a sponge, drinking in everything, thirsting for more around every corner; I felt electrified. I wanted to see it all, and was fortunate to have a mother with my same desires, as she was more than happy to wander these cities with her only daughter, beginning to introduce me to the wonders of this world. Standing outside our hotel, gazing out at Ponte Vecchio while trying to come up with the answers to my eldest brother's seemingly endless, seemingly impossible riddles.

Sicily—the land of my paternal ancestors. After a day and night spent meeting my father's uncles, aunts, and their children in Messina, the next morning we left for a visit to the "old town" where both my father's parents were from. Out of the city we drove—bundled into a car with people who didn't speak English—along the north coast, turning onto a smaller road that led up into the mountains. After many twists and turns up the steep mountain road, frightening but with heart-pounding, breathtaking views of the Sicilian mountain landscape with Mount Etna's smoking peak towering over it all, the town came into view. Galati Mamertino sprawled majestically upon the top of a mountain, its arms opened wide to welcome in the American cousins.

It seemed half the small town was outside their doors, waiting to greet us with cries of "My name is such-and-such and I am your [insert number] cousin, [insert some other number] removed, let me show you your home!" I had never had so many people all in one place claiming ancestry so far down the line. The house where three of my aunts lived was large and made of stone, built to withstand the years and nature. We were shown into a large dining area and my eyes opened wide at the sight of the long table filled with traditional Sicilian antipasti, just waiting for us.

I had never seen so much food! My amazement would grow as the afternoon went on; the first course came with two types of pasta, followed by a second course of three types of meat, followed by a vegetable course of various items. Just when we didn't think there could possibly be more, out bustled the aunts from the kitchen carrying palate-cleansing salads. We tried to taste a little of everything, but our American stomachs had never handled a meal such as this. We begged for mercy when out they came again from the kitchen carrying plates of amazing looking traditional Sicilian sweets, and were given a reprieve as it was suggested we indulge in a time-honored tradition: the passeggiata. Nearly groaning with gratitude, my brothers and I hoisted ourselves from our chairs, thinking we couldn't possibly move, let alone walk, and were led by our nearly-equal in age cousins out the door to a warm evening, dusk just settling in. As we began to walk up the small street to the main piazza, they led us first to the bar for a *digestivo* (an after-dinner drink), and then asked if we'd like to see the town cemetery where our ancestors were laid to rest.

As we entered the gates, various headstones were pointed out, all with our two family names on them, many with pictures. All the various years and names and faces became a blur as I took it all in as if in a trance, surrounded by the resting sites and faces of so very many of my ancestors. Night settled in and stars began to shine in a perfectly clear sky. My blood seemed to course more quickly through my body; I felt a warmth flow through me, bringing with it a sense of . . . calm. I felt I was being enveloped in the peaceful and quiet, loving embrace of these long-dead relatives. They seemed to be joining in the town's welcome, whispering "welcome to where it began, welcome to what created you."

Later that night, after we all clambered into our respective beds, couches, and mattresses and fell asleep to the sounds of the village doing the same, I was struck by the silence that ensued. Way up there in the mountains, there were no sounds except those of nature. It was incredible, but almost unnerving at the same time. How could anywhere be this quiet? No sounds to disturb my thoughts of, "How is it possible that we are sleeping in a three-story home built of solid stone, in a small town on a mountain in Sicily?"

The next morning we were woken by the aroma of fresh espresso being brewed, and greeted by a breakfast of prosciutto, mozzarella, croissants, and even chocolate ones. Later, after long goodbyes and cries of "please come back soon," we piled back into the cars and started the drive back to Messina. After a bit of exploring of the city, looking out over the channel, watching the lights of the ships and seeing the welcoming beacon from the harbor statue, I found I was beginning to look forward to going to our new home in Rome the next day. From somewhere in me came a feeling, a realization that it just might all be okay. There would be many new things to learn and see and do, and I no longer felt a great fear of this new country, its language, people, customs still unknown to me. I would have two months to get used to everything before starting school; I was starting to feel like I belonged here, like maybe I was supposed to be here.

❦ ❦ ❦

Life as a teenager in the freedom and wildness of the 1970s, attending an international high school in Rome, is a story all its own and one which, in all honesty, I don't remember everything about. The Overseas School of Rome, grades one through twelve (changed years later to the American Overseas School of Rome), was very small; three small buildings in total. The graduating class sizes ranged through the years from five to thirty (my 1976 class had twenty). Individual course classes never held more than maybe fifteen. Our English classes are perhaps what I remember most of all—they were where I began my love of writing and the language, and created a lifelong love of Greek classics.

The experiences living and immersing myself in Rome and the education I received by doing that and traveling around were priceless and, without a doubt, life-altering. We had school trips both locally, inter-country and even an annual trip to another country from a choice of three or four—the only one my parents were financially able to send me on was when I was 14 years old, and I chose Greece from the list. I made friendships that are still there to this day.

The '60s and '70s were for Rome and Italy itself glorious

years of *la dolce vita*, the sweet life. Though there were, and always have been, serious mafia and governmental problems, not to mention the *Brigate Rosse* (Red Brigades, a far-left, armed, extremist organization causing violence and terrorism), it was still a time of hedonistic, wild, free-for-all life. The type you see in the movies: strolling down Via Veneto, carefree, hanging out at the cafes, life is easy with no cares.

We didn't know guns and knives or teenage gangs. There were groups, certainly, of trouble-making, bullying idiots, but I don't remember gang fights or shootouts (again, unless it involved the mafia or the brigades or some other terror group causing havoc). If there were any, I probably didn't know about it, as my father was massively protective, being of Sicilian origin, and I was always surrounded by three older brothers. Though I didn't have much freedom to go places in the city itself to stay out for hours running around, my teenage years were mostly filled with hanging out at a few friends' homes. If I ever tried doing anything like skipping school (only once, and I still think I can feel the belt and the welts from the punishment!) or staying out until late at night or past midnight, the payment was fierce and swift.

My family lived in a relatively small apartment complex of six three-story apartment buildings in a u-shape, with a rectangular building topping it off, containing a hairdresser and management offices. Entrance was closed off at night with a gate controlled by two men who hung out in their little guard shack. A very small playground next to the shack contained swings, a slide and a small sand pit for toddlers. Under each building was a garage and laundry area with a few washers and lines to hang clothes on. We didn't have dryers, but plastic or metal clothes-drying racks in the laundry area or on the balcony of each apartment. Our apartment was actually two-in-one, with a middle wall removed, and perfect for a family with four kids. It was huge, with five bedrooms, two living rooms turned into one, a "maid's bedroom", our own small laundry room, a nice-sized kitchen, and a balcony that wrapped around three-quarters of it. The view of the hills and land surrounding Rome holding their tiny villages, was incredible, because the land in back and to one side hadn't been built up yet, as in later years. Last but not least was the aroma that would come wafting over from the restaurant/pizzeria next door, with its wood-burning oven.

The complex was on the Via Cassia, about eight or ten blocks from the school; only a five-minute walk away was a small, Italian-style strip mall, having a small grocery store with everything we could ever need, plus one or two small clothing shops, and of course the bar/café. Back then, "the Cassia" was a two-lane road lined with apartment buildings and shops, but easily navigated and only rarely clogged with traffic, as it became in later days.

Probably everyone who lived there during those years would remember the no-drive Sundays. They were awesome. During the 1970s gas shortage years, each Sunday was either odd- or even-day, going by the final number of the license plate, and traffic was obviously much less. Better still were the total no-drive Sundays—there was nothing better than being able to walk down the middle of a street that was normally packed with cars. Now *that's* la dolce vita.

Water conservation Sundays were fun, but pretty silly in its attempt to conserve water. We knew in advance which Sunday it would happen, and Saturday nights were spent with families everywhere filling up as many jugs and bottles and containers as possible with water, including filling up every bathtub and sink. That little conservation tactic didn't last very long, if I remember correctly.

High school was like school anywhere, I think—Rome was no different. Though we lived in an age-old city full of wonder and amazement around every corner, typical high-school bullying existed to the same extent as anywhere. Due to other things happening at home, I was a loner and shy introvert, the perfect target. In later life, as the years went on, I moved long past that and didn't let it rule any part of my life or brain, though still being a bit shy; but also known to dance-walk down the street with headphones on, not caring one bit! Perhaps overcoming and living my best life is the best revenge?

They say, though, that all good things must come to an end, and so my family returned to America for financial and business reasons; by then, I wanted to stay, but there was no way to make it happen. After seven years of immersing myself in Italy I had become Italian, living and breathing Italy, and that land had become my home. I had lost my heart and left it in the gloriousness that was Rome in the '70s when my plane left Fiumicino to return to America.

On the plane that day in 1977 (the day Elvis died), I was 19 years old and my heart was breaking, leaving a place where I felt at peace; I was leaving home, and at that moment when the wheels left the ground, I made a vow to all the spirits of every Sicilian ancestor of mine who had gone before me—one day I would come home.

CHAPTER 2

LIFE'S 25-YEAR INTERLUDE AKA LIFE IN THE US—1977–2000

Over the next twenty-five years I traveled around America, always seemingly looking for somewhere that felt right, somewhere that felt like home, but I could never seem to find it. I would stop into an "Italian restaurant" occasionally, but the food was never quite right. I would feel a longing, sending me searching through boxes looking for pictures of those Italian years. I would look through pages of my high school yearbooks that had a collage of candid shots of the streets of Rome; the vegetable and fruit markets, an old woman dressed in black unknowingly caught by the camera holding a tomato up to her nose to catch the scent of its sweet ripeness, perfect for the simple pasta pomodoro she would whip up for her family that evening. I would close my eyes and remember the sights, the sounds, the smells, and I would smile because for a moment, just a short moment, I would feel at peace again.

The years I spent in the US from 1977 on were spent in what I know now to have been a floundering search for what I had; really it was a search for the only life I really remembered. I had changed, and didn't know how to climb over or break through the walls that were put up by the world. Finances were tough at home and with one brother in law school, one in aeronautical school, and one at Loyola, the only option available to me was a short course at an inexpensive secretarial/business school. As was typical in the US, I had a part-time job during those months, working at a laundromat near our apartment, giving all the money to my mom for rent and bills to help out. My Dad was no longer in the picture, and they ended up divorced shortly thereafter. Nine months after landing back in the US, I was a certified legal secretary with superb skills and speed (I won second place in a city-wide typing speed contest, losing by only two words per minute, my claim to fame), and employed by a high-caliber law firm in Chicago.

I was such a fish out of water. Co-workers my age would talk about "cruising the main street" in cars during high school, and I still didn't even have a driver's license—the legal age for driving cars in Italy back then was 19. They said I sounded like an "uppity" snob because when they asked what I'd done in high school, I would reply that I climbed around thousands-of-years-old ruins like the Forum and Colosseum, hopped on a train and boat and went to the Parthenon in Greece, walked around on cobblestone streets, kicked a bottlecap around in a faux football game in front of the Vatican because a friend and I were bored. I didn't want to sound "uppity" and I truly had no desire to sound like a braggart, but drawing the line is pretty difficult at 19 when your life has been turned upside down, and when someone your age asks what you did last Christmas, responding that you took a quick trip to a Christmas market in Germany or France just doesn't sound normal.

It seemed that every three years I would get the itch to see something new. I would get antsy, picking apart wherever I lived and finding a hundred things wrong with it that were making me unhappy. My middle brother, Arthur, would call me, saying "You would love it here! Come on!" and I would, moving to Texas and then to California for a year each. It was fun seeing new places—until the day my three-year-old niece, Lara, said to me on the phone, crying, "I miss you, Aunt Maria." And I went back to Chicago where she was.

Shortly after going back, one day on the L-train the doors were closing at the station and a man came running, squeezing into the car. When he smiled at me, I had no idea just how much my life was about to change. A few months later I married him. Unfortunately, these were the years before domestic violence became understood; eyes were still at this time being closed, while police and even priests were telling women to "go home and be a better wife/clean the house better/make a better meal and he won't hit you." It wouldn't be until three years later that shelters would be started that actually protected, and police began to slowly learn that women needed help. It took a close brush with death one night for me to swear that if I woke up the next morning, that was it. Fortunately I worked for some great lawyers who took one look at me the next morning and said, "We're filing the papers today." That was mid-May of 1988.

For the next five or so years, I moved around in an attempt to make a new life, but then a phone call would come, with his voice on the line asking how I liked whatever city I was in, and I'd leave again. I moved to Arizona, where life was basically that—life. I've always loved the landscapes of Arizona, its mountains and deserts (and even huge green forests) and though I wasn't what you'd call happy, it did allow me a new direction in life; learning about and expanding my interest in Native American affairs, using my legal background to begin working with Indian judges and attorneys, learning everything

I could and landing my dream job at the time: court administrator on a reservation. I was in my element, working for Indian rights in the courts and living in a small log cabin in Pinetop with woods at the fence.

And then my mom, whom I can't remember ever having anything more than a simple cold, got a pain in her stomach after having come to visit me just after my birthday, from her home in Mesa. The pain didn't go away after a week, and she went to the doctor. One week later, after some tests and scans, the diagnosis came. Stage IV pancreatic cancer. My life at that moment took a turn I never imagined. I was still reeling from my father's death two months earlier, and was now being told we would be lucky if my mom lived more than three to six months more. One month later, my aunt (my mom's sister; they had bought their house together) called to tell me that she couldn't take care of my mom by herself any longer and needed help. I talked to the chief judge, letting him know what was happening, and he said "Go, and keep me informed. Creator be with you." I packed up some stuff, put my computer in the car (yes, we teleworked even way back then!); three hours later I walked into my mother's arms and held someone I barely recognized.

I've never regretted leaving that dream job and log cabin to care for my mother during her final seven weeks of life, as she deteriorated quickly and I home-cared her, doing things for her that she used to do for me as a newborn. It was the hardest thing I ever did, but sharing those final weeks with her, and laying wrapped in her arms talking to her a few hours before she died, knowing (believing?) she could hear me, holding her hand as she took her final breath—these things can't be replaced. She would be with me forever, I knew that. At 36 years old, I became an orphan within the span of four and a half months.

To say I was emotionally lost is an understatement. I tried going back to the court but my heart was gone, and after a long talk with my mentor, an Indian appellate judge, I resigned the job that I worked so long and hard to get, and left Arizona, choosing Oregon for my next move. I had met a friend in one of the AOL groups dedicated to Indian affairs issues who lived in Eugene, and she offered me a room in her home. Meanwhile, I finally found freedom upon being told by my ex-father-in-law that my ex-husband had died. I'll never forget that phone call, and think of it to this day sometimes when I need a shot of strength: "You never have to look over your shoulder again."

The move to Oregon found me discovering a new passion in life. Oregon in the late 1990s was beginning to blossom with wine, claiming about 100 wineries at the time. I began choosing four wineries each weekend from the state's "wine map," sticking to the smaller, family- or single-owned ones, and going to taste their production; I was fortunate to be able to have long conversations with the winemakers, learning more and more, and being invited to the cellars for barrel-tastings, and tours of the vineyards. It created a love for wine and all its nuances.

After leaving Oregon in 1999, I went back to Arizona, a place I always felt more at "home," most likely due to it being where my mother had been. And then I received a letter from my old high school in Rome: they had planned a reunion coinciding with my class's 25th year.

After receiving the reunion letter, I initially put it aside and dismissed the whole thing. It kept nagging at me, though. I'd always made excuses about not going back overseas or taking a vacation to Italy; it was too expensive, there was never the money. I told a couple friends this was happening, and after hearing far too many reasons why I had to do this, I realized this was, of course, the perfect chance for me to see again this place that held such a peaceful place in my soul. I was still treading water after Mom's death just three short months after Dad, stuck in a void of loss. But I knew the time had come to stop letting life dictate what was happening; I had been given a crash course in realizing our time here on Earth is far too short to not just take control and say, *"That's about enough of this floundering about treading water—time to swim!"* Or perhaps sink, but I couldn't know at that point.

After many sleepless nights with a brain that refused to switch off, going over the financial possibilities, running every *what if* I could think of, hours of conversations with trusted friends, I made the decision that I was going to do whatever was necessary to not simply visit Rome for the reunion—but it was time to start finding my way home.

CHAPTER 3

TEN DAYS THAT FOREVER CHANGED MY LIFE

Summer 2001

And so in June 2001 the preparations began. Just thinking about actually returning to Rome after so long away was an excitement all its own, wondering how much it had changed. Would I know and remember anything? Would I be able to find my old apartment? I wondered if they'd let me see it, or stand on the balcony and look at the view of the endless hills that were so much a part of my life each and every day for so long. Part of me didn't want to return because the teenage memories of what was home for seven incredible years were so vivid that I wasn't sure I wanted to disturb them.

But I started thinking . . . what if I could live there again? It had been such a struggle finding another place that felt so right, so much like "home." Should I go for it? My 40s were proving to be the prime of my life; though emotionally hurt, I was single with no dependents and nothing to stop me. I'd been wanting to go back; the reunion became the stepping-stone, a reason I needed to force my hand, so to speak, and to spend the money to make the trip.

I sent a couple "feeler" emails to some international law firms, just for the heck of it, to see what kind of possibilities there might be. Though I had left the legal field a few years before, I had been doing independent verbatim transcription work, so I was still surrounded daily by the world of legal proceedings, court proceedings, insurance investigations. It seemed like the stars were aligning when I received a response from one, setting up a date for me to talk to them, while an email arrived from the alumni committee with the link to Villa Miani's website where the gala ball for the reunion would be held, showcasing a breathtaking view. That did it—my mind was made up to kill three birds with one stone; go to the reunion, see what Italy was like now, go on some interviews. Sometimes decisions just seem to be made for you!

I hadn't spoken the language in 25 years; it was somewhere in my head, and I just needed practice. I began reading Italian websites, talking to an Italian friend, listening to Italian music; doing anything I could to try to fire up the memory and start getting the language back. My dreams were consumed by visions of a life lived so very long ago. The committee's travel agent was able to get two of us in Phoenix on the same flight; our alumni were scattered far and wide, and many of us were living in the same cities without even knowing it. Lisa and I had reconnected a couple months before the flight, finding out we'd been living a mere few miles away for a few years. Such a small world.

They say that planning is half the fun, and this was no exception. I hadn't decided exactly how and where I was going to spend my ten days. My thoughts were Rome, yes; north to Tuscan wine country perhaps; west over to the beach. The next two days were open, leaving the weekend for the reunion happenings. Ostia beach for two days was the last decision made, leaving the final night up in the air.

The final couple days before travel were a whirlwind of checks, checks, and a final check: got my lire (this was before the euro), passport, reservations on the airport shuttle, lots of room in the suitcase to bring stuff back. Everything seemed to be set as I thought, *I think I'm ready!* I prowled around the apartment the final night, trying to will myself to get some sleep, though I knew I wouldn't. But I also knew it would be a good thing, because then I'd be tired enough to nap on the plane. Arriving Sunday morning would mean staying awake all day, curing jet lag by immediately going on local time.

❦ ❦ ❦

On the airport shuttle, everyone asked each other where they were going. I turned out to be the only one going international—they were all so excited for me when I explained the reunion and return to Rome. Their excitement was contagious, which helped a little bit with my fear of flying and upcoming long trip; though I wasn't sure if the butterflies in my stomach were from the fear, or the intensity of my emotions. Watching the planes while on the moving sidewalk, my old friend and now travel companion, Lisa, called out my name. As we stood there, suitcases in hand, being slowly propelled along the sidewalk, it occurred to me—it was really happening.

With storms outside and chaos inside at Alitalia's check-in desks, it wasn't a great way to start the trip, but we had a little fun looking at all the people to see if anyone looked familiar and occasionally loudly mentioning OSR, though no one responded.

As I looked at the in-flight screen Sunday morning about an hour out of Italy, watching the little plane start to go over Sardinia, I almost couldn't contain myself. As we neared Fiumicino, I leaned over and looked out the window and saw the land. I felt like I was on fire. I wanted to jump out of my seat and run up and down the aisles, dancing all the way, there were so many emotions bursting at the seams to be released.

We landed and my heart skipped a beat in anticipation. My face felt flushed and I wanted to push these people out of the plane who weren't moving fast enough. Come on, come on, go, go, GO; just get the bag down out of the overhead bin, put it on the floor and move your feet; that's right, one in front of the other, that's the way; now do it faster!

I knew from the moment I stepped off the plane that this was what I wanted. It felt right and I was content. The sounds were familiar and part of me.

With two international flights landing within minutes of each other, passport control was mobbed, taking an hour and a half to get through. The pre-arranged driver had left as we were three hours late, leaving us to share a taxi, and off we went. As we entered the highway to Rome, I began to forget that I was hot, tired and cranky and tried to talk to the driver in Italian, even though he spoke English. We told him why we were there, and he constantly smiled and laughed at our exclamations of "Look! It's Luna Park!" and "Oh I remember this road!" As we wound through the streets from the outer area called *EUR* and on into the center, he nearly flew through the streets—I was amazed at the number of cars, motorcycles and Vespas, and everyone using cellphones while driving! It was all so familiar, yet so incredibly different.

I don't think I'll ever forget walking into the Hotel Tea and being greeted with sounds of screaming celebrations coming from the TV in the lobby. The desk clerk with a huge grin yelled to me, "Forza Roma! Giallorosso!" ("Go Rome! Yellow and Red!") All of a sudden, the world outside erupted into pandemonium—horns blaring, whistles, yelling; a city gone wild. Wide-eyed, I asked him what was going on and he said, "Rome just won the championship!"

My room was up on the fifth floor, overlooking the street, church, and park. It was small by American standards, but perfect for one person. Opening the window, I breathed in the air, still in a disbelieving state. The church bells were ringing across the street, and I was in absolute heaven listening to the people running in the streets yelling of the victory, hurrying back to offices too, living their lives. Looking to the left, I saw a small bar (which in Italy is the name for a coffee shop, a cafe) with its requisite four tables in a row. Feeling an urgent need for an espresso and to sit at one of those tables, it came over me strong—I needed to get out there.

I decided to go in search of some aromatic memories stuck way back somewhere in my mind, things I hadn't tasted in 25 years. Would anything taste the same? Would I even care? Taking a deep breath, off I went into the celebratory chaos; out the hotel doors and left to get to that bar a few feet down for the much-needed caffeine jolt. Standing at the counter staring into the tiny espresso cup filled my brain with, *Am I really here? In Rome? Have I truly made this trip?*

Then my belly grumbled and there was one thing on my mind. Pizza. Pizza rustica. The rectangular pizza with a multitude of toppings, crispy on the bottom and fluffy airy inside, sliced in whatever weight amount you want. And I wanted a *suppli* with it, a Roman *suppli*, fresh and piping hot, the mozzarella simply oozing out and stretching into what resembles a telephone cord, what we used to know as *"suppli al telefono."*

Two lefts out of the bar which faced the Borghese Gardens and I was wandering down Via Veneto. Memories floated around in my brain as I walked. The Red Banjo would've been just down this street and over, down one of the small side streets; there was the "church of bones," and Piazza Barberini. Even though I was hungry, I kept walking, as if something was directing me. Where in hell was I going? Something about this route was very familiar . . . as I turned my head at one point and saw a tunnel, all of a sudden it hit me. The side street on my right led directly down to Trevi Fountain, and on that street was the hole-in-the-wall pizza place. Every Sunday after my family went to church at Santa Susanna, my high school best friend and fellow guitar player at the noon mass would go to the pizza place and giggle at the adorable, 19-year-old Angelo. He of the flirty smile, sparkling green eyes and a head full of dark, ridiculously curly hair. That was a memory I wanted to keep perfectly intact, so I stopped in my tracks and turned around, knowing full well the Piccolo Buco pizzeria might still be there, but wouldn't—couldn't—be anywhere near what I remembered. There are some memories you just don't want to destroy.

Down one more side street on my meandering and I saw a familiar sight, one of a thousand small doors with a vertical sign stating simply *pizza*. As I looked inside, it was just as I remembered these fast-food pizzerie to be; the simple counter with tray after tray of different varieties of pizza, just waiting to be cut and weighed. The aroma hit me of warm bread, baked yeast, cheese, tomatoes, the heat from the ovens mingling all the ingredients into a tantalizing smell all its own. I also recognized in the air the flavor of the fried coating of the suppli. I couldn't stop smiling as my stomach rumbled again in anticipation. I heard *"Prego?"* (roughly translated *"May I help you"*) and without so much as a thought, said, *"Mille cinquecento di margherita per favore"* ("One thousand five hundred lire of margherita please", equivalent to about one euro). I watched him cut the fresh-out-of-the-oven piece in two, put the pieces back to back and wrap them in a piece of butcher paper. I was sure he thought I was a total lunatic as I held it and just smelled—they say smell can trigger a memory, and they're absolutely right. I looked to the left part of the counter and immediately said, *"E anche un suppli"* (*"And also one suppli"*), and just sat down at a table, simply enjoying, savoring every single bite while occasionally slightly shaking my head in disbelief, unable to stop smiling.

Why did I wait so long?

The jet lag had started to set in, and I made my way back, walking in the general direction of the hotel but taking little side streets here and there as the sun slowly began its descent. Stopping in again at my little bar, I wanted to relax with a glass of wine to wind down from the excitement and feelings buzzing through me. As it was a Sunday, sitting outside at the bar's table was prohibited, but this was Italy and the city was bursting its seams in celebration. I pleaded with them, saying this was my first day back in 25 years and next thing I knew the woman behind the bar was winking and gesturing with her head to the table outside. I can be pretty persuasive when I want to—I didn't grow up as the only girl in my family with three older brothers without learning a thing or two. I laughed while watching young men and women in groups take over the streets, arms linked and singing *"Siamo noi! Siamo noi!"* (one of those things that can't be directly translated, but basically means *us* or *we, we are the champions!*), team jerseys on, carrying flags of yellow and red, the streets a sea of these bright colors streaming from scarves and hats; it hit me like a brick how very right this felt.

A short while later with the windows of my room wide open, the celebrations outside a type of white noise, my entire being relaxed into a very peaceful sleep, the kind that happens when one feels at home.

❧ ❧ ❧

Sometime during the night I awaken. It's pretty much pitch dark and I lay there slightly confused. What's going on? It's impossible for it to be this chilly at night in Phoenix in June. I see the outline of the window and in a slight panic I get up and look out at the skyline, the outline of the church and the trees of Borghese Gardens. The confusion dissipates and I remember. This is not a dream. Of course, the echoes of far-away continued partying help me remember too! I flop back down onto the bed and just laugh as my heart relaxes.

❧ ❧ ❧

The sun shone through the window about 7 a.m., waking me up long before I really wanted to. My first thought was: cappuccino, baby! A fast, refreshing, hot shower and off I went downstairs for breakfast.

Walking through three beautifully furnished tea rooms took me back in time with their huge, overstuffed cushions on antique sofas, chairs with soft seats and high curved backs and arms, gilded mirrors on the ceilings, the rooms in hues of reds, blues, browns and gold, with intricate carpeting. A door in the final room led outside, where the only sound was chirping birds in the warm sunshine and soft breeze. As I waited for my coffee, I was drawn to the TV tuned to an Italian news channel. There had been an explosion on a train, bringing me back to too many memories from the 1970s, with various terrorist groups doing something to someone every other week. Some things just never change, do they?

The buffet breakfast included an item that made my day—rosette. Those amazing rolls, crispy on the outside and barely a bit of bread on the inside, are standard fare in Rome; the bread counters at supermarkets overflow with rosette, as people buy bags full. Whether sliced and stuffed with prosciutto or mortadella for a wonderful little panino (one panino, and two or more panini: you cannot have a panini and absolutely not paninis!), or ripped into pieces and slathered with butter and jam, or dipped in oil, they have a crunch and airiness that is all their own. My little plate held thinly-sliced prosciutto wrapped around succulent, wonderfully ripe slices of melon, a rosetta with a little marmalade and packet of Nutella, and my espresso—which would be followed by a cappuccino later because one little espresso wasn't going to cut it on this jet-lagged day. Time seemed to stand still as my brain registered all the tastes that had been long-hidden.

Out I went again into the bright sunshine, destination clear in my mind as I walked by instinct down Via Piemonte, over to Via Boncompagnia, turning left on the Veneto again to the bottom of the hill; at Piazza Barberini I had a choice to go left up the hill to Santa Susanna Church, Piazza Repubblica and Termini, or go right towards Piazza Navona and Trevi Fountain. I had to know, I had to see it, so of course I turned right. All around me in this chaotic, crowded, noisy area full of blasting car horns, the revving motors of vespas and motorcycles, were still signs of quiet beauty. Buildings with incredible architecture sporting curving designs of cement, brick, tile and mosaic; pieces of terracotta and ceramic here and there incorporated into the design. It was clear to see the Etruscan influence from building to building, in the arches and doorways, windowsills and balconies. You'll never go thirsty in Rome, I thought, passing street-side fountains on just about every corner, fresh, clean, drinkable water flowing. You might have to wait your turn to drink, though, as there is probably someone already there, filling up plastic and glass bottles to take home.

I knew I was close to Trevi Fountain and the small side street that held Il Piccolo Buco. The time had come to see if it was still there, that tiny hole-in-the-wall pizza place with one small room holding six tables. Down the street I went, passing restaurants and tourist shops, until something told me to stop. And there it was on my right, its door open with the smell of pizza wafting through the air. I peeked in and saw a room frozen in time. The same six tables, the same counter in front of the wood-burning oven; yet now there was another room at the back with another six tables. On the walls were photos from its early days, including all I remembered from the '70s—except for a curly-haired, green-eyed, flirtatiously smiling waiter, face breaking into a huge grin as he turned and winked, his strong voice quick with a *"Ciao bella!"* I talked to the owner a little bit, telling him that I was so happy to see it hadn't changed except for the one back extension, and that all the photos on the wall just made my heart swell. I promised to come back.

Stopping just a half block away at Trevi, I remembered having thrown my lire—actually I think it may have been a *gettone*, an old phone token—into the fountain. Perhaps the saying is true: if you throw a coin into Trevi Fountain, you are sure to return to Rome, the Eternal City, forever there. The legend and tradition continues according to how many coins: one to return, two means not only will you return but you will fall in love, and three means all of the above plus you'll marry. Choose your coin number wisely before tossing your luck into the fountain.

I sat for a bit and then continued on, winding my way up Via due Macelli and Via Babuino over to the Spanish Steps where I plopped myself down to sit and people-watch, just soaking it all in; listening to the chatter, the laughter, the hawkers, the noise and utter chaos that is Rome. I have to admit that at this point, I wasn't exactly sure what to do.

I wasn't really a "tourist," and knew deep inside that this was a trip with a special purpose: to reclaim memories of days long past, to see if this was where I wanted to be again. With a nod of the head, I decided to start at the beginning, so to speak, and headed to the metro that would take me to EUR.

EUR stands for *Esposizione Universale Roma*, and was chosen in the 1930s as the site for the 1942 world's fair, which Mussolini planned to open to celebrate 20 years of fascism. It's now a commercial suburb, a residential and business district, busy and bustling with international business, hotels, restaurants, huge high-end apartments. The hills which hold the ruins of a time long past, dotted with old houses, all seem to surround this new, modern area. But it is also the location of the American Palace Hotel, where my Italian adventures began.

Exiting the station, I looked to the left and saw it. Obviously it seemed much smaller and there was nothing palace-like about it. I stood at the entrance and easily conjured up images of that shy, awkward 12-year-old girl that I was, just four months short of becoming a teenager. Saw her standing in nearly this same spot, suddenly living in a foreign country, not speaking the language, knowing she will start at a new school soon. She hasn't been told what type of school it is, and her fear of attending an Italian school without speaking the language is nearly petrifying her. She is in a land she knows nothing about, except that it is her ancestry. Her voice has a full Georgia southern accent, and she is acutely aware of how it sounds when she speaks. "Ciao y'all. Comè stai y'all."

I knew it made perfect sense to go in and make a reservation for my final night there, to end where it had begun.

Going back to my hotel, I decided it was time for a *vino* break. I went to the same café and sat outside with my glass, perfectly legal this time since it wasn't Sunday, just breathing it all in—the whirlwind of sights, sounds, memories and emotions; everywhere I looked, every sound I heard, familiar yet strange. Each breath filled me with the air and emotions of my old life, creating a battle with this older, more mature brain trying to make sense of what in hell was happening. Even after a wonderful, simple dinner later at a little family-owned osteria, Zii Umberto, I was still a bit keyed up and wanted to just walk in the night air, thinking about trying to find where the Red Banjo used to be. I found the place, going on some type of memory instinct, giggling a little bit as my eyes wandered over the door, the windows, remembering the myriad of times I had been there listening to the band mostly made up of teachers from our school. Of course it was closed, long closed, as things change—and well they must. But oh my, how very many memories were locked up behind those closed doors, the nights spent doing things I probably never should have. Testing boundaries, both parental and personal; rebelling and pulling back; making mistakes and learning; unrequited love or crush; somehow getting through the angst-filled teenage years while living in a foreign country.

 I decided not to go up to Toscana/Umbria after all, but stay in the city until the reunion. There was some huge convention going on and finding somewhere was definitely not an easy task. But with the help of my hotel, we did it. The next day saw me wheeling my suitcases over cobblestoned streets to the Hotel Edere by the Colosseum. It was small and simple, but as I walked through the lobby I found it had a pretty little courtyard boasting swing chairs, tables and chairs, all surrounded by a garden with lush plants and three fountains. I was instantly immersed in its quiet beauty, fountains trickling, the building buffering outside noise. I knew I would have to revisit this tantalizing courtyard at night so I could lie on one of the swings and stare up at the stars. They say you should never judge a book by its cover—some of these little places with nondescript outsides hold such gems inside.

I went to explore after check-in as I was near the Colosseum, and entered a large park with many benches and fountains, and enough trees to keep it shaded and cool. I found a fountain with a semicircle stone wall, just high enough that it was a nice jump for this short person to get up on it and kick back against a tree trunk. What is it about people-watching that is so interesting, yet calming and relaxing? I enjoyed again the simple sounds, the voices, everything about it. It was always in the front of my mind that I was utilizing this trip to find out if this was somewhere I wanted to live again, and much of my time was spent attempting to do the things I would in normal everyday life were this to be my home. Okay, not that lounging on a park wall was going to be my everyday life, but . . . Closing my eyes and enjoying the warmth, I heard a dog barking and saw a black lab run in front of his owner, leash dragging, and jump into a drinking fountain, happily splashing away, lapping at the water coming out of the faucet. It was a great Kodak moment.

Turning my head, I watched three young Italian soldiers, looking quite spiffy in their uniforms, enjoying some time off, talking and laughing, flirting with all the young women purposefully tossing their hair as they sauntered by. How easy it was for me to travel back in time and remember the handsome, young, curly-haired, green-eyed Adriano (what is it with me and curly hair and green eyes?) on the train to Vicenza that summer in 1974; he on his way back to his base and me with two friends going to visit a cousin. I still blush and smile every time I open a certain scrapbook that contains a certain postcard . . .

I was so lulled that I nearly fell asleep, so I got up and walked over to the Colosseum. Having visited many times in the past,

I was content to simply walk around it, trailing my hand along the worn stones, feeling the simultaneous coolness and warmth of them; the history contained in every nook and cranny. While the upper part was now open, leading to an amazing view, the bottom part was completely closed off—the part where we used to climb over the fence and run around as teens, pretending to go into where the lions had been kept.

I kept walking towards the Forum and found it just closing; never mind, I thought, and spied a pretty tree surrounded by a square stone bench in front of the Arco di Costantino, where I sat to take a breath, as it had been pretty hot all day. My eyes fell upon a row of various national flags. I felt my chest tighten; my heart started pounding and I started to tear up, suddenly almost unable to breathe. I realized I was looking straight through at the FAO building where my late mother had worked for seven years, basically supporting our family. I would go and hang out with her there so often, having lunch together many times, meeting her co-workers. This was when I realized why it had seemed so important for me to make this trip. Sometimes something seems to just pull at you, forcing your hand. It had seemed so damn important for me to do this, and suddenly it came to me while sitting there. It was June, and I was the same age that my mother had been when we first moved to Rome in 1971. June was the month when we had seen these things for the first time, all those many years ago. I felt I was seeing everything again for the both of us. I tried to imagine what it was like for her to move here at this age, a stranger in a foreign land, with four teenaged children. Both of my parents loved it in Rome, and that love transformed itself in me. I took a photo of that view through the arch, felt my mother's love in me, and pictured her smile as I began walking down the street towards the hotel and its peaceful courtyard.

I had a special mission to get back to the hotel for—I had to call the law firm to set up my interview. It was an exciting moment and got scheduled for Friday afternoon, right in the middle of some reunion goings-on. But no matter, this was far more important. I stopped at the café by the hotel for their homemade *gelato*, and found that speaking Italian was becoming second nature by this point. I hadn't spoken a word of it for 25 years, which meant that I missed many things, and stumbled on others, but I found people to be exceptionally understanding. They loved that I was at least trying. Returning to the hotel, I sat in the courtyard, reveling in its peace, exactly as I had imagined it. The evening quiet, stars shining above, and a gentle breeze meant the swinging sofa needed no help to rock me nearly to sleep.

❧ ❧ ❧

I think this trip showed me the joy and peace of solo travel. It's not for everyone, but, for me, I never felt lonely at any point, and it gave me the alone time to decide what was real, and what were merely memories of "good times past." And I needed to do it myself, by myself.

I grew up watching my mom pack for vacations with four kids with one small suitcase. Time was taken every night to wash out the clothes; it's a travel habit that's stayed with me. Filling up the hotel room's bidet with water and soap, letting a few dirty clothes soak for a bit and scrubbing out the travel grime took me back to a Saturday night sometime in 1974: I was sixteen and my high-school best friend and I decided to make a cassette tape for my brother, who was stationed in Ft. Rucker. My eldest brother had moved out of our apartment by then, and I got his room—the huge one with the private bathroom. After all, I was the youngest and the only girl, and it made perfect sense to me at the time that I should have my own private bathroom. My friend and I had decided to get a six-pack of cheap beer, sit in the bathroom with our guitars because of the great acoustics, and make a hilarious tape for my brother, full of talk, jokes, songs, etc., over the course of a few hours of drinking. Have you been in a hotel in Italy, or any Italian apartment? You know there's always a bidet that's perfect as a child's own personal sink or . . . the perfect cooler! Fill it with water and ice and it keeps your beer cold and handy in that acoustic playground.

I took time to walk now-familiar streets to visit Santa Susanna, the main English-speaking Catholic church. Though I'm not particularly religious and gave up Catholicism years ago, I still wanted to see it as it held a hell of a lot of memories. Santa Susanna served as the American expatriate community parish, specifically from 1921 to 2017, when it was overseen by the Paulist Fathers, its priests and deacons generally from the North American College up on the Gianicolo hill. Historically there has always been a titular church (during the time I was there, it was assigned to a cardinal priest, the Archbishop of Boston) on this site since the year 280 AD, sitting on the Quirinal Hill.

I walked up the steps of the Baroque façade, its columns, curving lines carved into its outside walls, its statues, all familiar to me and forever etched in my memory, as I opened the doors and became transported in time. I stared in awe at the paintings and carvings, the windows of stained glass, the walls frescoed with scenes depicting the history of this church, the beheading of St Susanna and scenes from the Old Testament. How could nothing have changed? I walked the length of the inside, up and down its aisles and pews, standing by the alcove where that same friend and I used to play guitars to accompany the singing of a couple of the deacons from the North American College at the noon mass on Sundays. An hour before that mass, we would hold a babysitting service in the church office, making ourselves some playtime money. It seemed so much smaller as I looked out at the pews, remembering the people, and standing there in our flowered maxi skirts, rocking down the house. That was the only mass that was that progressive, even in the '70s. It hit me how opulent that church was. I stopped at the parish office next door and spoke to the woman working there about some of the changes I noticed; she excitedly pulled out photo albums, and rectory and parish family listings. We spent a fun couple hours talking about the people and what the church used to be like. She loved hearing about its past and especially the music we used to play.

It hit me later, while enjoying a simple dinner of pasta pomodoro, veal scaloppini, and a dessert of banana cut into small slices covered with a dusting of sugar and a dash of lemon, that the next day I'd be changing hotels to the northern parts of the Via Cassia and my days would be filled with reunions, happenings and people I hadn't seen in 25 to 30 years. Yikes.

⚜ ⚜ ⚜

Moving to the area of the city where the school and my old apartment were felt a bit strange. It was the area where so very much of my life had been spent: I took the Via Cassia every day, whether to school, or over to the road which led to what we called the round church and friends' homes, or up by Marymount and the area where my best school friend lived and half my memories were made. The seemingly infinite number of trips on the 201 or 301 buses to the Ponte Milvio for *gelato* or the Saturday market, where we would be given a flower by the flirtatious vendor each time; or where we changed to the number 2 bus and spent many a weekend night going to Piazza del Popolo, getting off the bus at every other bar—drinking a cheap beer and getting back on, more giggly and crazy after each. In those days, the buses had ticket-takers who sat in raised seats with a little shelf in front of them, to give out the tickets and to push a small buzzer if someone wanted off. If there was no one on duty, the buzzer was disconnected, leaving the seat open for some tipsy teenager to take the seat, pushing the non-working buzzer very covertly because it squeaked. If you timed it right and pushed it rhythmically, it would match the movement of someone's footsteps, making them stop and gaze at their foot, wondering why their shoe was squeaking. I'd sit still as a statue, looking at my friend, the two of us trying not to burst out laughing.

The long-awaited reunion was set for 5:00 p.m. at the school. It'd been so many years; I knew I'd changed immensely, would I recognize anyone? Though I had only kept in touch with perhaps one or two people from those days, there were some on the attendee list that I imagined would be great fun to see. Hey, we all change, it'll be great! Before this could happen, I needed to get to that side of town, so the now-familiar pattern began, *bump bump bump* as I noisily wheeled my suitcases up the street to the metro, changing at Flaminio (Piazza del Popolo) to the #2 tram, to get to the 201 bus at Ponte Milvio to take me up Via Cassia. Whew. On the 201 for the first time this trip, I'm sure people wondered who this crazy person was sitting and grinning from ear to ear. The route goes by the old Via Flaminia, turning down the new Via Flaminia (because confusion is fun!) where the real traffic always began. This time, the congestion was heavier than I remembered. I easily spied where my late aunt's and grandmother's apartment was—look! There's the building! And the hill I walked up to get to the apartment! We turned onto the Via Cassia and I eagerly looked front, back, side to side.

I really didn't recognize the road. Where'd all those buildings, apartments and stores come from? We passed the small hospital I got rushed to when I walked into a door in the dark and nearly broke my nose. I almost didn't see the school because there had never been so much around it. I practically jumped up out of my seat, twisting and turning to look at everything. A woman whom I don't think was having a very good day glared at me and wasn't impressed when I said, "That's my old school! It's been 25 years!" I got the "Whatever! Go away nut" look. A little bit further we passed Via Grottarossa, where I had spent my first summer making Italian friends and learning "street slang." My heart began to pound because I knew I was less than a mile from "home." I couldn't believe it was happening; would I recognize it? Would it even still be there? I looked to the left where the small strip-mall should have been. Where was the bar? Where was the grocery store I went to countless times? And then I saw them. The grocery store was much bigger now, tucked off behind the stores. The blood seemed to rush to my head and I started to feel hot. I'm sure people could hear my heart beating so hard as I whispered, *please please let the apartment complex still be there*. I looked to the right and I could see myself walking, holding schoolbooks or a grocery bag.

My breath nearly exploded from me as, unbelievably, the traffic slowed down right in front of the apartments. There was 1020 Via Cassia in all its glory. I saw a new gate at the entrance and wondered when that had happened, or whether it was a mis-memory. Otherwise it looked the same. The small playground still on the right, surrounded by seemingly the same trees, the same sign for the hair salon located in the back of the complex. I gazed over at the small maintenance building, a hut really, half expecting to see the same two men relaxing in their chairs, smoking cigarettes and thinking about fixing whatever broke. I considered getting off the bus, but it started to move and so, wiping the tears I hadn't known were there, I stared straight ahead, unsure what to feel. It gave me some measure of comfort to know that part of my life was still there, and I could go back and see it again any time I wanted on this trip.

Two stops later I clickety-clacked, bump-bump-bumped down a winding gravel road through what looked like the entrance to a convent. It was Hotel Villa St. Dominique, a three-star hotel, tucked away off the main street. I became immersed in a quiet that overwhelmed me as I looked around at hills rolling to the horizon in front of me, behind the villa. An old chapel sat serenely among trees; the view familiar—just like the view from the back of the school, it seemed endless.

∽ ∽ ∽

With just enough time to splash some water on my face and change clothes, I piled into a van along with the few others staying at the hotel. Within a few minutes, we were driving through the gates of the Overseas School of Rome. OSR (now with the word 'American' in front, a change made many years ago) is an international school, with nearly 20 nationalities represented at any one given time. It covers K-12, but with only a few hundred students for all those grades when I attended; my own graduating class had had under 30. There were children from all walks of life, from daughters of kings to kids of actors and actresses. The school taught us many things, most importantly how to appreciate other cultures and respect differences; one couldn't attend the school and have prejudices.

That education has stayed with me and nearly everyone I've spoken with over the years.

As I walked up the stairs from the parking lot to the quad, my eyes followed the square of buildings: the single-story, L-shaped elementary school along two sides; the two-story high school building along a third; the gym along half of the fourth; and finally the four-story villa that houses the middle school and business office.

A moment after our arrival, the air filled with sounds of laughter, excitement, cries of "Is it really you?" Tables were set up with so much food and wine, cheeses, fruits and vegetables and pastas and meats. Oh, we were being so spoiled. The wine flowed as we ate while walking around or sitting at tables, the sound of glasses clinked in toasts amidst the background of music playing; all around were the sounds of people laughing and talking—"How are you?", "Where do you live?", "This is my husband", "This is my wife", "Here are pictures of my kids", "Do you remember when we used to . . . ?", "Yes, I do!", "Remember when we went to . . . ?", "Of course!" Well into the evening, the air was electric.

So many memories were brought back as I wandered the high school building; nostalgia kicked in as I made my way down the stairs into the cafeteria where, impossibly, nothing had changed; through the dining and assembly stage area and out the door to the back where there's a view that probably none of us had ever forgotten. Hills and trees that stretch forever, cut by wooden benches in the ground in amphitheater-style with the small stage at the bottom where our plays were held with perfect acoustics. Back up the stairs I went and walked down the high school building hallways, passing the rows of lockers and down to the girls' bathroom, where we would congregate and sneak cigarettes while having countless "girl talks". In the library, I opened the window onto the back hills and heard nothing but birds chirping and a gentle breeze. Across the hall the open window in the old science room gave me the soft buzz of many voices laughing. The contrast was startling. I gazed down at where the smoking shack used to be—it seemed impossible that some of these things had never changed. Over to the middle school villa I went, walking up the tiny, winding staircase that leads up to the classrooms; I felt so small and young and yet so old at the same time.

It filled me with a certain sadness. Where did the time go? Looking out at my old schoolmates on the quad, I thought about my own life and everything that had happened in the last 25 years. The good, the bad, the joys and pain, the loves and losses. Something came over me as my mind whirled with all the memories. This is probably when my decision was made, a decision that would change the rest of my life.

As I made my way back to the hotel, I decided to get off the bus in front of the old apartment complex. Part of me wanted to leave it alone, keep it in my memories—but the other part of me said, "Oh, do it!" Across the street from the complex, I sat on a low wall, just looking: there was building number 3, third and top floor. I was mesmerized as a thousand images ran through my mind. I saw myself standing on that wrap-around balcony looking out over miles of unobstructed view to the back, or waiting and watching on the front part of the balcony, anticipating that the beautiful blue X19 would soon come roaring in, signaling the arrival of two or three handsome young army men from Vicenza, who had become like brothers to me and adopted sons to my parents, come to visit for the weekend; or waiting and watching for my eldest brother to return from university in the States, or another brother coming home for a visit from wherever he was stationed; or sometimes my maternal grandparents visiting from the States as well. Needless to say, even that balcony held a lot of memories.

Back at the hotel, I cajoled the night clerk into giving me a glass of wine even though the bar was closed, and I sat in the little breakfast nook overlooking the hills outside. The summer sky blanketed with stars overwhelmed me with emotions. A couple of guests came in, an alum and his wife, and we got the night clerk to give us more wine and spent a couple hours talking—he was from the '60s while I was '70s, yet we talked of teachers past, of life in Rome past, of being teenagers growing up in a foreign country.

◈ ◈ ◈

I don't think I'd ever been so nervous about an interview before; though I'd been in my position for nearly 20 years, I'd never thought about what an international law firm would be like here, other than very different. I wasn't sure how to tailor myself for it, or whether to just act like I would at any other interview. Basically, all I did was succeed in freaking myself out and become even more nervous.

But it all went relatively well; the hiring partner asked my level of Italian fluency and I honestly told him that I had not spoken the language conversationally in 25 years. He agreed with the personnel manager that once I was immersed in it, it would come back quickly, and so they didn't see it as a problem. They let me know that they were opening a satellite office and needed it staffed—my qualifications were exactly what they were looking for. But then the next question stopped me in my tracks: "Do you have your working papers?"

I did my best to formulate my next statement as professionally as possible. "In your email you stated you would sponsor the work visa if the interview was successful." "The laws have changed," he said. My heart sank. "The government is cracking down on businesses and the sponsoring of work visas, because of issues with fraud and other things. We haven't been able to sponsor any new-hire visas for the last few months, and have some attorneys waiting in the wings to be hired because of the changes."

I would be lying if I said I wasn't a tad frustrated that I hadn't been told this information in their last email to me. After suggesting to me that I return to the States, get either a work visa or regain my dual citizenship status (or find out if it was still valid), and then email them when the papers were in order, I thanked them for their time and the opportunity, and left.

On the ride back to the hotel, I had time to think and consider. Maybe this was a blessing in disguise. I was feeling a lot of things, from relief to disappointment. At the same time, I thought it might be for the best—I could do some things I needed to, get my language level back, put some money away, get my papers in order and find out the status of my citizenship, and then come back and do it right. It occurred to me that I had set my life on high-speed, supersonic, and I wasn't ready. By the time I walked up the driveway to the hotel, the quiet and peacefulness of it calmed me, and I began feeling a lot better about everything. A message awaited me, telling me a group was meeting at the bottom of the Spanish Steps for dinner and to be there at 7:00 p.m. After relaxing for a while with a glass of a nice red wine, I went just down the street to a small grocery store; I wanted to connect with local life and meandering the aisles of a grocery store just seemed to do it for me somehow. It's something I've always liked to do in every city in every foreign country I find myself in. There's something about the connection between food and culture, and you can find some of it when you wander a local supermarket, small grocery, or of course an outdoor market.

The evening turned out to be quite a feat. I met up with the group, and when it looked like we were all there, our fearless leader Jimmy simply said, "Follow me." Picture it—a group of 20 middle-aged Americans going down one street, then another, then over to another one, then another and then another. "For Pete's sake," we kept saying. "How the heck much further is it?" In our little crowd were constant cries of: "Remember this place? Remember that place? I remember this street. Oh, look at the stores! Oh, look at that balcony!" On and on we went, laughing and having a blast, but wondering—after what seemed like 30 minutes of wandering the streets—if we would ever get to this restaurant Jimmy was taking us to. Finally, we reached Piazza Navona, turned down a side street and saw other alumni at a table at one of the many restaurants in the piazza. We kept going (the general consensus was that we were meant to truly work up voracious appetites), and I believe at this point we turned down Via S.M. dell'Anima and saw a wonderful, small, quaint trattoria. "We're here!" we chanted. "Let the wine begin! Yay!"

I wish I could remember the name of the trattoria, but as I sit here and write, it's just impossible. I do remember that it was gorgeous, with three large rooms, very high ceilings and about six ceiling fans. I suppose we sometimes got a bit noisy at our long table, but we were a group of old friends who hadn't seen each other in far too many years. Our connection seemed to have never left though. I've heard this from many people of varying schools (called overseas brats, sometimes known of course as military brats)—it seems no matter how long the separation is, there's a connection among us. Maybe it's the growing up in foreign lands, moving around, getting too used to saying goodbye. I don't recall even using that word very often—it was always "see ya." The wine flowed, carafe after carafe; food was ooh'd and aah'd over, the various bruschette were exceptional, and there were never enough of the ones with melted gorgonzola, the ones so exquisite that someone would invariably ask "You going to eat that?" if one sat on a plate for more than 30 seconds. Our laughter expressed so many feelings. Who's doing what? Where have you been? Tell me of your life. Questions heard up and down the table, everyone joining in.

It was nigh on midnight when I remembered the last bus for my hotel left Ponte Milvio at midnight. The hotel was too far away for me to afford a taxi, especially at midnight rates. "Good night all, until tomorrow. See you at school!" Somewhere in my wine-befuddled brain I knew there should be a bus on Via Risorgimento that would get me to the tram and, though a good starting thought, I seriously couldn't focus much—I had the attention span of a kitten as the thoughts sped by: midnight . . . last bus . . . oh look, Piazza Navona . . . oh, pretty fountain! There were still many people of all walks of life out because, after all, Roma had won the championship. I smiled at a guy doing some type of dance interpretation; on the other side of him someone was painting something beautiful, his hands interpreting whatever his mind's eye saw; further down, someone was drawing caricatures; and everywhere, people still sat out at the cafés, enjoying the gorgeous night. It felt like every Roman was on the street where I needed to get the bus: walking, riding mopeds, in their cars. It was chaos! *This can't be normal traffic*, I thought, and so I asked someone, who explained that this was one of the streets chosen for the victory celebration. The noise was deafening and the traffic was at a standstill. Buses weren't moving anywhere.

After about 45 minutes of waiting, I decided to follow some of the crowds walking. If I could find my way to the Spanish Steps, I would be okay—I remembered it being the start of the number 25 night bus that goes up the Cassia. I looked at my trusty map that was always in my pocket, folded precisely to show the city and the bus routes, which was a saving grace. "Roma—The Happening City". It was very aptly named. *Okay, I thought, let's see, if I go down this street in front of me, then over another one, then down two more, I should be there. Easy peasy!* Following the crowds, I asked one police officer for directions, and kept going. I found myself recognizing some things, but my mind and sense of direction wandered as I continued on. I wasn't paying the greatest attention because the eye candy was too great to ignore. Well, perhaps the amount of wine I had drunk was contributing somewhat.

Soon, I found that there were few people around me anymore. I looked at a street name on a building and didn't recognize it as one I should be on; the celebratory voices were gone and it was quiet, so quiet. I looked at the watch in my pack and saw it was 1:30 a.m. I was lost. Not a soul around.

Interestingly, I didn't panic or feel frightened. This was a city that I remembered inside of me; the streets felt familiar and I had always felt safe; I have always known the general travel precautions to take (money for the day in my front pocket, valuables in the hotel safe, hand over the zipper of the pack) and even in a tipsy state, I knew to stay in the general area of central Rome because this was no longer the 1970s. My brain triggered some knowledge that I couldn't be too far off the mark and that, if I just kept walking towards anything that looked like more light than just streetlights and listened for noise, I'd get somewhere close. Shortly after, I turned a corner and heard what sounded like water; I saw a few more people and, as I turned another corner, I couldn't believe it. Trevi Fountain, jam-packed with people at 2:00 a.m. I must confess, I breathed a small sigh of relief and sat on the closest stone bench to the fountain, the beauty of it flooded with lights, the water blue-green, coins twinkling in the pool; the breeze coming off it cool and refreshing. To my right was a young couple, their arms wrapped around each other, the adoration in their eyes as bright as the lights.

Knowing where I was now, I got up and walked one block over to Via del Tritone, just a short distance from Barberini, where the stop for the night bus was. Seeing the number 25 listed, Via Cassia by way of Ponte Milvio, I suddenly remembered too many nights of immense trouble I had gotten into from my Sicilian father each time I missed the last 201 at Ponte Milvio and had to wait for this bus. *Shhhh*, I admonished myself once, *don't make noise. Walk quietly. Please don't let Dad be awake. Please.* I had put the key in the door, and then nearly fell inside the apartment as the door jerked fully open. "Gah!" I had yelled, as Dad's hand clamped onto my arm, yanking me inside and shouting: "Where the hell have you been? We have been worried sick! Your curfew is midnight!" I had tried to speak, "The bus . . .", but it was too late. Dad believed in not "sparing the rod", and he was already pulling off his belt . . .

I stood up from the memory of how much that belt had hurt. Looking at the schedule on the sign, I could see the next one was due at 2:45, so I did the only thing I could: I sat and waited. And waited. And waited. Because of the traffic and all the routes backed up from the celebrations, the bus finally came at 3:20 a.m. In Rome, chaos reigns supreme! There were more people on the bus than I would've thought possible at this time of morning. All in all, I was quite happy when we got onto the Cassia and passed my old apartment complex. Up the hill, I hit the button to get off the bus, but the driver flew past the stop. I yelled out, "Hey! *Ferma!*" (Stop!) The last thing I needed was to get even further away. Fortunately, he stopped the bus and let me off, and so I crossed the Cassia and backtracked down to the hotel, feeling thankful that they had left the light on the driveway. It was quiet and cool out and I relaxed as I rang the night bell to get in. The desk clerk worriedly asked if I was okay. Smiling tiredly, I simply said: *"Ma certo, grazie, e buonanotte."* (I sure am, thank you, and goodnight.)

◈ ◈ ◈

That night was the big fancy ball where we got to get all gussied up. But, before I went, I wanted to relive another memory, this one involving *gelato*.

Cool, creamy, delicious, hand-made at the mom-n-pop shop that I remembered, and hoped was still there. My destination was Ponte Milvio, the meeting place of a thousand times, a thousand days. As the bus meandered down the road, I watched the scenery and thought about a lot of things—I'd always wondered if the sensations I remembered of life here would fade, but I found they hadn't. They'd remained with me, buried but alive, just waiting to be let free.

I got off the bus at Ponte Milvio and looked for the outdoor farmer's market, needing a visual cue to help me find my gelateria. A lot had changed, the piazza had many new stores. I wandered the stalls of the market first, finding that I was looking more at the flower vendors than anything else. Why? Well, though it was impossible, it would still have been a kick if one of the vendors struck a chord of memory; the handsome man with dark hair, moustache and beard, wonderful teddy-bear body, crying loudly, *"Buongiorno bellissima!* Come, take this flower, though not as beautiful as you." Many times, it's the memories that can never change which are the best.

Yes, yes, *gelato*! Using the front of the church as my focal point, I closed my eyes and pictured the shop, two teenagers standing in my place, saying: "Let's get *gelato*," and it worked. I immediately went to the left side where the market used to be, walked past the bar that had the best *suppli*, and when the sidewalk curved slightly I saw a sign for a pharmacy. A slow smile came over me as the cool, sweet aroma hit. There, the small shop with a simple arched doorway, *Gelateria* written over it, *Creperia* on the side, the small balcony over it. I stood in the doorway, and crossed into the past. On my left were five wooden chairs, and I thought they must have been the same chairs that were there 25 years ago. On my right was the bar, numerous versions of heaven waiting to be sampled. Nothing had changed. Nothing. It was a very small place, and an older woman was standing behind the counter. When she smiled at me in return, I thought to myself, *it can't be*. To make sure I wasn't imagining things, I asked her, "How long has this shop been here?" She laughed and responded, "Oh, nearly 50 years my husband and I have been here. Though now our children run it much of the time." I explained as best I could how many times I had been in her shop all those years ago, and she ran out from behind the counter, giving me a huge hug, and saying she remembered "her" two crazy American teens who always had a smile for her and loved her *gelato*. She asked what my favorite flavor was and, without hesitation, I said: "Pistachio." After taking me for a little tour in the attached room where they hand-made all their *gelato*, she handed me a filled cone. I felt young again, the taste every bit of what I remembered, cold and creamy. I couldn't thank her enough for giving me this joy.

I headed back after talking a nice walk along the river, criss-crossing over a couple of the bridges and buying my little support for Rome's football (soccer) team—which is generally named *"AS Roma"* and has red and yellow team colors, hence their nickname *"i giallorossi"*—a simple red and yellow multi-string bracelet. I felt a part of it all then.

∽ ∽ ∽

6:00 p.m. and the van picked us up: six of us standing in our hotel lobby, five women in evening gowns, and one man in a tuxedo, excited about the ball and seeing old friends and teenage loves, crushes and rivals. The van drove seemingly out of the city, and began up a hill, up and up, curve after curve, the view around each corner more and more beautiful; partially hidden behind trees and the hill, giving only a glimpse of a prize at the top. We were let out in the courtyard of a huge, incredible villa and went inside; we were told to go up to the top floor where the party was being held on the huge outside veranda, surrounded by the view hinted at through the trees. Inside, we were immersed in marble floors and shining chandeliers, velvet curtains, richness all around us. Someone used to actually live here! We went up a small winding marble staircase and across a huge ballroom where we saw a band setting up. Following the sound of laughter and clinking glasses, we walked out onto a tremendous balcony terrace and nearly fell over from the beauty. All around was 360 degrees of the entire city of Rome; we were high above it as the sun began its descent. Still as a statue, I watched the changing colors over the hills and the buildings, the Sistine Chapel easily seen and high above everything else. I was in absolute awe and tears came to my eyes. Three of us stood there, old friends reunited, and our hands reached to each other, overwhelmed with emotion as we watched one of the most profoundly beautiful summer sunsets we'd ever seen.

Table after table held bottle after bottle of gorgeous wines to go with the ridiculous amount of amazing food. Before the band struck up its beginning notes, a screen appeared. The students of the video and art department gave us probably the best gift they could have—researching yearbooks and photos covering about ten years, they had put it all together and set it to music. There we were, in all our glory on the big screen: pranks carried out; a teacher's VW bug moved from the back parking lot into the cafeteria, silly black bars placed over the eyes of the culprits; cries of: "We see you, what you're doing!", "We recognize you!", "Oh, I remember that!", "Ahhh!" when shown a picture of a beloved teacher now gone. Laughter full of memories of times gone by floated from the tables and out over the city, the music of the video quieted us for a moment as we watched and heard the words of the song . . . "there are faces I remember, places I remember, all my life though some have gone." The band struck a chord and the announcement was made—let's dance and celebrate! From the depths of our memories we rose, wiping tears from our eyes, letting our dancing say it all. They played "oldies" that took us back, completing the evening. We felt young and alive.

As the night wore on, people gravitated to each other, catching up on lives not spent together. Rejoicing in good things, a touch of the hand upon sad stories. For some, this was the final night before leaving; others were staying for the Sunday final brunch. It was 2:00 a.m. and buses were ready to go. Tears flowed freely during goodbyes and promises to keep in touch. Phone numbers and email addresses were exchanged. "It was so very good to see you again, be well my old friend, be happy."

❧ ❧ ❧

Philosophical moment here. Staring out the windows at the hills the next morning, I thought about my plans to leave the city that day to go exploring other areas. Rome was my little anchor, this area of town held my memories, my reason for venturing out of the box I'd been in for 25 years. My heart seemed to skip a beat, and a momentary tightness gripped my chest; there was still a part of me that feared this could be my final afternoon there ever. What if I never got back? What if it just didn't work out? I found myself getting sad, and tried to pick up a bit by convincing myself that I would still be in Italy; this city was not why I was there, nor was it what provided those amazing feelings in me. This area was simply, what . . . a small particle in the desert of my memories, a drop in the ocean of my mind, a single strand of the web that enveloped—me.

Either that, or I just needed some coffee after all that wine.

It didn't take long until it happened—that old familiar feeling of excitement at seeing and doing something new started flowing through me as I thought about the remaining three days of my journey. Sometimes we just need to stare out a window and let the philosophical musings do their thing.

Driving down the Cassia one last time that afternoon on my way to Ostia, I took a final look at the old apartment complex and it tugged at my heart. Though I wanted to walk around inside, I didn't ask the driver to stop because I wanted to keep going—life is a circle, we must always move forward, always keep going. I loved what I was seeing, sitting back in silence enjoying the ride to Lido as the countryside just rolled by, and it strengthened my resolve.

Hotel Sirenetta, fronting the boardwalk, was a cute little place; the whitewashed building reminding me of Greece.

Through a pretty little entrance was the lobby with a few comfortable couches and chairs, bright with the afternoon sunshine, leading to a cute little courtyard perfect for enjoying the smell of the sea across the street. After dumping my bag in the room, I was off to wander the boardwalk and just let the water's view do what it always has for me.

As an aside, I do recommend this cute little hotel. Its simple restaurant overlooks the sea and the boardwalk; rooms are large and comfy, and if you get the top floor, your room will have a huge terrace overlooking the sea. Perfect for relaxing with a bottle—sorry, glass—of wine.

Football being crazy-important in Italy and Europe, the winning of a championship, long overdue, takes noise to an unheard-of level. I stopped in the restaurant bar for a bottle of water to take with me on my walk and a glass of wine for fortification, where the bartender was watching a television program on loud—loud being the operative word here. Watching the chaos as I waited, he told me it was streaming live from Circo Massimo in Rome, where a bazillion people were gathered for a celebratory concert by one of its hometown singers, Antonello Venditti. Years ago, when Roma won their last championship, he had written a special song called *Grazie Roma* and he would be singing it again tonight. The crowd was going ballistic in a sea of red and yellow, everything the color of the home team, the joy palpable. I couldn't stop the few tears as Antonello began singing *Grazie Roma*—the bartender came around the bar, reaching over to put his arm around me as we sang it together, swaying to the tune, congratulating our team.

It was at this moment that the realization hit: my life was no longer in the US. The fact that there could be no other decision jumped up and smacked me upside the head at that moment.

❧ ❧ ❧

It was an absolutely beautiful night out and the town came alive with people taking their *passeggiata*. Walking down the boardwalk towards the pier where it looked like half the town was, I reached the pier's entrance. It was circular there with a huge tree in the center and some benches. People were strolling the pier—the young boys and girls doing what young boys and girls do best on a beach at night: preening for each other. It was such fun to watch them; there are many cultural differences throughout the world, but when it comes right down to it, some things are the same wherever you are. Lovers strolling hand-in-hand, elderly couples arm-in-arm, seeming as one from their many years of walking side by side. There was something about the clear, cool night, with the sky blanketed in stars and the moon high and huge as I stood at the end of the pier, the sea behind me, people in front of me, stars above me, the moon to the left, and the boardwalk to the right. It was as if the moon and sea were working in concert to tug at my heart. I breathed in deeply the smell of the sea and it mingled with the smells of the food, various perfumes and colognes. I didn't want to move; I couldn't seem to get enough of turning to stare out at the sea; the stars seemed to mingle with the darkness of the water; the moon seemed so huge. It felt like all the forces of nature, every entity, had come together to put on this show especially for me. Breathe . . . breathe . . . I couldn't get enough.

I soon tore myself away from my seat on the wall. It was getting late and had been a long day, filled with many emotions that began with bidding farewell to all those old friends at the final reunion brunch that morning. Taking my time walking back to the hotel, I watched a juggler and then a clown thrilling children of all ages with their shows. It was great fun to watch and I found myself laughing right along with everyone. When one show stopped, the performer would pack up his little bag, and another would take his place. Each performance was unique to the previous. Although it could probably be a pier in any beach town anywhere in the world, I knew there was something special about this one, at least to me. On a bench near the front of the pier sat a young man strumming a guitar, his strong voice serenading a young woman gazing at him with loving eyes. You didn't need to understand the language to know that he was singing of his love for her. On another bench an elderly couple simply sat, their enjoyment of each other's company radiating as she rested her head on his shoulder. He sat tall, ever the protector of his love beside him. Others sat, stood, walked around; there was something in the air, pulsing with electricity fueled by the depths of the emotions of so many. I watched it all, taking the images and feelings deep inside me to remember.

∽ ∽ ∽

For my next-to-last day I wanted to simply enjoy walking around an area that wasn't Rome, because who knew where I might end up in the future, and I wanted to know what it might be like. I stopped at the front desk where the receptionist was standing doing something, his back to me; I just watched his body move a little bit as he sang along to the radio. He turned around, and I swore I was gazing upon my old Alessandro from the *Piccolo Buco* in Rome. I couldn't stop the slow smile as he winked, singing in a strong, deep voice, "*Solo tu, sempre tu*" ("Only you, always you"). I don't think any more words registered with me at that moment, but I quickly recovered and asked what song it was and who sang it. I was momentarily taken aback when he said, "Pooh." Okay, I'm a huge Pooh fan and Tigger is my favorite, but at that moment I thought I had had too much wine the previous night. He wrote it for me, and asked why it seemed strange to me. After attempting to explain who Pooh is in America, he so very seriously responded: "This Pooh is not a bear." I doubt I'll ever forget the look on his face. He gave me directions to a small music shop where I could buy Pooh's CD, and the explorations began!

There is a distinct difference in this smaller beach city of Ostia, with a ton of city noise but nowhere near the ear-splitting-decibel level of Rome. Though a hugely popular seaside city, there were still a couple weeks before the summer crunch. I stupidly hadn't written down the directions to the music shop, so instead of asking someone, I decided, "I don't need no stinkin' directions!" Yeah, you know what happened next. Keeping my eye on the basilica of a church that sits nearly in the middle of town, I just took off down one street to the next, turning left on one, right on the next. I knew that if I could see that church and aim for it, it would be a straight shot down the street to the beach. Easy! I continued on my merry little way, stopping at every other water faucet to fill up my water bottle. Here and there along the streets were small, simple shrines, honoring those who had died. Candles set in beautiful decorated glass sat inside the small indentation, the flames gently dancing in the slight breeze, shadows flickering and playing on the flowers surrounding the candles. A beautiful testament to the life and loving memory of a father, mother, husband, wife, son, daughter; known and loved by someone unknown to the one standing in front of the shrine silently honoring the unknown memory, acknowledging the beauty in its simplicity.

I found myself at the train and bus station and, after crossing up and over the bridge across the tracks, I laughingly thought to myself: "I just came from the other side of the tracks." Okay, so it was funny only to me—sometimes you just have to amuse yourself! After wandering around for another hour or so, completely and totally lost, I turned a corner and saw the word "hi-fi" over a tiny shop, music wafting out over the quiet afternoon. I walked in and a man in his 40s with old jeans and long hair was sitting behind a counter desk. After asking about a Pooh CD, he explained they had many and if I sang a little bit of it, he might recognize it. This was not a very good idea—when I try to sing, dogs come running from all directions. But I figured, heck, I'm on vacation, I'll never see this guy again, and I want the CD. So I sang the four words and he just smiled and said he didn't know the song, but it sounded like a good one!

Disappointment clear on my face, he pointed to a chair by the wall, telling me to sit as he'd made a CD once of the band's greatest romantic hits that I might like. How can I explain what it felt like to sit in a small shop on that hot June day in a seaside Roman suburb as a music lover played five seconds of each song on there for a tourist who'd fallen in love with one song? I agreed that they were wonderful and told him I would love to buy a copy of the CD. He said, "How much time have you got?" and proceeded to tell me how music was his passion, and how he had taken on a project of putting all the "old greats" onto CDs from their old scratchy records. He brought out what looked like a suitcase full of CDs and proceeded to spend the next two hours playing snippets of song after song from the 20s through to the 90s. Before nearly every song, he said, "See if you remember this!" Most of them I did, and for those hours we played music, sang along, swooned at the romantic ones, and just had a wonderful time together.

We talked of Italy and America, and he commented that when

I spoke Italian, he assumed I must be living there since I spoke the language so well. I sat a little straighter when he said that, amazed at how much had come back naturally. I bought the Pooh CD and he gave me a copy of the Circo Massimo celebration concert to go along with it, telling me that when I played the CDs, I was to have a glass of wine, dim the lights, close my eyes and remember him and his little music shop in a far-off country and to smile—I'm sure the smile on my face and in my eyes assured him I would. Some would probably wonder why I spent nearly three hours in a small shop in a small town listening to old music, when I had spent so much money to go overseas, but if they could have seen the light of happiness in my eyes from the slice of life I had just experienced, I believe the answer would have been clear.

With a hug and kiss goodbye, I headed back towards the hotel with a new little bounce in my step and a smile that wouldn't stop. After some more boardwalk time and a wonderfully simple dinner with a couple glasses of wine, I took the rest of my bottle up to my terrace to kick back and enjoy the beautiful show put on by the sea and stars once again. As I leaned my head back, I was rewarded with a gorgeous huge moon, hanging out with the stars. Lulled by the cool breeze, the sounds of the waves and voices that seemed so far away, I found myself humming *Grazie Roma* and *solo tu, sempre tu* as I fell into a peaceful sleep.

≈ ≈ ≈

It was nearly time. Technically my last day, I walked onto the balcony and stared out at the water as images of the past days played through my mind and a small ache began deep inside me. The sea—normally the one force that can calm my mind and soothe my soul—now seemed to hold the tears I couldn't allow myself to shed. Not yet.

At Ostiense I took a few minutes to go up the stairs to the part of the station where I would get the airport train. To save time, I bought my ticket in advance. But, as I stood at the window handing the woman my money, I didn't want to take the ticket. That ache came back and I thought somehow she seemed to know—she looked at me and the harried look on her face melted for a moment as her face softened into a small smile. With a deep breath, I smiled in return and took my ticket. Walking down the long corridors with their moving sidewalks, I pretended I was on the airport's walkways, coming in to Rome. Getting off the metro at the end of the line at EUR, outside I turn and walk to the American Palace Hotel for my final night. As I stand at the entrance, I see my teenage self again . . . This was a fitting end.

Walking later around the EUR lake, I passed a market that was closing up, and watched the tired vendors packing up their wares and placing them into small trucks, visibly and deeply sighing, their eyes holding the hope that perhaps tomorrow will be a more profitable day. I ended my wanderings lakeside at a place in the park that was shaded and cool; seeing an empty stone bench next to the water, I laid on my back, face to the sun peeking through the trees as the leaves gently danced in the slight breeze. Closing my eyes, the sun warmed my face; for a while I forgot that I was just a visitor, and became part of the life and background. The atmosphere served to calm my spirit and soothe me.

Sadly leaving my bench later, I felt I was leaving a piece of my soul there. But that was okay—because I knew that, perhaps one day, someone else will lie on that bench, enjoying long-ago memories, and he or she will leave a piece of their soul. And maybe one day far into the future, a lost soul seeking peace and solace will rest on that bench on a cold day, and suddenly, somehow, a warmth will radiate through them, chasing away the chill as their spirit is soothed. Maybe they will gain a little strength to keep going.

At the hotel's bar enjoying a glass of wine later, I chatted easily with the bartender about this circle I had made, from staying there my first night in Rome 30 years earlier to this, my last night. He said it was a testament to the hotel that I chose to spend my final night there. As I stared into the glass, every moment of these past nine days seemed to swirl together with the wine, becoming one memory to drink in. After packing quickly and easily, I stood on the balcony of my room, gazing at the stars, feeling the breeze gentle and cool on my face.

I am content, I thought to myself. As a tear silently made its way down my cheek, I smiled and whispered a silent plea to the spirits of everyone I've loved and lost, to allow me to come home again.

❧ ❧ ❧

It was now time. This journey was over and I had to go. Tired from not having slept well, I stayed as still as possible in bed—if I did, maybe it wouldn't be real and wouldn't happen. I knew realistically I had to get up or lose a large amount of money on the plane ticket. Besides, there were things I had to do, and from somewhere deep inside me, I heard my mother's voice: "It's never over; you will be okay." With a heavy heart, I got up to begin the day.

Going through the motions, numb, I changed trains at Ostiense, walked the four long moving sidewalks to the next train. I couldn't shake the feeling that what I was doing was so wrong.

The flight boarded late and subsequently took off late. As I heard the engines go full throttle and we lifted off, I closed my eyes and allowed the tears to flow. I had my hands on my chest because it felt as if hands had reached in and were squeezing my lungs, not allowing air to get it. My soul ached; I felt lost again. I wanted to go to the pilot and tell him, beg him with everything that was me, please, please turn around and take me back because I can't do this. I don't want to. Please take me back home.

∽ ∽ ∽

The lights of Phoenix and the desert were immensely beautiful as we glided in on my flight from JFK, but it didn't serve to soothe me. While standing outside the airport doors, waiting for the Super Shuttle, the noise seemed to assault me. It was no more noise than Rome, but it was different. The voices spoke English and Spanish. I was drained, and all I could do was stand nearly motionless outside and wait for the shuttle. Arriving home, I fell exhausted into bed.

Did I sleep? Not much. I knew where I was and that I wasn't in Italy anymore, but the air didn't feel right, nor were the sounds the same. I got up a couple times and stood in the back yard, gazing up at the Arizona desert sky, clear and blanketed with infinite stars, and Superstition Mountain. I love this sky and view, and have loved it my entire life, and it always calms me. But not that night; it only served to remind me of where I wasn't.

The next morning I woke up with the decision firmly made. I would do whatever it took to get back home.

Chapter 4

Am I Going to Become an Expat?

For the next year, I was a woman on a mission. I had one goal, and I was going to move every mountain, climb every hill and swim every ocean to get back there for good. The days and months were filled with making contacts online on various message boards devoted to Italy travel and living, with expats, international companies, and old friends who still lived there. I kept running into the brick wall of: "Your skills are wonderful! But how's your Italian, and do you have authorization to work here?" Well, I had started working on regaining my language fluency through various means like music and magazines, so I wasn't overly concerned with that. The biggest goal, and hurdle, was the citizenship.

I wanted to do everything to the letter of the law, and decided to attempt to make the move there using my ability to live and work in that country based on my dual American-Italian citizenship. Due to our ancestry and residency, and of course our father having Italian citizenship and his parents being Sicilian, my mother, three brothers and I had all gotten citizenship too. Because the only question I was constantly asked was about my legal status to work there, my new mantra became: "I think I do but I don't know, I have no idea where the papers proving it are." I knew that somewhere in all of my parents' paperwork were the documents I needed—but as the years had passed, things had got lost, papers were thrown out for not being necessary anymore, and there was no trace of anything I needed. With the help of an Italian friend in Phoenix, I wrote emails to the citizenship office in Rome and had people in Rome calling the same office. Their mission was: "Just ask them if they can tell you if I do indeed hold dual citizenship." But their answer to my friends was always: "You are not Maria, we cannot tell you."

Countless emails and letters later, one day out of the blue in May I received a letter in the mail. The return address read *Comune di Roma, Ufficio Cittadinanza*, Italy. What was it? A letter from the office of citizenship in Rome? My hands were shaking as I opened it as gently as possible (just in case I tore something important), removing a single sheet of paper containing a short, two-paragraph letter. I immediately copied the words into an email to my Italian friend living there in Phoenix and asked her if it said what I thought it did—I understood many of the words but I didn't want to be too hopeful. Later that evening I received an email back from her: "Congratulations!" it said. "From now on we speak nothing but Italian because you need the language if you're going to move there and work!"

※ ※ ※

The next few months were a whirlwind of excitement, plans and decisions. An opportunity arose for a house to rent for a reasonable (or so it seemed at the time) price in the small town of Piedicolle in Umbria. The owner had assured me I could easily survive for five or six months on the amount I was going over there with; that Piedicolle was a small, charming town where hardly anyone spoke English, and where they had just built a brand new bar. Pictures she sent showed a wonderfully quaint-looking piazza right by her house. It sounded perfect and seemed the perfect way to ease myself back into Italy, without going right smack-dab into the chaos that was Rome. And besides, research into rents in Rome were proving quite high, and it felt better and smarter to start off somewhere smaller and affordable, while trying to research Rome or other cities while there and while looking for work.

I had gotten all my paperwork together and sent it to the Italian Consulate in Los Angeles in order to get my Italian/EU passport—the physical proof that I could legally live and work in Italy. The application was bad enough to fill out but I got it all together and sent it to the Consulate. "Perfect!" came the reply. "It shouldn't take more than two to three weeks since you have your letter stating you have citizenship." I let the consulate in Los Angeles know I had a place to rent and that's why I needed my EU passport so quickly, they for some reason just didn't care and weren't going to budge from behind their bureaucratic wall. As a side note, not all the Italian consulates in the States are that bad, but the LA one is known for this and has this reputation. It was just my luck that they oversaw my area. One day not too long after, they called to tell me they didn't have enough paperwork from me. She then felt compelled to grill me about why I didn't already have my Italian passport and why I didn't get it when I was a teenager, and why I didn't get it ten years ago, or fifteen years ago, and why I waited until this close to leaving time—I must say I so very much enjoyed that conversation! They concluded with informing me they were sending me back my pictures, money order, and letters and suggested that I wait and apply in Rome as they had my "file of information" and the LA consulate would have to create an entire "life" for me. Lovely.

Chapter 5

Making a Decision

Early 2002

Some may think this was a pretty easy decision to make, a no-brainer. But the decision was to give it all up, to leave everything one knows, all that is familiar, to leave all remaining family and friends, to take a flying leap out of the world that has become a safety net. I had become estranged from my brothers after our parents' deaths, had no relationship with my cousins, and had only my aunt there in the States—but life in Arizona was relatively comfortable, and it was a life I knew. I was safe in this little bubble. I had my few wine-tasting acquaintances with whom I'd share an evening at the wine shop and discuss our passion for the wines of the world. Travel on a vacation was one thing: picking up and moving was something entirely different.

Those ten days in Italy had felt so good, and I was still holding those feelings, flying high. I wanted to be back there; it filled my mind, my heart, my senses, everything that is me. At the same time, my stomach churned when I thought about it. It was a really scary idea, and I was full of thoughts: could I do this? Would it work? How in hell was I going to make money and support myself? Would my little savings even get more than a couple months? I constantly asked myself these questions as if I was some kind of idiot. Even though I didn't like being in the States anymore and it didn't feel right, I kept thinking I was being a fool to leave, to even think about it. I should just keep saving money and travel there occasionally, like others I knew. It was okay to think about it. But to actually do it, that was another matter altogether. It ran in my head—Stop it. *Okay*. Breathe. *I can't*.

I needed to talk about this, to bounce this idea off people. I needed to hear pros and cons. This sounded like a job for the wine shop group. I had discovered a wonderful, small, husband-and-wife-owned wine shop in Ahwatukee, an upscale suburb of Phoenix. Marla and Sam's passion for wine was contagious, as was their knowledge. They held regular, guided tastings every Friday and Saturday night, and you could usually find me there every single time. Whether a guided blind tasting, or a country night, or a varietal night, it became my second home. At the regular Friday night tasting was the same group of people, the ones I'd gotten to know through our commonality and the sharing our love of good wine.

After walking in a couple weeks later, I nearly lost it—"No, this can't be," I thought, "it's Italian night and Maurizio the wine importer is holding the tasting. This isn't what I'd call fair." Maurizio had moved to Phoenix from his native Italy only a few years before, and was eagerly asking me about my trip. He was the main importer for Italian wine that the shop chose to do business with. The paired food was from the Italian-owned deli down the street. Breathing deeply as I sat down with the group, I silently said to myself, *"Settle down, Maria. This is where you need to be right now."*

The Italian night group is a wonderful, amazing group of

people with whom I got along and usually had great conversations. We were all joined by our passion for the wines of the world, learning as much as we could through these tastings. Most everyone who joined these weekend tastings were middle-class people with decent jobs, all living in the various suburbs of Phoenix such as Ahwatukee, Chandler, Gilbert. Charlie and his wife, Carol; Tom and Sharon; Suzanne and Clarence. I made a conscious decision to make sure I ate enough and didn't go nuts on the tasting so the wine wouldn't go to my head—after all, a decision made while even close to being drunk often leads to a decision you're sorry you made.

As I heard Maurizio talk about all the wonderful Italian wines, in an accented English that was so familiar to me, the feeling began to come over me. At the end of the tasting, most left except for the group that usually stayed and started tasting the hidden stuff with Marla and Sam. Some were travelers, others not so much. Good. They were the ones I wanted to talk to. We had all previously talked about my trip when I was planning it, and our conversation naturally led to me revealing my feelings, and my thoughts. Taking a deep breath, I said, "Tell me, what should I do?"

One after the other, sometimes together, they told me.

"Go!" Marla said. "Are you kidding?"

"You have to take this chance," Charlie added.

"But what if it doesn't work?" was my only reply.

Sharon tilted her head, flipped her hand, and said, "Then you come back."

I sighed, closed my eyes as my head dropped, and said, "But if I give everything up, I won't have anything to come back to. No home, nothing."

The table was silent for a moment, until I heard Sharon's quiet voice: "Maria." Lifting my eyes, I looked at her as she said, "Can you live with not having taken the chance? Can you live with always thinking to yourself, for the rest of your life, 'if only I had tried it, just tried, made the attempt.' You've got the offer of a roof over your head for a few months, you have enough to live on there for six months. You don't have anyone to worry about or be concerned with except yourself, single, no kids."

"Well hell, when you put it that way," I laughingly said, as we all clinked glasses. Part of me was getting excited while we talked about this; at the same time my stomach began to churn again, and not from the wine.

It was from the fear.

The awful, overwhelming fear that it might not work out. And what if it didn't? I'd be in a foreign country, albeit a country known to me, but foreign nonetheless. How would I get back if I had to? Though I've flown a few times in my life, I am actually petrified of flying. I knew that if I got on another plane, I wanted that flight over to be the last one I took.

The conversation continued. "You really think I should do it?" I said. "Would you do it? In all truth, in all reality, knowing the uncertainty of it all, the not having a lot of money to live on, the not knowing what will happen in a few months when the rental time runs out. Would you give it all up, give up everything you know, leave everyone and everything that is familiar to you?"

The response was unanimous. "In a heartbeat," one said. "I would love it if someone gave me that opportunity," said another.

"I need to go home and sleep," I said as we finished off our glasses. "To think about everything all of you have said. You're my go-to group, and I knew I needed to bounce this off you all."

⸙ ⸙ ⸙

A few days later my dear friend Brent, a captain at a major airline, called me to go out to breakfast. Yes, I hate flying even though I have a very good friend who is a pilot and one of my brothers is a pilot. Brent had spent hour upon hour trying to get me over my fear, but it never worked. I can still hear him. "Just imagine a rock in a river, the water rushing over it, around it, this is air and this is a plane . . ." I would always respond, "Yeah, okay, whatever! I pretty much flunked all that science and gravity stuff." As we sat in the coffee shop, over a couple coffees and breakfast, we talked about this major decision I was trying to make. Though the place was busy, I didn't really hear any of the background chatter. I was focused in on trying to get some wisdom and trying to make a life decision. Though breakfast has always been one of my favorite meals, I don't think I ate much or tasted much, the food getting cold as I wrapped my hands around the warm coffee cup.

"Talk to me," Brent said, "What's going on in your head?"

"I'm not even sure I know myself, but I'll try," I said. I spent the next fifteen minutes just spitting everything out that was in my head, the fear, the doubts, after which his pearl of wisdom consisted of one line, one sentence. "I'll miss you so much," he said, "but if you don't take this chance, my whole opinion about you, your strength, your determination, your dreams and desires, will have been wrong."

I smacked my cup down with a loud exhale, not paying attention to the looks I know I got from the other diners. "Shit. Brent, you suck and that was so not fair and you know it!" I continued, "I am so scared, my friend. Do you understand me? Can you understand? What if I am still afraid when I get there, what if I get lonely, what if . . ."

"What if what?" he calmly replied, "I'm here, and always will be. You will always have your friends. When you get scared, you call me. When you get lonely, you pick up the phone. I will always be just a phone call away."

I felt small and young as I replied, "Really?"

With a nod and a huge grin, Brent set down his cup, took my hands from around my own coffee, and said, "Yep. Now that we have that settled, can I come with you?"

And I smiled. I even began to laugh a bit, telling him he could come with me if he was the one flying the plane, because somehow that would make a difference to me and my fear. As we toasted each other with our coffee cups, he gave me his oh-so-familiar wink, saying how he admired me and my ability to take such a chance. With a slow intake of breath, I simply shook my head a little. Never having been good at taking compliments of any kind, I softly said, "Please don't admire me, because truly this little show of bravado is simply that—a show." At that moment, I wanted him to come with me, because I wanted someone, anyone, with me. To hold my hand and make me feel secure about this. But I knew it was something I had to do on my own. It needed to work only because I made it work, by myself. With only my own strength, only my own determination.

As I looked in his smiling eyes, while thinking also about everything that was said to me at the wine shop, a small part of me began to relax a little, just a little. I felt like I'd been holding my breath. I wanted to exhale.

∽ ∽ ∽

The next morning when I woke, I was feeling excited. I went to visit my aunt, my mother's remaining sister and with whom she used to live, and as I walked around her house my eyes found all of my mother's collections that made her happy when she was alive. I lightly ran my fingers over those things and it was as if I could feel her. Her spirit that was still so alive in me, in my heart and mind, in my own soul, the blood coursing in my veins. People have always told me my eyes are so like hers were, even with so much of the same color. I felt like I was looking at these things of hers with her eyes.

I looked at a photo of her and, as always, talked to her in my head. "What should I do, Mom? I need you here with me, to help me make this decision." Clear as a bell—though it was probably my own mind knowing precisely what she would tell me, no ifs, ands or buts about it—I heard her reply, "There's no decision to be made, my girl. I taught you all your life to be strong, to use your head. Mostly I taught you to take chances and grab the opportunities that are offered, to live your life for all it's worth. I instilled in you a love for discovery of the world; for the journeys; a love for seeing everything there is to see. You may feel alone in this, but recognize the fact that there are people holding your hand through this fear. They're not going to let go. The most important thing I tried to teach you was to listen to yourself, because you know what's best for you. You know what to do."

An amazing thing then happened. Finally, I exhaled.

After all those years, after all my searching and all I had been through, my heart was glad and I felt an amazing sense of peace. In a few short weeks, a month at most, I would be going home. While I knew it wouldn't be easy and there were many hurdles ahead, I knew that this was right, and all the walls I hit and frustrations with bureaucracy had all been worth it, for they were bringing me peace. They were bringing me my roots, bringing me home. Italy had given me back what was buried deep inside me—my life. She was in my heart and soul, and had always been a part of me.

And so the preparations began, as I researched and purchased tickets, sold my old, junky car, packed up a few boxes of old yearbooks and knick-knacks, and packed three suitcases.

Now, I thought, *let the games begin!*

Part Two

Chapter 6

The Dream Happens

Piedicolle, Umbria, Italy
September 4, 2002

I sat in the main park there in the small village of Piedicolle, perched on a high hill way up in Umbria as the sun set, turning the vastness of the rolling hills of that green land into shades of golden orange and red. All I could see were the lights of Perugia way off in the distance, and a few lights dotting the few towns perched on their own hills. The park there is small, too small even for a soccer match, with no swings or playthings for children. A few benches sat here and there in the small space below the bar. Staring out at the quiet vastness, I reflected on the last year that had culminated in the past couple weeks. It had been a road of myriad emotions, excitement, joy, happiness, doubt, frustration, but through it all an underlying constant peace. All around me were the sounds of my new home, with few cars up on the hill and people speaking in the language that used to be mine but which was inherently different. This hill town, while physically close to Rome, was linguistically a long way from the Roman dialect I spoke so long ago.

Piedicolle is a small village and of course that "Piedicolle chatter" began as I checked out the bar that first evening, nodding and saying *buonasera* to the townsmen standing around in the bar. The question in their eyes was clear: who was this unknown woman walking in?

"Ah, it must be the Americana we saw getting out of the car and walking up the street with suitcases," one whispered to his table of companions.

Taking my *gelato* in hand, I walked up and down the two streets that formed a horseshoe shape, marveling at the stone houses, each connected. There were about thirty or so of these houses forming the horseshoe around the central church serving as the village square, all built around 400-700 AD. Inside the church the stone walls immediately blocked out any sounds from outside and I could suddenly understand why so many found sanctuary in a place such as this. The air cooled the skin and it was so quiet one could hear themselves breathe. It was typically Catholic; the walls lined with the Stations of the Cross icons in gold. On each side of the aisle were about eight small pews that looked to hold perhaps ten each comfortably. The altar was understated and simple with its few candles and icons, and made for a very inviting sanctuary. The bell in the tower broke the silence of a day, calling the faithful to enter. Two large stone plaques on its wall were dedicated to the brave men of this village, called to serve their country, and lost to various battles. Reading the names reminds all who come here, that even a village this small has its story.

The street I lived on ended at a curve that led to the second street of houses; on the curve was a wall, perfect for sitting and gazing out at the amazing view of the Umbrian countryside. There were lights scattered where villages with their own stone houses surrounding churches and bell towers dotted the hills. The air smelled crisp and clean from the day's rain showers, with a slight cool breeze gently blowing. I breathed in the cool, clean air and marveled at the quiet. There was no noise, save for an occasional dog's bark and cat's mewing, and the quiet footfalls on the cobblestones of someone returning home. I found it nearly impossible to believe that two short days ago I had left the oppressive heat of a desert city of asphalt where quiet was impossible to imagine, as police helicopters flew overhead constantly, looking for someone, and sirens became a background noise and part of everyday life. High up in these hills, nothing else seemed to exist.

With the bedroom window open later to catch the slight breeze, the air had cooled somewhat. The quiet was intoxicating: it filled my ears and soothed my mind. I could feel my spirit beginning to calm.

The followings days of the first week were spent attempting to get used to these surroundings, getting my computer hooked up to the Internet, stocking up on some groceries by getting a ride from the owner, and starting to get to know my new town. As I had never met the owner of the house nor seen it or the town before coming here, I had relied on, and trusted, what she related to me about both. Although some of what she had told me was true, most was not, such as the rent she was requesting for her house being reasonable for this area; how large (or small) the village was; and the fact that while there was a bar, it was quite small, not open every day (and when it was, it was open only in the evening for two to three hours). It would've been nice to have been told that the road leading to the village was long, steeply twisting and turning (as you get close to the top, newer homes line the road, where most of the population of 60 live); that there were no buses that come up here and that the road was far too steep to walk, except for the young and super-fit, or those with a car or motorbike. Which every villager had. Or that, even more important than anything else, a car was necessary because there was no market or shop in the village. Surprise! Live and learn, I suppose!

Chapter 7

A Comedy of Errors: the Non-Shakespearean Version

So you think you want to move to Italy, eh? Well then take heed, dear reader, for this is what you may have to contend with. With all due respect to Shakespeare, who would turn over in his grave at this, I'll share with you my travails of getting from Arizona to Umbria, featuring bureaucracy at its finest. Though the moral of a story always goes at the end, I'll cheat and give it to you now: patience, grasshopper. Our players are:

Maria—she who just wants an apostilled birth certificate

LA—she who started this play due to incompetency

Rome—the bureaucratic experts

FS—all she wants is my apostilled birth certificate

Q—the Questura, city police

Mun—Municipio, Municipal office in each county

* * *

Act 1, Scene 1

Open on a beautiful spring day in Phoenix, late April. The sun is shining, the sky is blue, Maria walks to her mailbox, expecting bills. Upon opening it she finds a letter addressed to her from Rome. Barely able to breathe, she tears it open. On the official Comune of Rome letterhead is a statement of citizenship. It tells her to send the letter to LA, who will then issue an EU passport based on said citizenship.

Act 1, Scene 2

Cut to Maria in May compiling a package of both the original and a copy of Rome's letter, both the original and a copy of the application for the passport, originals of a letter from the Vice-Consul of Phoenix attesting to authenticity of documents, two pictures for the passport, copies of her US passport and secondary identification, and everything else listed as required, and then mailing said letter overnight via FedEx to LA. Italian music plays in background.

Act 1, Scene 3

It is June 2002. The phone rings.

Maria: Hello?

LA: Is this Maria?

Maria: Yes it is.

LA: I have your package in front of me.

Maria: Wonderful!

LA: But there's a problem.

Maria: Oh? I included everything that was listed as required.

LA: I can't issue this passport.

Maria: Why not?

LA: Where did you originally receive your Italian citizenship?

Maria: In Italy.

LA: When?

Maria: 1972 or thereabouts.

LA: Why didn't you get a passport then?

Maria: Pardon?

LA: Why do you not have an Italian passport already?

Maria: Because I was 12 years old.

LA: So?

Maria: Ma'am, I was a child—my parents took care of all that.

LA: Do they have your passport?

Maria: I don't believe so, or at least I've never seen one.

LA: Have you asked them?

Maria: I can't, they're both deceased.

LA: Well, why didn't you get the passport later?

Maria: I didn't need it, I had returned to the States.

LA: Why didn't you get one after that?

Maria: Because I wasn't going to Italy then! Could you please explain what any of this has to do with my request now?

LA: Well I can't issue it because I have no history on you and there is none on our computers.

Maria: You have a letter from Rome stating I have Italian citizenship.

LA: This letter means nothing to us.

Maria: It's from the government of Rome, which oversees you, and it means nothing to you? *Maria is beginning to get sarcastic, probably not smart when talking to a consulate who can issue her passport.*

Maria: The letter said to simply give you the letter and that was the authorization you needed to issue the passport.

LA: If your citizenship was issued in Rome, then they have your history information.

Maria: I'm not presently in Rome. I'm in Phoenix. You're my area Italian Consulate.

LA: That doesn't matter.

Maria: Why not? *(sound of fingers beginning to tap on table)*

LA: It would take at least a year for you to get this passport because we would have to create an entire history for you from the day you got here.

Maria: Ma'am, I leave for Italy in three months and have the possibility of a job, and need the passport to legally work there.

LA: Why did you wait so long to request the passport from us?

Maria: I sent you the letter and documents as soon as I received them from Rome, and besides that I'm in Phoenix and you're in LA.

LA: The only way you're going to be able to do this is to wait until you get to Rome and then get your passport there.

Maria: But they told me I had to get it from you.

LA: Well they're wrong.

Maria: They're the government of Rome.

LA: I don't care. They're wrong. This letter from them isn't authentic. I'll send you the documents back, using your prepaid overnight mail that you included, and you take them with you to Rome. We can't help you anymore.

Maria: Even though I'm an Italian citizen and you're the Italian Consulate?

LA: Do not get rude with me.

Maria: Ma'am, I'm not being rude, but I am a little frustrated. *We see a stuffed animal being thrown across the room.*

LA: You should have your documents by tomorrow.

Maria: Okay. (said to dead air as click of phone hanging up by LA is heard)

Act 1, Scene 4

It is September, 2002. Maria moves to Italy, believing what LA told her about where to do this paperwork, and spends a week in Rome to get paperwork done. She learns the new term "playing with the government."

Maria: (handing letter to passport worker) I have this letter . . .

Rome: Are you in the computer?

Maria: I don't know.

Rome: I should check.

Maria: Thanks.

Rome: Well here you are!

Maria: Yay!

Rome: But there's a problem.

Maria: Why doesn't this surprise me?
Rome: You were granted Italian citizenship in the 1970s.
Maria: Yes.
Rome: But you have zeros in front of your number.
Maria: And this means . . .
Rome: This means you are not here.
Maria: I'm not where?
Rome: Here.
Maria: I am.
Rome: But you are zeroed out.
Maria: I think I'm confused.
Rome: *(speaking to co-worker)* Go to the archives and find the original application card.

Maria waits with her Italian friend, speaking quietly, while Rome stares at his computer screen. 15 minutes later the co-worker arrives, faded yellow index card in hand.

Maria: Oh look, it's a card filled out by my father and someone here.
Rome: Ah.
Maria: Ah?
Rome: Here you are. You arrived in 1971.
Maria: Yes.
Rome: And emigrated to America in 1977.
Maria: Yes.
Rome: But we have no other information on you after that.
Maria: Because we were living in America.
Rome: Which means we essentially lost you.

Maria: But I'm here.
Rome: And now we've found you.
Maria: And . . .
Rome: Now I'm not sure what to do with you.
Maria: (*wishing she had a stuffed animal to throw*) Give me a passport or identity card maybe?
Rome: No, we can't do that.
Maria: Because . . .
Rome: Because there are zeros in front of your number.
Maria: Remove the zeros.
Rome: Can't.
Maria: Why not?
Rome: Because you're blocked.
Maria: Unblock me. I'm right here.
Rome: Are you a resident of Rome?
Maria: I've only been in Italy a week. I'm living in Umbria.
Rome: Then you need to do this in Umbria.
Maria: Am I in their computers?
Rome: No.
Maria: So how do I do this?
Rome: You need to register, then get a *permesso di soggiorno* (*residency permit, good for a year*), and then apply for your identity card.
Maria: Aren't *permessos* only issued to foreigners?
Rome: Yes.
Maria: Are they issued to dual citizens?
Rome: No.

Maria: Then how do I get a *permesso*?

Rome: You can't.

Maria: ....

Rome: You must apply on your American passport.

Maria: How do I apply for the Italian identity card if I have an American *permesso*?

Rome: You will be able to do it.

Maria: How?

Rome: Ask in Umbria.

ACT 2, SCENE 1

January 2003. Maria applies and receives, four months later, certification of rental residency in Umbria. She decides to leave Umbria, staying in Rome for six weeks and then moving on. Umbria tells her she must do all paperwork in Rome.

(At Questura (police) office)

Maria: I've been told to come here for my passport.

Q: *(taking rental residency paper)* This is not a certification of residency.

Maria: But I was told it was by the questura in Umbria.

Q: It is not.

Maria: *(producing Rome letter)* This states I have citizenship and am in the computers of Rome.

Q: We need a certification of your citizenship.

Maria: This is all I have.

Q: You need to get a certification. Are you a resident of Rome?

Maria: I just moved here yesterday from Umbria.

Q: Go to the Comune, get the certification, do a new rental residency for Rome and take both papers, along with two witnesses who will swear you are you, to the Municipal offices and they are obligated to give you an identity card.

Maria: Really.

Q: Yes.

Maria: You're sure about this.

Q: Absolutely.

ACT 2, SCENE 2

On telephone to Comune, next day.

Maria: Help. *(fade to three minutes later after full explanation)*

Rome: If you are in the computers in Rome, you need only go to the municipal office and they will need nothing else to issue you an identity card.

Maria: Really.

Rome: Yes.

Maria: You're sure about this.

Rome: Absolutely.

ACT 2, SCENE 3

At municipal office, same day.

Maria: I'm trying to get an identity card or passport based on my Italian citizenship.

Mun.:   You have Italian citizenship?

Maria: Yes ma'am.

Mun.:   Your passport please.

Maria: *(produces US passport)*
Mun.: This is an American passport.
Maria: Yes.
Mun.: Where's your Italian passport?
Maria: I don't have one.
Mun.: Why not?
Maria: I'm trying to get one!
Mun.: You have dual citizenship?
Maria: I do. If you look in the computer, you'll find my information.
Mun.: *(pounding on keyboard)* Is this you?
Maria: It is.
Mun.: I can't issue you a passport.
Maria: Why not?
Mun.: Because you have no address on file.
Maria: I've just moved here.
Mun.: Have you received residency?
Maria: I just moved here two days ago.
Mun.: Wait.
Maria: *(sound of head pounding on wall while waiting for woman to return from talking to supervisor)*
Mun.: Okay we have the solution.
Maria: Oh good.
Mun.: We can issue you an address as a foreigner.
Maria: Okay.
Mun.: Fill out this form, and bring it back to us with a copy of your birth certificate, a certification of your residency in America, and take it all to the Comune.

Maria: I don't have a copy of my birth certificate.

Mun.: The American Consulate can help you get that. They have procedures for obtaining them. Just tell them what you need it for and they will print out a certification of your birth and residency.

Maria: And once I get this?

Mun.: The Comune can issue you an identity card.

Maria: Really?

Mun.: Yes.

Maria: You're sure about this.

Mun.: Absolutely.

ACT 2, SCENE 4

On phone to Comune with same person as before, same day.

Maria: Help.

Rome: What happened? *(fade for three minutes of explanation)*

Maria: So now what?

Rome: Go to municipal office and fill out a declaration that you live here. They will send the police out within 10-15 days to check to see that you live there. They will then fill out a form with your address, stating you live there. Take that form to the Comune and they can insert the address into the computer.

Maria: And this will work.

Rome: Yes.

After hanging up phone, Maria returns to Questura since it's only five minutes away, to ask if she can fill out the form there instead. They say no because the municipal police are a different branch from the

Questura. In an attempt to help, cut to activity between Questura and Maria trying to figure it all out.

Maria: They said I needed to get my birth certificate and other documents.

Q: You don't need all that.

Maria: They said I did.

Q: Let me call them. *(fade as police call Comune)*

Q: Okay.

Maria: Okay what?

Q: You need the birth certificate and other documents.

Act 3, Scene 1

Rome Comune, citizenship office, February–March. Maria decides to go to the source of the initial citizenship letter.

Maria: Hello. I have this letter signed by an "FS," and I was wondering if this person exists and if I could speak with her.

FS: That's me. And you are?

Maria: The Maria you sent this to.

FS: Hello! How can I help you?

Maria: Well, since you wrote the letter, I figured perhaps you may be able to straighten out the ridiculous mess of paperwork I seem to have become entangled in.

FS: *(smiling)*

Maria: Easier said than done?

FS: Let's see what we can do.

Many moments later, after lengthy discussion of the convoluted mess:

FS: LA should've done all this for you. They said we didn't have the authority nor the knowledge?

Maria: Mmhmm

FS: *(Maria hears for the first time in a long time some choice Italian words . . .)*

* * *

This is the end of this part of our play, as the remainder involved getting a copy of my birth certificate, having it translated into Italian, sending that copy to New Jersey to get an apostilled copy of it and having it sent back to me. This involved FedEx, people at the New Jersey Secretary of State's office, an old Slow Travel friend living there who helped me out, and then getting everything sent back to me. *Spoiler alert: this little play possibly could have been resolved shortly after its first six months, but bureaucracy just doesn't work that way; after much more back-and-forth that even involved yet another small town, it did finally get resolved in December of 2008.*

    Thanks for attending the play! Exit stage right.

CHAPTER 8

BACK TO THE HILLS AND LIFE IN A SMALL UMBRIAN VILLAGE

Though the little play above spanned a few years, the second part's trip to Rome for documentation began only a mere two weeks after arriving in Piedicolle. I had known I'd be knee-deep in frustrations that would cause me to question why I had ever taken this leap, but with the help of others to keep me calm, grounded, and not lose hope, I was determined to make this work.

While waiting in the train station to leave, I sat and watched the life going on around me. Train stations are always wonderful places to people-watch, where people from all walks of life come to use these services. Rome Termini of course is huge, an absolute hustle-and-bustle den of activity, with people coming and going from everywhere. As I waited for my train, I watched them, thinking about what glorious adventures they were coming from or going to. Was theirs a trip filled with joy or sadness? I wondered if they wished to ever return to where they were coming from. My own trip had been one of old memories and old friends, and I'm very happy to say that it included some new friends I met at my small hotel: a husband-and-wife reception/

cleaning team, who invited me to their home in a country I'd never been to, Romania, and the region of Transylvania. I was shown pictures of their home, family, friends, and even a traditional wedding, of which they explained the details of the ceremony and clothes. Maybe one day I will be able to take a little trip sometime there, and see the land described to me as clean and beautiful, the forests thick and lush, the mountains numerous amidst clean air.

Entering the hills of northern Lazio and southern Umbria, I was glad to be returning, at least for a while, to the smaller towns and cities. There is a bit less stress, it's less "touristy". I was pleased with the progress my language had made in the week of dealing with officials, and felt I was beginning to get into the groove of my new life. Having no car, I was basically relying on public transportation and the occasional taxi/car service, or new acquaintances to help out. It wasn't an easy three months, but I found, and made friends with, a wonderful car/taxi company in Marsciano, the nearest city to Piedicolle, called *TAM Autonoleggi*. Owned and operated by brothers, Raniero and Luciano, I used them constantly, as they drove everywhere throughout Umbria, Tuscany and Lazio and both spoke English. Luciano really helped me out a lot in my months there, ferrying me places I needed to go—in turn, I helped him with his English. A good trade-off. Even though he would sometimes just pick me up from the train station if I'd gone somewhere, he remained professional throughout, always showing up in a suit and tie. I was so happy to have found them; they were life-savers.

~ ~ ~

It didn't take long to discover some new things about my adopted home—I learned that although the elders have an entirely different dialect than what I knew in Rome, they felt I spoke and understood the language well. That one sentiment would always bring a huge grin to my face and made me feel that I just might, indeed, be okay in this new life. They were forever patient with my attempts to speak the language, and when I would begin to show frustration at not being able to find the correct words, they never got impatient, merely telling me to go slowly and the words would come. I also found out that the elderly man who brought water and other drinks up to the main piazza was, although a huge flirt, completely harmless and so very helpful in correcting my language errors. Without him I wouldn't have found the village house that doubled as a market of sorts, carrying most daily food staples and easily walked to.

I began to get more comfortable, though not happy, as I learned that in many of the not-easily accessible hill towns, two delivery vans/cars arrived a couple times a week; one bringing various breads, the other various canned goods and vegetables and fruits. These deliveries are vitally important to those who live up the long hill and cannot simply walk to "the closest store." The various "adopted moms" all promised to not only yell out when they arrived, but to also knock on my door to let me know—just in case I didn't hear all the yelling. While that was enough to make me feel a part of the town, it was when three different people offered to pick up some cheese or eggs or anything else I might need the next time they went to the store that I felt a renewed sense of belonging in this country that I had adopted so long ago. With it came a sense of acceptance in this small village, not an easy feat. Thought I doubted I would ever cease to be *l'americana*, I kept on learning and, with time, realized that this just might turn out to be one of the best decisions I had ever made.

Mid-September 2002

As time went on in this small village, I seemingly became everyone's daughter, needing to be taken care of, even though I was in my 40s. The women remained my teachers of the language, forever patient and always proud when I said the same sentence later correctly without help. They had asked previously if I was here alone and somehow this resulted in my transformation into the 'town needy project,' as this was a situation foreign to them. Going off on your own, especially as a woman, leaving the family nest and home, just didn't happen here. If I went away for a day, they asked how long I'd be gone and when I'd be returning. When I returned from a day-and-overnight trip to Verona, one remarked to me that she thought I had left without saying goodbye; others gave me pure hell for getting into Luciano's car and not telling them where I was going and what I was doing.

"Maria! Maria!" I turned and saw Flavia, one of the older village residents, ambling towards me quickly.

"Yes ma'am? What's happened?" I said as I closed the door of Luciano's car and waved while he drove away.

Grabbing me in a bear hug, Flavia cried. "You're back! You had your suitcase and I thought you'd left and didn't say goodbye to me!"

"Aww, no, I'd never do that. I only went to go visit a friend for a day or so in Verona."

She looked at me in horror and said, "Alone?"

I think Luciano began to get used to waiting for me. There were plenty of other times when the village women would stop me from getting in his car, look him up and down as he held the door open for me, and ask me questions.

"Where do you think you're going, Maria?" Daria asked me once.

"Just going to Deruta to visit a friend," I replied, putting my hand on the car door.

"And when will you be back? What time?" Daria placed one hand on the door handle and the other on her hip. I knew this was going to take a minute. I could see Luciano calmly waiting, a little smile on his face and humor in his eyes, as he winked at me.

With a sigh and a smile, I said "Daria, mama, I love you for caring about me."

When answering their questions about what I was planning for lunch and dinner one day, and replying that I was going to have a sandwich for lunch and perhaps a nice steak and salad for dinner, I was promptly told (a bit forcefully) that I was to start eating like an Italian—steak or pasta was for lunch, and sandwiches were for dinner. In my mid-40s, I had no alternative but to reply, "Yes ma'am."

Daria lived two doors down and had adopted me almost from the day I moved in. She patiently helped me with my Italian and made sure I had anything I needed. Though she constantly worried about me, just as she did with her actual daughters, I think she actually admired what I had done. I don't think she fully understood it and wasn't too keen about the whole "alone" thing, but there was something she admired. While sitting outside enjoying the air one evening, she came to me and asked if I was able to get to the grocery store. When I responded that I could if a friend was available, she replied that she was going the next morning and would be happy to take me with her. I think this caring concept is normal for small village life anywhere in the world. In all of the various shops we went to, Daria seemed to be having a great time helping me choose which products were the best in and from this area, which oil, cheeses, olives. It was great to learn of the regional treasures. The protection could get to be a little bit much sometimes, honestly; she remarked that I was coughing a lot and maybe should get some medicine from the pharmacy. I explained that I was simply getting a bit of a cold and would be fine. I swear for the next week I was constantly asked how I was doing, if I was okay, making numerous suggestions for making sure I ate and drank right and got enough sleep.

A tip: while in a small town in Italy, do not ever go sit outside in the sunshine to dry your hair after washing it. Never do this! It will result in a group of women coming out to you (that old Piedicolle chatter-line) insisting that, if you weren't sick before, you definitely will be now. You must never ever go out with wet hair. This then became a major discussion of how I was feeling, how my cold was, did I sleep last night. I begged them to stop fussing over me as I was an adult, which resulted in them basically ignoring what I said as they commenced to discussing what they felt was best for me. I could do nothing but smile. Oh, but I did get my patience rewarded with a freshly baked, piping hot pizza made with parmigiano reggiano on a plate wrapped up for me. They knew I liked the fresh pizza brought by the woman who delivered the fresh bread, a simple pizza dough with a light dusting of tomato on top that kept well for a couple days. This homemade pizza with the parmigiano mixed into the dough seemed to me more of the consistency of an American cornbread, very light and airy and the aroma of the parmigiano was absolutely heady when hot. It was heavenly, soft and moist. When I remarked how incredibly tasty it was, the biggest smile I've ever seen burst onto the woman's face, followed by a group discussion of everything that would taste good on top of it, in the middle of it, and even alongside it. I merely listened to it all, wishing I hadn't eaten a fresh mozzarella and prosciutto sandwich on ciabatta bread a half hour earlier for lunch.

October, 2002

One evening a few days later, when I walked out of my door to take a stroll, I was hit with a cold slight wind; when I looked up I was immediately held in awe as I gazed at the clearest of skies. The stars were already coming out, bursting forth in all their glory, the Big Dipper, the Little Dipper, Orion's Belt, and many others I cannot name. They were brightly lighting up the sky as if to say: *see us! Gaze upon us! We have been here, you just haven't been able to see us for the nights have not been clear enough, the breeze not enough to blow away all the clouds keeping us from you.* I walked down to the park and was again taken aback by the lights from the city of Perugia, as bright as the stars, trailing down the hills. *Look at me, see how beautiful I am situated here in these hills,* it whispered into the wind. Looking to my right, I saw the smaller towns, their bell towers lit, dotting the hilltops. *We have been here all this time,* they seemed to say to me, *waiting for nights such as these to make your spirit soar.*

It was a fitting end to a gentle day that had shown me a very personal slice of life, as Daria and her husband had invited me to go with them to make a few stops in a couple towns and then to journey to the town of Daria's birth. She wanted to go visit her parents' and ancestors' gravesites and place some flowers. I was honored, a foreigner, to be invited to observe such a personal ritual. After stopping in a few places and not only practicing my language but getting many impromptu verb lessons in the process, with people looking on and laughing as I stood beside the car repeating verb conjugations with Daria, we drove up into the hills to Casalinga. The bulk of the village sits seemingly quite precariously on a hill, the attached stone homes tumbling down the hill.

We stopped beside a beautiful grove of trees and vineyard and, gathering up the flowers, entered the gate to step inside the wonderfully kept cemetery for this and the surrounding couple villages. I followed them to the family crypt with a small, decorative gate. Inside held two families; on the right side, Daria pointed out and explained who each person was to her. These village cemeteries usually always have a picture of each person buried there, and as I looked at each one, I saw Daria's kind eyes and gentle smile. As they began to arrange flowers, reciting quiet prayers, I quietly and respectfully retreated and walked around the grounds, reading the words and putting faces to names. It suddenly came to mind that I had done this exact same thing so many years ago, wandering the cemetery in my ancestral home in Sicily, seeing my own eyes reflecting back. I heard Daria call to me, waving me back over; she took me then to her husband's family's crypt, explaining all his relations as well. As we left and drove away, I felt honored that they had shared this with me.

We stopped in Marsciano as it was market day and for some reason Daria decided I needed some thick, warm socks for the coming cold weather. How did I ever make it to my mid-40s? It was a definite lesson watching her at work, bartering for those socks! Something as small as this seems silly to write about, but coupled with the atmosphere, it simply served to make me feel a part of it all. A part of life here in these small towns in Italy.

Late October, 2002

It was olive harvest time in Umbria, and a couple days before I'd been out taking a walk on the road out of town that led into the hills when the most amazing thing happened. I stopped and stood looking up at Collazzone; hearing my name called, I turned to see Daria standing underneath an olive tree. She waved me over and, without really seeing what she was doing, I innocently asked if there was anything I could help her with.

For the next two days we stripped all eight of their trees of all the olives . . . it was certainly a sight that first day, having no idea what I was doing as I tried to match her experienced movements. "Take a branch in your hand and pull quickly downwards, releasing all the olives into a bucket," Daria said as she demonstrated, "it's easy." She almost couldn't continue because she was laughing too hard at my continued "Ouch," "Oh!" and "*Managia!*" I commenced to merely picking them one-by-one by hand as I couldn't tolerate the continued sticking I was getting.

After trudging back up the hill to the house as it started raining, I was amazed at how good I felt—though I couldn't remember having ever been that tired. It was wonderful to be out in the cool air, performing a time-honored yearly tradition, the picking of the olives. The following day, she took pity on me and gave me a little hand-held rake specifically designed to take the place of the hands pulling downwards on the branches. As we walked down to the field, a few of the village women stopped us to ask where we were going and after she explained that I was helping her pick the olives, I think I may have inadvertently promised to help another of the women with this or some other chore—everyone was talking in dialect and I just kept saying "*Si*" and "Okay!" I figured I'd find out if someone knocked on my door and asked if I was ready. It wasn't as cold or rainy; with a smile on my face, I felt like a pro as I stood underneath each of the two trees I was assigned, feet planted firmly on the net on the ground so as not to crush any of the fallen olives, and expertly raked each branch, causing all the glorious olives to fall. The work was fun and I found myself thinking, "Am I really standing here underneath these trees picking olives in Italy?" The best part? She told me she would give me the bottles of the oil made from "my" olives, and I couldn't wait to taste it.

A couple days later I went with them to take the olives to the small, family-owned press to produce the oil. Inside the small building was a fireplace where we cooked a little meal while keeping an eye on the olives being cleaned, stripped, chugged up into the crushing machine; after a little while, we held bottles under the spigot to be filled with the most headily aromatic, indescribably green, pure Umbrian oil gold. Running my finger under it, I knew I had never until that moment tasted anything so delicious. Walking into my house later that evening with three bottles made from my olives, I realized my previous not-too-great mood had entirely vanished; I fell into bed with a light heart full of wonder at the last few days. These people had welcomed me, included me in their family dinners. All the times I had gone next door for coffee, Daria had listened to me whenever I was feeling lonely, scared at the magnitude of what I'd done, or helped me work out my recent decision, or given me her untiring help with the language. Without it, I wouldn't have been able to stay there for as long as I had.

I still to this day smile when I remember . . . I hand-picked olives, in a little village up in the Umbrian hills!

Early November, 2002

From early 2000 I had been a member of an online travel board dedicated to slow travel, appropriately named "Slow Travel." Through that message board I met so many amazing people with whom I remained friends throughout the years; in the beginning, they were my sounding board as I bounced ideas about where to go if I made the move, and they followed my daily journey to my school reunion also. During November, I'd gotten word that two fellow ST members, Barb and Art, were coming to Piedicolle and staying in the same house I'd rented. Then, a few weeks or so after, a woman named Deborah and a couple of her friends were going to Umbria— she was planning on coming to the village where we'd meet up. It was so cool that people were coming to my little part of these hills, and really helped get me out of my little funk.

While Barb and Art were not actually my guests, they had been booked in as renters for two weeks, and we ended up being co-renters and sharing the house, due to, why mince words here, a greedy landlord not cancelling either reservation. I didn't mind much, because it was great fun meeting and spending time with them. I was fortunate that we got along so well that they took me nearly everywhere with them as they searched the towns of Umbria looking for their new home. I was like a kid in a candy store as I saw more of Umbria's treasures in those two weeks than I could ever have hoped. Medieval villages and towns galore, some old and small, others larger and more modern.

Sunday, November 3, found us in yet another medium-sized town watching the Remembrance Day parades (the day itself is the 4th, but as it was a Monday that year, all ceremonies and parades were being held on the Sunday before). It was a sight to behold, like the same parades held throughout the world, as everyone stopped in respect as the procession exited the town church and weaved its way out the center walls, the Italian flag held high as old soldiers, still able to fit into their uniforms, albeit a bit snugly, walked proudly in front of the younger ones—every button shining in the sunlight, eyes staring straight ahead. What were they seeing? Perhaps their staring eyes were simply remembering. As I watched them go by, each drumbeat seemed to say to me, 'you may not agree with the reason for the war, but you cannot help but feel respect for these men and women.' I remember those that I had lost, and I think that's what they wanted all of us to remember. That morning I felt fortunate to see nearly this same procession in my own little village, though much smaller. Every town and every village has its story.

I loved Umbria in all its glory before those last two weeks, but found that I had become entirely enthralled with its beauty as I saw more and more of it. It is, after all, called 'The Green Heart of Italy'. The incredible shades of greens of the hills, sunflowers, vineyards and olive trees stretch seemingly forever, rolling into the surrounding mountains. Small winding roads where tiny villages rest in the curves and valleys, their vistas take your breath away and nearly bring tears in their beauty. You think, who are the people living there? How long has their village been there? What are the stories tucked away inside their walls? I wanted to know.

After Barb and Art left, Deborah arrived. Though not staying in Piedicolle, she came up to see me, bringing with her a much-desired new pair of sneakers. I have always had sort of large and wide feet, and it is next to impossible to find comfortable, affordable sneakers that fit in Italy. After showing her around the village, we got into her car and went to a great little trattoria nearby, spending a wonderful few hours laughing, talking, drinking wine, and making a lifelong connection. I love my Slow Travs, as we all think the same about travel and seeing the world. Even long after the website and message board closed down, we have all remained friends on social media.

Late November, 2002

The past few weeks had been filled mainly with doing what I came to do, speaking as much Italian as possible and learning, getting back into the Italian way of life. Being there and seeing those friends also helped to cement some decisions that I had made. So much that happened in the last three months not only sent my mind to spinning, but also produced clarity, if that was even possible. While I very much enjoyed this small slice of life in this village, and had been happy to be adopted by them as one of their own, I decided to leave Piedicolle and take an apartment in a larger town or city. It was fun gathering with the other villagers and waiting for the bread truck every other day, the vegetable and fresh produce truck once a week, and walking down to the staples market in a villager's garage. I feel fortunate to have participated in, and been a part of, these people's lives.

There is something exceptional about small villages like this—the inhabitants are born here and will die here. Most marriages are inter-village in this tiny part of the region; the husband or wife being from the next hill village a couple miles away. Their daily lives are a routine of cleaning, cooking, eating, sitting outside and visiting with each other in a large group twice a day, bouncing each other's grandchildren on their knees, caring for the village stray cats. It seems mundane and boring to many, but there is a fact that remains; they are content. Their village is tranquility defined. Their lives are free from the stress and strife of the city. I found I couldn't fault this, and even envied it in a way. However, it was time to move on. To a place where there was more to see, more streets to walk and people to talk to. I knew I would enjoy not having to plan ahead to a time when I could get to a butcher shop for meat, and enjoy not having to find the woman with the keys to the tobacco "shop." Going to a bar at any point in the day would be a treat as well. It had been a wonderful couple months, and I'd done what I came to do for the first while, but there comes a time to move on and branch out, using what I'd learned about not only Italy, but myself as well. The fact remained, though, that I would miss my little village, my little slice of tranquility. There would be no more nights of silence so heavy as to be near-deafening, but there would be more chance for more adventures.

Lessons from Small-town Italy

Before I leave off describing this area, there are a few lessons I learned, good and bad, that I took with me and that, perhaps, you can use if you are thinking about calling a small Italian village home.

Never refuse when someone invites you in for a coffee—it's considered rude, and is a part of life.

Life in a small Italian village is not always as romantic and wonderful as it seems. Like any small town anywhere, there are problems and frustrations. There is nothing so interesting as a piece of gossip to occupy people's minds. I found that everyone seemed to know when I left and came back, and the first things out of their mouth were always: 'Where have you been?' and 'How did you get there?' When I responded that I had gone with a friend, the next question was: 'Who?' A simple visit from a male friend gave fuel for a couple days' worth of gossip.

These small hill towns are often quite remote, and while the peace, quiet and tranquility seem ideal, one is far from the mental stimulation of a larger area. A car is essential and to leave the town requires its use. Depending on its remoteness, one must be prepared to do a lot of driving. Because so many are born and raised in these small towns and never leave, minds are seemingly often closed as a result.

These things are difficult for a generation used to being mobile, with minds eager to see and do and experience. I do not fault the life lived in these small villages, as their tranquility is admirable and even enviable. I will always look back on my months there with kind words and fond remembrances of those who took me in and made me a part of their community. I will remember being addressed with terms of endearment, dinners in their homes, invitations for coffee, and knocks on the door from people standing there holding something homemade as a gift for me. I will also remember those who were not so kind, as there are mean-spirited people everywhere, those who do not accept "outsiders."

But such is life in a small town, even in a country as beautiful as Italy.

Chapter 9

And the Plans They Keep on a'Changin'!

Mid-December, 2002

I'm sure it's probably clear by now that I really shouldn't even attempt the whole "plan" thing. This time, I'd decided to go visit Rome for six weeks—inside, I was a little concerned as it was a long time to be in a huge, bustling and hustling city when I'd been in such a small village for so long. I wondered if I would miss the quiet; I wasn't sure because there's something to be said for the noise of many people living life. However, I had decided that after my little six-week break I wouldn't be returning to Piedicolle but going a bit further north to Florence for three months. How did this come about? Well, the same friends who had the apartment in Rome also had one in Florence and offered it to me to rent. This couple was the same one I knew from Phoenix, and were the ones I turned to when I received the letter from the Comune about my citizenship. Their Florence apartment was a big two-bedroom, two-bath place and I wouldn't be renting it alone; Lynda, a woman I met on an Italy expats board, had done the same thing with her life that I had done a few months before, was about my age, had led an almost parallel life as mine, and we got along great. The perfect person to share a place with. (As I write this so many years later, she and I have remained great friends.) I'd decided to only rent it for three months to start because I wasn't sure what would happen after that. I did know that I'd have better options in Florence, and that the probability of work in Rome—not to mention affordable rentals—was pretty slim. In a few months the tourism season would be starting, giving me more options for work. After that—who knew?

    Anyway, needless to say I was about as excited as could be. Christmas time in my vibrant and beautiful Rome, and the start of a new year in wonderful Florence—which I hadn't seen in nearly 30 years. I love change!

Chapter 10

Greetings from Florence!

February 2003

Ah, Firenze—what an ageless, timeless and glorious city! Its quiet beauty calls to all those who wish to partake in the incredible bevy of art in all its forms. Around every corner is another hidden treasure; those who wish to escape the maddening crowds of the more famous sites are rewarded for their forays down the narrow side streets, don't close your eyes or you may miss an old convent-turned-school, now closed down, where as you enter the door to the garden you feel you have stepped back in time. The noise of the city outside is gone and you understand why this was a place of refuge; the garden is well-maintained and the columns surrounding it reflect its age. A large door beckons you to enter the simple chapel where, once inside, your senses are almost assaulted by the simplicity enmeshed within the detailed art that fills the ceiling. An ancient organ's pipes spire towards the colors of the ceiling.

Tourist season was not yet in full swing and the streets were manageable as I decided to play tourist in my new home for a while before "getting down to business." Lynda was set to arrive in a couple weeks, and it was fun to try to get know this little neighborhood so I could play tour guide when she arrived. Walking first around the neighborhood itself, I cut down to the long street leading to the center; the Duomo can be seen down many of the small streets sitting gloriously in its piazza. I stood in awe while staring at every intricate detail contained on every inch of its walls and door. What an amazingly colorful piece of architecture. My wanderings took me to a place with a long-held memory, Ponte Vecchio, Florence's most famous bridge, an icon of the city itself. As I walked across it, I found there was almost nothing there as I remembered it. It was so crowded now with jewelry shop after jewelry shop down both sides. I felt sad as I walked the bridge; having seen the changes of Rome, I was well aware that thirty years will change any city, and yet armed with that knowledge I was still somewhat disappointed that this symbol I remembered was now just a teeming mass of cheap, overpriced knock-offs, trash everywhere, and featuring a "lock of love" part with hundreds of modern locks chained together on this centuries-old, beautiful bridge.

Or was it just misguided memories? From the bridge I could see the hotel where we stayed those many years ago, and could still picture our family standing in front of it by the bridge, my eldest brother zinging us with riddle after riddle that he had recently learned at university; the street lining the river seemed so much smaller now and more compact. I was continually amazed that much of the changes were more perceptual than anything else.

Each day I wandered, partaking in the sites, and filing various things away for my nightly emails to Lynda. As if she wasn't excited enough and time moving slowly enough for her, she wanted to hear everything, every single day! The apartment was in a zone of the city, away from crowds, where the hills containing the town of Fiesole were easily seen, and a tributary of the grand river ran alongside my street. My emails were filled with details about the little shops in our neighborhood, the wonderful fresh pasta shop next door, the little *trattorie*, the *gelateria*; hers full of excitement to get there and wander around to see it all, to meet the neighbors I'd met, a few of the various shopkeepers who already waved as I passed by, the daily produce market in our piazza, Le Cure.

Some of my observations from being there for a week are a bit obvious in nature. Things change even for those born and raised here; when I asked someone where the train goes that stops in this piazza, I would get the response, "What train? There's no train station there." Maybe that's the same no matter where you are; the changes in your own small town are invisible to you. Florentines consider their dialect to be the purest and original form of the Italian language. Eyebrows were raised when I spoke my Roman dialectal slang and it made me laugh. The city was quieter, even though it was very noisy. I found this world to be an incredibly small place, as I stopped in a bookstore and ran into an old friend from high school who had lived there in Florence for many years. Not all items bought in the piazza markets were of the best quality—I sometimes felt a little like Hansel and Gretel as I left a trail of little black fuzzies all over the apartment from the five-euro pair of sweat pants I bought. But that's okay, at least I'd never get lost in the apartment! I found my language skills were coming back at a rapid pace and I was communicating well. I bought a few children's books to help me out—a tactic I would end up using years later as an English teacher.

Out the apartment building door within ten steps was the wall of the river, and I found it quietly calming to listen to its quiet gurgle as it flowed; occasionally a few ducks lazily floated along. The stars seemed to shine very bright there during the chilly nights, trains went by frequently but the walls of the apartment made them seem to be off in the distance. I've never minded hearing trains and their whistles; it's never noise to me but a representation of what I love most dearly in life—the train is going somewhere, its passengers going to new places, new adventures. Maybe they're off to meet the love of their life, or a new traveler on their first big trip, or maybe someone is going home. Whenever I hear trains it always brings a smile with the memories, reinforcing my yearnings that have brought me to my own adventure.

Firenze . . . I knew I was going to like it there, even if it proved to be only for a very short time, the three months I'd originally planned.

Chapter 11

Never Say "I'll Do Anything" to a Sicilian

Mid-April, 2003

"It's with a heavy heart that I bid farewell to you, my beautiful city of Firenze. What a wonderfully enchanting time I've had here; your timeless beauty has surrounded me for these three months and has helped to soothe my spirit and calm my restless heart. I have gazed upon your architectural wonder, the Duomo; have discovered precious treasures tucked among your myriad of side streets; have stood open-mouthed with incredulity while gazing upon the tombs of such geniuses as Michelangelo, da Vinci, Galileo; your streets have quieted me. I will miss you."

Back in mid-March I began a correspondence with an expat who had lived in a large town called Motta Sant'Anastasia in Sicily, not far from Catania, for eleven years. David told me, "I fell in love twice those many years ago—once with the beauty of the land, and once with a beauty from the land." Now firmly entrenched in his town, he had made many contacts, knew half the people, spoke not only Italian fluently, but had also mastered the Sicilian dialect. It's truly like an entirely different language, and is a dialect I had heard for most of my life from my Sicilian father, grandmother and aunt. Lynda was staying in Florence and going to attempt to make it there finally, but I was struggling financially with only a couple hundred euros left and no way to pay the rent, no work in the tourism industry due to tourism almost halting because of the war, and had many emails and phone calls with him about life in Sicily. Not too long after, he texted me one day on my cellphone (I felt like a real Italian!) to let me know I was to arrange a trip to Sicily because a friend of his had work available and wanted to meet me.

The joint US Navy and Italian Air Force base, Sigonella, is in that town; it's one of the main local employers, with in-town, off-base TLAs (Temporary Lodging Apartments) being secondary. The lure of work, and an Excel spreadsheet he previously sent me outlining the average cost of living there, was enough to start my research on the Trenitalia site. As I mentioned, the work was just not there in Florence, due to the decline in (make that, pretty much stopped) tourism; with only 300 euros to my name (and an open-return ticket), I was faced with making some serious decisions. Sometimes I think I may be just a little too independent for my own damn good, as I was adamant that I was not going to call anyone to help me out, and would figure out a way. A few days later, hugging Lynda tightly, tears of fear filling my eyes, I was on my way.

Overnight sleeper trains are a great cheap way to travel long distances in Europe, and this time was no exception. My excitement to see Sicily again had me drifting in and out of sleep, waking me fully as the train was being loaded onto the ferry to cross the Strait of Messina. The lure of being able to get a nice espresso helped some as well! As soon as we were allowed to, off the train we bounded like so many caged-up monkeys, all racing towards the bar.

I've always loved ships and one of my greatest pleasures is to stand on deck watching the water and the outline of a coast, in this case two, the one I was leaving and the new one that was to hopefully become my future home. As I saw the welcoming Madonna statue at the port, my heart did a little flip-flop. I could easily remember seeing it the first time as a girl of twelve, the unknown shore of my ancestors welcoming me home. It gave me the same feeling this time, beckoning me to gaze upon its shore, see the second city of my blood—*"come to us,"* it seemed to whisper on the wind, *"come home."* On the shore I saw the same hotel where I stayed so many years ago. It was amazing to me that the city still looked so very much the same—the huge autostrada that had been built seemed out of place, but its importance was obvious. Somewhere in those hills was Galati Mamertino: the thought made my heart beat a little faster. A short time later our train raced down the shoreline past Messina and into Taormina; I was amazed at these views—on one side was the sea, on the other were the mountains and the glory of Mount Etna. It was, for lack of a better word, simply awesome to behold. Smoke plumed from its heart, its sides covered in snow; alone in its dominance of this side of the island. It commands, and even demands, respect with its show of force and power.

Catania is huge, crowded and chaotic, but has its own beauty. The symmetry of the train station being directly next to the huge port held a certain fascination with its ability to take you to, or bring you from, wherever you wanted. How many stories those two places must hold, how many hellos, tearful goodbyes, excitement as people board its trains or ships to go find adventure, love, new lives, old lives—if you listen closely, you can almost hear it.

After being picked up, we drove to my small bed-and-breakfast in Belpasso (only 20 euros a night, already I was loving the prices) and one of the next towns over from Motta Sant'Anastasia where I was to meet his friend Silvio. Suitcase-dump and we hit the ground running, driving around Motta. I liked the streets and town itself—it sits a bit up on a small hill made of lava rock and is formed entirely from an eruption of Etna too many years ago to count; a large stone church, as always, sits at the end of the town on the edge of the hill impressively towering over it. The general atmosphere of the town made me think I could be okay there, and maybe even like it. Though the initial person wasn't available for me to see, I was taken around to meet other people he knew who owned/managed other TLAs (a big business there, as Sigonella was a very large base, and home to a huge, international, yearly military exercise), being constantly introduced as "the half-Sicilian woman I was mentioning to you who's looking for work."

Back to Belpasso, a nice enough little town; nothing, in my mind, much to it except its four churches and incredible view of Mt. Etna. Most of the small towns in that area are considered "on the slopes of" Etna, the years of eruptions clear everywhere you look; the lava rock in the buildings, lava stone in various places, and ash packed into the crevices of the cobblestone streets. Europe's most-active volcano, it is always smoking, rumbling deep within as she decides whether to erupt. The people of this area are used to it, and have learned to live with this frightening aspect of life. But they always—*always*—remember that no matter how hard we may try, we cannot change this awesome piece of nature and must always respect its power. Though right near the base, tourism is not huge there, and I enjoyed that aspect of it as I wandered around.

In one small odd-'n'-sundry shop, I ended up escaping the heat a bit while having a leisurely conversation with a young woman barely 20 years old. It hit me deep inside as she told me about her love of travel and desire to see the world, but was fearful of doing it on her own because she knew no one in the places she wanted to go. I think of her as I write this book, and think sometimes that that's why I decided to do this. To let other young women, or women of any age, know that it's okay—you have the strength to do it and to make your dreams come true. Make the plans. Take a deep breath, maybe even many, and take the first step.

I happened upon a street exhibition of artwork made from lava stone and mosaic tables, sinks and the like. It was a great way to spend an hour looking at the works that would rival those I've seen in centers of art such as Florence. It's amazing what one's hands can do with a piece of lava; when you touch it, you can almost feel the essence of the earth, of life, that is represented from that piece of the volcano.

∽ ∽ ∽

Finally, after a gorgeous motorcycle ride up the long, winding path leading to the craters of the volcano, we met up with Silvio. Over a coffee, he asked me what kind of work I was looking for, and when I responded, "I'll do anything," I learned immediately from raised eyebrows and choked-on swallows of coffee that that is one phrase you never say to a Sicilian! I quickly qualified that, while I wasn't averse to selling squeaky motorized rubber duckies in some tourist area, I drew the line at some things. Having broken the proverbial ice, we got down to business. Yes he had work, yes he could put me to work as soon as I got there, and yes he knew of many apartments that would be available for me to rent at a mere 100–150 euros per month, and yes if they were unfurnished things could be very easily gotten for me to use. I felt a little of the tension of the past month or so begin to leave me . . . a little.

I'll tell you a quick story and give you a tip. If you ever get the chance, make sure to drive any of the roads leading up to the top of Etna. It is a sight and experience that will not only leave you breathless, but will remain with you forever. The morning had been chilly and cloudy as we climbed up, riding curve after curve, up and up, my mind a flood of emotion. Surrounding me was a landscape of black dry lava scattered among green trees; everywhere the land was nothing but thousands of years of lava on top of lava, with snow everywhere. At one curve is something that has almost become a tourist attraction of sorts, even though just the thought of its history can bring a racing heart. There in an indentation of the curve sits an old house, buried to its top windows in lava. I was awe-struck by the incredible nature of it all, the power in that mountain we were riding up. It made me truly understand the precariousness of life here. At the top, I was struck by the odor of fire that still emanated from a destroyed building from the most recent eruption. The cable cars ran no more as they had been destroyed as well. My "piece of Etna" that I took home? A discovery of *Fuoco dell'Etna*, a tantalizingly fiery concoction of pure-grain alcohol and berries. Two sips of this and you're unaware of the cold outside; this stuff gives the smoothest of grappas a run for their money! Good stuff. Remember, though, that taking anything from Etna's ground, ash or lava stone, is highly illegal and not taken lightly. Don't even try it.

❦ ❦ ❦

Standing on the ferry deck after my return train had been loaded on, I watched the lights in the dark and looked at the welcome statue/beacon shining. I followed all the lights along the coast and up into the mountains and said to the air, "I'll be back soon, I know it." I didn't want to leave, but also wanted to go back to Florence; in a way I wished I could've already been on this boat crossing back to Sicily. Maybe it was because I hadn't been there in so long, maybe it was because it was new, I don't know. But I do know it felt good there.

Back in Florence, I began my preparations to leave, deciding which would be the best way to get there with way too much luggage and when would be the best time to go. Leaving my buddy and housemate Lynda was so difficult, and though I would miss her very much, somewhere in us we knew this day would come and the plans for working in tourism just weren't going to happen with all that was going on in the world at the time. This city I'd called home for three months was beginning to get very crowded, and that was helping to make me want to be back in the hills of Sicily. I told my neighborhood bar that I was leaving and they wondered out loud why I would do this, insisting I must return and visit. Stopping in to my favorite neighborhood wine shop, where the old man who always kept me in there for an hour as he brought down onto the counter at least ten bottles for me to choose from—while showing off special prizes even though he knew I simply wanted one little bottle of inexpensive wine—told me he understood the pull of the ancestral land, but, like the others, he implored me to return for a visit to say hello (and also to enjoy the amazing Sicilian wines). I assured these people I would do so. Because after all, Florence has a pull all of its own, in its skies, its warmth, its ego, and its beauty.

And so I was left to wonder. Will this work? Will all be well? Will Silvio really have something, work and an apartment, for me? I didn't know, but it would be fun having a go at it. However, if you're walking through a Sicilian square somewhere, sometime, and you see a woman who looks half-Sicilian and half-American selling squeaky motorized rubber ducks, stop and buy one or two, 'cause you never know.

Chapter 12

Little Snippets as Life Begins in a New Home

A City with a Reputation
Early September, 2004

"So what'cha doing today?" she said.

"Got the day off, thought I'd just relax. What about you —going to study?" I replied.

"Blah. I'm tired of studying. I've retained everything I'm going to."

"You know what this means then . . . ," was my natural reaction.

"I'm thinkin' I do . . . Pick you up in 30."

Road trip!

Three months prior, a woman named Kim and her daughter, Devra, came sauntering down the walkway of the TLA I managed, and with a simple "Hey, what's up," Kim became my traveling-and-general-get-in-trouble cohort for the next three years. She would become my lifelong best friend, the yin to my yang, my soulmate, my travel buddy.

I was the general office manager of the TLA handling check-ins, check-outs, making sure apartments were cleaned and ready for individuals or for large military groups coming in. At times there were international military exercises, and each TLA in town was handling upwards of 50 or more people—we'd take the list of officers and enlisted people, grouped by ranks, and create a board showing who would be in which apartment; officer ranks would live alone, while we would lump together two, three or even six enlisted ranks to share an apartment. It would be chaotic and confusing, and I loved every second of figuring it all out. From the time I'd started at the TLA, I was always interacting with the Naval reservists who came through, helping them understand some things in their new home while making various suggestions of where to go and what to see. One day, one of the commanders invited me to go to their weekly dinner, and I wouldn't have said no for love nor money! We had a wonderful time, full of food and wine, and more wine, and laughter and general silliness. A short time later, this would become my way of introducing reservists and new families, whatever the rank, to Sicily—I became known for organizing 'get to know your new home's food and wine dinners' every couple weeks. People who left and then came back another time always asked if I was still organizing them.

Anyway, during one raucous, hot Sicilian evening, four of us gravitated outside to cool off from the heat of the restaurant, which was located inside a cave/wine cellar, ending up tipsily reciting line after line from *Monty Python and the Holy Grail*, laughing until tears were running down our faces. There's always a special connection when you meet someone who immediately responds to: "It's just a little rabbit." At some point, one guy started talking about Corleone because his favorite movie of all time was *The Godfather*. After many groans from the rest of us, he also said he'd heard they had some phenomenal wine there as well. Kim and I immediately perked up and tipsily yelled, "Roooooad triiiiiip!" We decided on the following Sunday since everyone has a three-day weekend and I was off that day.

Road trip! Destination Corleone. A/C on, some fantastic '70s CDs blasting, zooming down the highway cutting through the middle of the island of Sicily with no real plans other than seeing this town. The driving plan was to first take the road towards Caltanisetta and Enna, turn north to the sea, head west along the northern coast for a little bit, south on the winding road that would take us to Corleone. After lunch and a little, okay hopefully a lot, of wine tasting, back on the road to cut across east to the highway, south to Agrigento, east to the coast road through Licata and Gela, and finally north to Motta. Got all that? We had all day, it's not that big of an island, and so why not hit the northern sea, the internal mountains, and the southern sea, all in one fell swoop?

As there had been nearly zero rain most of the year, all around us the hills were shades of brown interspersed with huge rock hill/mountain outcroppings. Along the road were further results of no rain, large burnt patches of grass. One spark and the entire hill would just about blow up. While some were clearly controlled burns with their lines of burnt grass, it was easy to see others weren't. I could've been back in Arizona!

Before we knew it, we came around the curve after a huge hill and there it was: stretched out before us was a beautiful, sky-blue body of water, the summer sun shimmering off of it, and no one on the beaches. The summer holidays were over. Rolling down the windows, the fresh, salty air poured over us in cool, clean waves, perking us up and getting us ready to check out this town-with-a-reputation. Turning west and south down a small winding road that would lead us to Corleone and our lunch coupled with wine tasting, I have to admit that both of us were pretty curious to see whether the town would be anything like it was in the movie. Round and down kilometers of windy little roads, there it was; the large town of Corleone. It was nearly deserted since it was siesta time and just after lunch, though its main park was set up for a wedding. Corleone was, in essence, a small Sicilian town with a certain known reputation that had little to do with the movie and everything to do with its own sordid little past and present as the birthplace of (and still home to) the mafia. It has its place in history, and said reputation is abundantly clear throughout the town. Since we were stared at by the few men hanging around—Kim is tall, blonde, gorgeous, and in excellent Navy shape—we felt unwanted and distrusted. Frankly, we couldn't wait to get out of there. We walked around for a little bit on a couple streets, but were so uncomfortable that we decided to just go. (As a side note, in the future this town began to clean up its act through the newest, younger generation, standing up and taking back the city; it's a breath of fresh air to see. Check out "Libera Terra" on the Internet.)

After more twisty internal roads later, we had a wonderful lunch with wine-pairing at *Agriturismo Casa Mia*, run by the owners of the Corleone cooperative winery. We wandered around outside waiting for a table to open up, checking out the picnic tables full of tomatoes, sliced and lying on wooden slats to soak up the sun and become delicious and flavorful sun-dried tomatoes used in various recipes. Yummy! Out around the other way were wonderful views of lush hills, plentiful with acre upon acre of full vines ready for harvest very soon. Out among the hills you could see Corleone a few kilometers away, spread out along the hillside.

I loved the scenery around this *agriturismo*, and would recommend it for an overnight trip, a lunch or dinner, and of course a winery tour complete with tasting. It's got plenty to keep kids busy with a pool, mini-golf course, and playground. The tasting lunch was done quite nicely, as three of their wines were brought for tasting along with each course of the (normally) set menu; a basic red, a pretty and fruity native-to-Sicily-and-only-in-Sicily varietal called *inzolia* (in my opinion, it had the nose and palate of a *pinot grigio* and Oregonian *pinot gris*, crisp and pleasant on a late summer day), and a *rosé*. Our lunch was a plate of wonderful antipasti, typical Sicilian style, with olives, mushrooms and croquettes of potato and prosciutto, and a delicious pecorino that was soft and pleasing; we opted to skip the pasta and went straight to the main course of three types of meat—lamb, homemade sausage, basic thin steak—alongside roasted potatoes and vegetables. As Kim is a vegetarian, they added on some salad with extra vegetables, tomatoes and cheese.

The *cantina* was open as there had been a tour group, so of course we meandered over there to do some (more) tasting. They were just closing up but after I explained that wine was a huge passion of mine, a young apprentice winemaker named Luca looked around, then waved us in for some special tasting. As any wino like me knows, if you're taken for special tasting into the cellar where the barrels are, then you know what's coming—three barrel tastings of Cabernet Sauvignon, Nero d'Avola, and Merlot. Probably a very good thing that Kim was driving and not doing anywhere near the amount of tasting that I was. The Cab and Nero were wonderful, but the showstopper was the Merlot; though extremely young, it showed a world of promise, and made me want to pre-order a bottle for the next year's bottling. In a year or two, this was set to knock your socks off, a beautifully deep burgundy, with a nose full of tobacco and chocolate, spice, the typical lava-rock pepper, dark mature berries, and absolutely luscious.

Making our way back home meant going south towards Agrigento, east along the coast road and then cutting north—I think I mentioned before we never did road trips in any straightforward manner! The sun was about an hour from setting as we came around a curve to the sight of the grand temple sitting high up on the hill, alone as it shone in that near-setting light. What a sight, as it commanded that hill! Reaching the southern coast road was pretty amazing in its own right, giving credence to the mantra Kim and I had: "It's not that big of an island, you know." Just a few hours before, we'd been at the northern shore, had lunch, and now here we were on the southern coast.

After a short stop to walk along the beach and admire that beautiful view of the sea in the setting sun, off we went for the last leg home. It was a wonderful trip, and felt immensely soothing to have been able to do this for a day. I felt as if I had been given a reprieve from my ridiculous working hours—as Kim put it, given a day pass—and really helped me relax. Something I hadn't been able to do in far too long. We made plans during that drive for other road trips; maybe a full coastal drive, or putting the car onto one of many ferries either to the islands north of Messina or maybe to Malta. We never made concrete plans, as these spontaneous road trips were much more fun!

Everyone Has Roots Somewhere
Mid-October

How can I possibly explain what happened to me Sunday; will I succeed in finding the words to explain the whirlwind of emotions, the kaleidoscope of images, the peace and joy and excitement? Along with, surprisingly, an overwhelming sadness that was admittedly a bit tough to shake. Why? Well, I'll try to explain.

Into Kim's car we went, taking off on a little road trip. Starting out peacefully enough, we took the scenic route north through the mountains around Mount Etna, braving the gorgeous hairpin windy little roads through the many small towns: Adrano, Bronte (of pistachio fame), Randazzo. Town after town, village after village, dotted the hills of breathtaking scenery as we entered the Nebrodi forest. Leaves were beginning to turn and the air was cool way up there; breathing it in and looking out over the mountains, I felt as if I breathed in my very life. My eyes took it all in and my blood seemed to rush through me. I could tell we were close. Something in me changed at that moment.

As I sit and write this, I find it difficult to concentrate. I want to describe everything about the trip leading to the town and afterwards, and yet I'm having a hard time doing that. I'm reaching deep inside to find the words to describe the experience—one that I recommend to everyone, for there is nothing quite like looking into the eyes of your ancestors, and finding far-removed relations that remember you from so many years ago. The feeling of reconnection.

But I'll try.

◈ ◈ ◈

Nearly immediately upon entering Galati Mamertino, we came upon the main piazza, looking the exact same as it did all those years ago. I knew it wasn't, as it was just perception, a 12-year-old's memories. Looking around, I was drawn immediately to the war memorial and I found many names with both of my surnames. Remember when I mentioned people in small hill villages had a tendency to marry those in the same village or from one immediately surrounding? Well, this was no different. Both of my paternal grandparents were born and raised in Galati, meeting, marrying and raising a family, never leaving until years later when they boarded a ship in late 1921 full of their compatriot migrants bound for New York.

As we stood in the center of the piazza, I tried my best to picture the walk there from the family home those 33 years ago. I turned in circles, but my perception was so distorted that I just couldn't picture it. The streets all looked the same. I gave up and thought maybe if I walked around I'd find it. We decided to stop in the main bar, *Bar Carcione* (related somehow down the family tree), for directions to the town cemetery. Asked if I was from there, I told him my grandparents' surnames and also asked if he by any chance knew where my aunts' home was, or used to be. From a nearby table, a man immediately came over and began asking questions, explaining that he was a cousin something-removed and rewarded my efforts by saying, "I know exactly where the house is." He offered to take us on a walk to the house, to show us the best place to eat in town, and then to the cemetery. I was flattered but not really surprised. This was the "family" mentality of my ancestral home.

As we walked, he continually introduced me to anyone who had either of my two surnames. Of course they did, there were only five family names in this town, and I had two of them! We got to a small hill street and he asked if it was familiar, if anything was coming back to me. I admitted that there was something familiar about it; in just a few more steps, he pointed out a door and said, *what about now?* I knew it immediately, though it seemed so much smaller! How in the hell did all those people fit in there during the huge town party that day in the

'70s? I just stared and stared, drinking in every inch of it, even the side that seemed to be crumbling. He (as did a few others, later in the day) told me that none of the remaining family living in Messina ever came, and it was now abandoned with a big lock on it. I felt like my ancestry had been abandoned—this house that contained my blood, my life, my beginnings. Behind that door, locked away, were a 12-year-old's first memories of this town and country, crumbling with the years.

I wanted in. I wanted to see the big dining room where my aunts bustled around, fawning over the American relations coming to visit. I wanted to stand on the balconies of each floor and look out over the mountains where there had been such quiet like I'd never before known, and such peace. I wanted to feel the life. He told me that my cousin in Sicily had the title to this home (through her father, my grandmother's brother), but never once in the past ten or more years visited either the house or anyone in town. She came only once each year to visit her father's gravesite, nothing more. It made me so sad—and even mad—that this was happening to my grandmother's home.

I wanted this house. Would it give me the sense of "home" that I had yet been unable to find? I didn't know.

He then said he wanted to show me something very special, and we piled back into Kim's car, where he directed us down a steep winding road that led to a house that looked like a warehouse was attached to it. As we were still sitting in the car, a little wary of the three dogs, and not sure even where we were, I saw our little guide gesturing to a woman and an older man standing outside. They waved us out of the car and she—Giovanna—promptly and excitedly told me her mother was a first cousin to my grandfather! I began to understand why the man had said there was something special. I turned to her father, quietly waiting, who immediately, without any introduction, took my hand in his, held on tight, and said, "I remember your father and all of you coming here to his family's home in the summer of 1971; we had a big party, and I was there." At that very moment, I nearly couldn't breathe from the slamming of emotions I felt. Standing before me was the husband of my blood relative, and he remembered us. He then softly said something to me that brought tears to my eyes, a very simple: "Welcome home." I could do nothing but squeeze his hand even tighter as he asked about my father and my family, and then listened as he told me of my other family in town. He asked questions and when I told him we had moved to Rome after visiting Galati, he laughed and said, "And you never wrote in all these years?"

They invited me in to see their little home factory, a coffee company where they roasted their own beans, producing some of the most aromatic and intense coffees and shipping them all over the world. We walked the grounds, tasted far too much coffee, and were more than ready for lunch at this point. I was a little concerned about Kim, as I figured she was probably bored to tears by all this and just wanted to get some lunch and get going to Capo d'Orlando, but she merely said, "This is your moment. It may not be as overly exciting for me as it is for you, but it's still exciting and fantastic to share it with you. I'm enjoying myself, believe me!" We all went off to lunch at a small trattoria, where we were treated as family, as Galatese who'd come home.

Some of the amazing Nebrodi specialties we had included, of course, its famed porcini mushrooms and black pigs. Over the course of an hour or more, we were served mixed antipasti of prosciutto, salamis, spinach squares, eggplant, local mushrooms, sun-dried tomatoes, sun-dried peppers, local Provolo cheese; followed by an area specialty of risotto with porcini alongside a plate of tagliatelle with sautéed porcini mushrooms and one of a simple pasta rolled with eggplant—both of these were served much as the same as spaghetti olive, olio e pepperoncino, which is family-style with a huge spoon and fork to take however much you wished. These dishes are served in this way in order to show their guests that they are friends, and considered family. All of this was accompanied by many glasses of local Nero d'Avola wine, native to Sicily and absolutely gorgeous. Deep purple, full-bodied with aromas of pepper, spice, tobacco and earth. Years later, it's still one of my favorites, and has a distinctive taste that can't be found in any other wine.

A few photos, hugs and kisses later, we drove to the cemetery. It may sound morbid to want to visit a cemetery, but like most Italian cemeteries, these are not headstones in the ground. Instead, row after row, stacked on top of each other, are crypts where the remains are stored. Nearly every single one has a photograph. Kim was a good sleuth, so armed with the two family names, off we went in search. I was thrilled to have her there with me to share this, and it was something I've never forgotten. There I was, reading name after name with my surnames. After a moment, Kim said, "What was your grandfather's first name?" I told her and she said, "I think you need to come here." I stood there and stared at his name, wishing there was a picture, but for some reason there wasn't. I knew the year he had died, a scant few months before I was born, so I knew it was him. Further down I was looking at the names on the larger mausoleums, and saw one with my uncle's name on it (the father to my cousin living in Messina). I remembered him as a wonderful man, full of life, intelligent, and I always remembered him. It read 'Family of Italo Carcione' and I looked through the door windows and saw my three aunts' names, and then, there it was—my grandmother's name, for whom I was named. I tried the door, it opened, and I was taken back in time through memory. Though there was no photo, as I looked at the date of death, it all came back to me. I saw myself, a few months after my high school graduation and only three days before my 18th birthday, standing beside her bed along with my mother, father, and aunt, kissing her a last time a few minutes before she died that day in Rome. Walking out of the cemetery gates, I stood with Kim and gazed out at the town in front of me, high on this hill. We looked at each other and all I could say was, "I found them all. This is where my blood is. This is where I started. Those were their homes, and where all of my generations are."

❧ ❧ ❧

I mentioned at the beginning of this story that all of my excitement also included sadness. As we drove through the mountains towards the sea to Capo d'Orlando, I didn't have it in me to even speak. It seemed to have hit me that they were all gone. I may be the last of this direct line because, and this is their choice and one I have accepted, my brothers are really not interested in these roots. Unfortunately, my ties with my siblings broke after the death of our parents. Without those ties, I've felt alone, and seeing the graves of my ancestors made the feeling even deeper. I realized at that moment that it is just me now, really. I knew also that I took too long to come home. (Years and years later, my second-eldest brother and I mended our tie; he visited Galati and took a wonderful, old, photo of him and our grandmother, and placed it on her crypt; but the feelings of this "home" weren't there for him. And that's okay. I am so happy there is now such a wonderful photo on her grave!)

Along with the sadness of the trip came also a feeling of pure peace, and of strength. I felt able to take on the world, able to deal with anything that came along. I could breathe deeply now, and breathe in everything of what they had all been. Their lives, their loves, their joys, their sorrows and pains. They are all in me, a part of me, and they are who I am. A thousand generations of power flow through me now.

Our hearts control the flow of our blood which is our life. They say home is where the heart is.

I found home.

November Interlude, or, Love Happens

So I guess it was bound to happen at some point, especially working in that job where so very many people, men, came through, whether for a one-, two- or three-year change of station move; or for a month-long military exercise; or a civilian contractor coming through for base work. In all honesty, I'm not sure I ever really gave this aspect of life any thought at all, at least not serious thought. And then one day, I realized what a mistake that was. A beautiful, crisp fall/early winter day in late October/early November, I was in the office on a normal day, just doing my work in preparing some documentation for a few incoming Navy reservists, arriving for just about two months. Sitting in my chair, head down rifling through a lower drawer of files, I heard my name yelled.

"Maria! You here? Where are you?" one of the guys staying there asked.

"Yep, hang on, just a sec," I said as I popped my head up quickly, hand on a file, not paying any attention to the fact that the top of the desk was right above my head, as I continued,

"Of course I'm here, where in hell else am I going . . . yow! Ow!" promptly smacking my head and rolling my chair over to the other side of the desk.

Hand on my head, I looked over at the guest. Who was not alone . . .

When I saw you standing there, I 'bout fell outta my chair . . .

It wasn't supposed to be like this, John; what in the hell am I going to do? What am I supposed to do now? So many changes. My big tough marine. You're not so tough, you know. God I could fall for you—the problem is, I could fall hard. You made, you make, me feel alive. Loved. Desirable. Beautiful. You look past it all and see me. You brought a passion in me that I never dared let out before. How did you do that? You took me to an edge that scared, scares, the life out of me. When you said you love me, I wanted to tell you no. Please don't. Because I don't know what I'll do if you do. We both have our lives, our plans, and they're 6,000 miles apart. You tell me you want to stay. I can't let you do that. I want you to. But I can't let you give it all up.

I don't want to go back. I gave up too much. Would I give this all up for you?

No. God help me, but no. What future would I be giving up? Which happiness? All that I've worked for, or all that I could have?

∽ ∽ ∽

I'm supposed to be used to this. In my life I've said goodbye to more people than I can possibly count. It's part of my lifestyle. I accepted it a long time ago. Ma quanto ti vorrei. I don't know how to do this. I feel sick just thinking about how I'm going to feel when you leave. I tried to explain last night to you that I can't go with you to the airport, and I nearly drowned in your eyes. You whispered sweet words of coming back here to stay, creating your incredible artwork here in my world. Will the thought of that be enough to make this pain of you leaving go away?

You were not supposed to do this; you see, I made a vow to never let anyone get this close to me in my job here. You guys come, and then you leave. Hello. Goodbye. Stay safe. If you ever get this way again, make sure you stop and say hi. You're not supposed to make me question this most important decision in my life.

Damn you, what have you done.

෯ ෯ ෯

Uh oh, I knew it the moment I first looked in your eyes; you're going to change my life, aren't you? You've decided you're coming back and will stay for a time. Yikes. When you told me, you started talking about all the things you wanted to do with me, and all the places we would go. I'm glad you're tuned-in enough to me to know or to have heard my slight hesitation. You knew enough to tell me, "but not all the time", because you wouldn't take away my independence because I have a life here. Thank you for saying that.

You still leave tomorrow. I wish I could be there today for the kudos they're giving you. I would love to see you standing there, accepting the commendations. The pride in your eyes as they ooh and ahh over your work—the work I watched you creating last night, the peace in your eyes and on your face as you worked your magic sculpting that wood in all its detail. You create such beauty. I love watching your hands do this, those same hands that have begun to break down my walls enough to make me fall fast and hard.

Your coming back will ease the sorrow that will come tonight when I lay, safe and warm in your arms, and feel your heartbeat for the last time. It will help ease the pain tomorrow morning when we say goodbye.

I Miss You . . .
Monday, December 29

Options, options, God, Buddha, every deity ever, please help me because I can't seem to do this anymore. It's almost like I'm getting that same familiar itch; I don't want to be here. I don't know what I'm doing. This isn't what I wanted for my life. This is not what I gave up everything for, what I left everything I knew for, what I left everyone I knew for. Every little thing that happens here during every day just serves to remind me that this isn't working for me. And I want to leave. I want to run.

I remember when I first got here and I told myself—no, demanded of myself—that I not allow myself to feel strongly about anyone here, and most certainly not to allow any relationship to go beyond a little bit of fun for a week or so. I didn't want to find myself in this position. I'm still young, free, have a travel-and-discovery itch in me that doesn't allow root-planting or staying in one place.

I was listening to a CD yesterday and a song froze me in my tracks while cleaning my apartment. I didn't want to need you, I didn't want to love you, I didn't want to fall, but I did. *And while it's a good thing, and I can't deny my feelings for him, it also makes it entirely difficult for me to stay where I am. I feel like I am merely existing, and that isn't what I wanted. The long phone calls and emails just seem to make it worse.*

These were the problems I was beginning to wrestle with, but there was an even bigger one: I absolutely loathed who I worked for. I'd been in the legal field for all of my working professional life. I'd always stood to uphold the law, to be honorable and honest in all my dealings. Part of me wanted to bust my boss, the TLA owner, for what he was doing with invoices, books and contracts. I also knew that I could simply go to any of the commanders, tell what I knew, and the business would fold, the contract pulled. Part of me wanted to do it, take the computer disk to a trusted commander; the vengeful part of me I suppose. Or was it the legal-minded person which I'd always been in every job I'd held? If I could figure out why I wanted to do it, then that would make my decision for me. There was a problem with that, though; if I did it, then I was out of work. Which is also why I stayed and took all the horrid, mean-spirited, spiteful comments and put-downs from the owner, instead of telling him to fuck off, that no one could talk to me like that, that no one could treat me like that. He had somehow succeeded in berating me to end up working 12- to 14-hour days, 7 days a week. No one else worked on Saturday afternoon or Sunday. But I was made to feel that I, as the American and "one of them", should do this for them, to be there always for them, whether at the office or always with my cellphone on.

If you're wondering why I continued to take it and be miserable, and not just go find another job, understand that I was in a small town with no viable transportation to larger towns/cities, I still didn't have my paperwork, and that TLA seemed to be nearly the only game around. All the others were staffed and no one was leaving. You might say, oh come on, that's not true, there's always other work. Unfortunately there wasn't there. There were too few jobs and too many people. Italy, and Sicily in particular, have exceptionally high unemployment rates and I was, after all, still a foreigner and always took second place in hiring. I could have "expanded my box," but that would have entailed being able to take a leap and get out there somehow to find the work, find a new apartment, etc. Without a car and with only one day off, it was tough to do.

I had always been a strong person emotionally and mentally—at that point in my life, for the first time, I didn't feel even the slightest bit strong. I felt like I couldn't make a decision, was close to tears constantly, and back to simply existing. I hated it. Mostly, I hated that I had allowed it to happen.

Ringing in the New Year, Coastal Sicilian Style

Kim and I and her daughter, who was visiting from university in the States, went to have the traditional New Year dinner, called *cena di capodanno*, at a wonderful small, family-owned trattoria on the coast of Acireale, to which we'd been a few times before. There was so much food, too much actually. We started with appetizers at 8:30 p.m. and it went on until about 12:30 a.m.; and we left when there were two more courses yet to come! On the coastlines of Sicily, fish is naturally a staple, so the entire meal was based on 12 types of fish, one for each month of the year. Interestingly, there was one course of meat-based pasta thrown in there. The menu was printed out, each course being a line on the menu, and we just kept looking at it, saying, "Oh my god, there are still seven/six/five/help lines left!" Although far too much, the quality was outstanding. Lots of wine, both white and red, with the traditional *aperitivo* before. I've never been able to get into those and just don't like them, at least the ones I've had, and that night was no exception. I know so many people who really like Campari, and it is always served, but not me. Nor Kim. But this was New Year's Eve, and we were served it by our restaurant owner friends, and so we looked at each other, took a deep breath, said "Okay, on 3 . . . 2 . . . 1 . . . salute!", me downing mine in one go to make it go faster and Kim holding her nose while she drank it (not hard to see why we're best buds!). We did the countdown at midnight, kiss-kiss everywhere; we were given sparklers and took them outside. There must have been a gazillion others and all with firecrackers and fireworks of some kind.

After staying for the traditional good-luck lentils, though passing on the final two desserts, we took our leave and ventured out into a clear and pretty night with stars shining over the sea; the lights all along the coast were simply gorgeous.

A Musical Interlude
Monday, January 5

That cool, crisp Monday morning found me a bit calmer as I waited for Kim to get off work so we could go to our favorite pizza and spicy-bruschetta place called Paradise Pizzeria. I think some of the calm came from an evening of listening to some beautiful music. I had been invited by Luca Burini and Daniela diPippo, a soprano and her pianoforte maestro, to attend one of their concerts in Francofonte, somewhere between Motta and Siracusa. They'd invited me many times before and I just hadn't been able to go, but I couldn't refuse anymore after hearing her practicing (they'd been staying at the apartments, and we all became acquainted, going to dinner or out for drinks), her beautiful voice carrying through the air as she stood on the apartment's balcony, giving everyone the gift of that voice. Though they mostly performed in Milan, they were quite well known internationally, so it was kind of fun to say, "Hey I know them!"

On that occasion, they were giving a charity concert at one of the Francofonte churches for the holiday season, and I have to say that I was absolutely blown away! Daniela is a phenomenal singer—no, she's exceptional, exquisite, magnificent. Most of her singing gave me goosebumps, and three times she brought tears to my eyes with her voice—it was that amazing.

When she performed *O Holy Night*, there wasn't a dry eye. At the end everyone stood and clapped and there were yells of *brava brava*! No wonder she had won all sorts of international awards. Luca's pianoforte was wonderful as well—and it was easy to see why he had gotten so many awards as well, and earned the title *maestro*.

After, we went to dinner at an *agriturismo* in a little town near Lentini called Carlentini. The cool thing about *agriturismi* is that all the food is produced and grown on-premises. The antipasti were wonderful, and the highlight was actually their fresh ricotta, light, a little creamy, fresh, cool. I could go on and on about their food, and I loved it so much that it became one of my go-to reservist dinner places.

I had also been thinking a lot during that time about buying my old ancestral home in Galati Mamertino, but had no idea how to go about finding out if my grandmother ever signed over her portion of the home, or how the title stood. My cousin's name showed up on a search as having that address in the town, although Giovanna from the town told me she never went to the house. It stayed in the back of mind, tickling my brain, as I continued to try to figure it all out. Numerous calls to her went unanswered, as did messages.

Also around this time I went to the town's *municipio* (municipality, government) to see if I could further the comedy of errors that began back when I started this journey. Unfortunately, nothing had changed and I started to feel like every *municipio* in every community in Italy knew my entire citizenship story. However, at least this small town office took copies of everything, telling me, "Okay, the answer is that we need to call Rome and find out all the details because this is confusing. Then we'll be able to move forward with this."

I can hear you laughing.

Breakdowns Happen... Fight or Flight
End of March, 2005

The following weekend was Kim's birthday and I was treating her to a spa weekend of absolute relaxation. I had gotten the full weekend off and was going to take advantage of every minute. With reservations made at *Terme Acqua Pia* in southwestern Sicily, we were off. The Terme is an incredibly beautiful place, with thermal springs and pools at 104 degrees, mud-bath treatments and massages and so much more. Set amongst green hills lush with forest, it was down a long, narrow, dirt road and quiet as a whisper. It was weekends and trips like that which served to remind me of all the good in my life, even during shitstorms of bad—the long driving trips along coastal Sicily, our standard road trip CDs ready and stacked so that we could roll the windows down and sing to our heart's content, doing the best-bud thing of talking out everything that had been going on with each other in the last weeks. Those trips were my sanctuary.

Though we had an absolutely, positively amazing time at that outdoor spa, it ended up being a precursor that probably, somewhere deep in me, prevented a very bad decision. I call what happened my *fight or flight breakdown*. I suppose it happens to every expat at some point. After all, when you've left everything and everyone on the basis of a decades-old dream and memory, and are just going day by day trying to make it—when you don't have the means to buy an old villa in a quaint Tuscan countryside village or one of the myriad movie and book stories—while dealing with crazy bureaucratic nightmares, I would think a little fight or flight breakdown is inevitable.

Something hit me a few nights after the spa trip and I couldn't shake the feelings of wanting out; feeling so uncomfortable like some impending doom; antsy and itchy; feeling like I had made the biggest mistake of my life and had to just *go*; no matter how hard I tried. I came to within moments of packing everything and leaving. Running. What prevented it? A phone call to an old and exceptionally dear friend of mine in Chicago named Hannah. Even though she was only a few years older than me really, she had always been almost like a surrogate Mom. She had such a unique outlook on life, a spiritual faith that blew me away in its simple strength. For six years, way back in the late '70s and into the mid- to late-80s, we worked side-by-side in a small office. She saw me through the worst of my life, the years I was married, the greatest pain I've ever endured. I was in the darkest place I'd ever been, torn to pieces emotionally and physically—with her calm and gentle spirit and love, she picked me up, helped me to accept myself again, and is someone for whom I will be forever grateful.

Over the ensuing years, we would talk a couple times a year, always on our birthdays which are two days apart. From the first time we'd met, whenever I find myself in dark, emotional times, it is Hannah I think to call. Kim was my rock, but at that moment I couldn't put all of this on her. Hannah and I had known each other for years, and she always had this incredible ability to let everything roll off her shoulders. She would find a way through and make me laugh until I hurt, usually by bringing up memories of when we worked together, our boss, our Christmas parties; she was able to do it again that Saturday night. It had been a rough couple days leading up to that point, with too many things happening piled one on top of another, over and over, again and again. The verbal and emotional abuse thrown at me by my boss; spreading rumors to his buddies who worked on the base, knowing they would spread those rumors to the commanders and reservists; doing everything in his power to blacken the fantastic reputation I had so carefully cultivated. I was being ostracized by my co-workers because they were afraid of the boss—both job-wise and physically—and didn't want to seem as if they were friends with me. Somewhere along the way I lost my grip. When I got home that night, I looked down at my hand where I wear my mother's ring, and all of a sudden I felt like I was drowning in her loss. I suddenly missed her with an intensity that's nearly impossible to describe. I needed her calm, her strength, her wisdom, and mostly her love. Somewhere in that, I even missed my father. I felt like I couldn't breathe, and I wanted whatever ton of bricks that was sitting on my chest to just get the hell off me. Usually I can handle the pain, for it has eased with time. But something about that night made it impossible.

I looked around my apartment and could see myself packing everything up. I even got my suitcases out of the closet. The thought then popped into my head to call Hannah. I walked to the office to use the phone; she wasn't home and wouldn't be for a couple hours. Damn. Since I was there waiting, I called my old friend Brent in Arizona. I had a few half-hearted laughs, smiles really, as I told him all about what had been going on, and he mentioned that he thought I was having just a smidge *too* much fun. I tried to explain to him that being there those last two years had changed me. I wasn't the same person I had been when I was living in the US. I couldn't say if it was that I was more free, or maybe just less inhibited. I was living my life to the fullest, always taking proper precautions in sexual situations, not hurting anyone in the process of anything that I did, or at least doing everything in my power not to. I tended to put others first, their feelings, but I didn't ignore my own anymore. I didn't know if it made complete sense, and I felt like I was defending myself; and I knew the call wasn't helping.

I went back to my apartment, sat down, and began to think. So many things went through my head. I learned a long time ago to not think when my brain and emotions and whole being is in such a confused and pained state. That's not a time to be making decisions. I started to think about leaving, where I would go, what I would do—hell, it was so cheap there that I'd saved enough money up that it wouldn't be a problem to just go—and then I started thinking about the people I had met there, that came through my life every day. If I left, I wouldn't see them again. That wasn't a good enough reason to stay though.

Enough time passed that Hannah would have arrived home, and I went back to the office. When she answered, she heard me take a deep breath and just say her name. She heard it in my voice, asked what was wrong, and I simply said, "I'm lost, and I miss my mom so damn much." She knew just what to say and how to bring me out of it. "*Weedee,*" she said, using her pet nickname that she had come up with 'way back when'. "I've told you 700 zillion times that your mama has never left you. I see that being overseas hasn't changed your inability to listen to your *Naner,*" she continued with a laugh, "You're as bad as my kids." We talked, we laughed, we reminisced. It was just what I needed.

The thing is, life wasn't all bad there; I was just in a bad situation. And I was trying to get out of it, but if I left, I would feasibly lose a lot. If I stayed . . . if I stayed, I could gain a lot, but also lose just as much.

I thought about how I was more in touch with my ancestry and heritage than I had ever been in my life, and that when I was alone, I thought and spoke in Italian. I was, and had been for a long time, more attuned to the European life and lifestyle. It was a part of me. Italy and Sicily are wondrous places, and the reality of it is that being there was not the problem. I enjoyed it and felt at home. The problem was I had ended up choosing the wrong job by making a fast decision, or rather the wrong employer, and ended up neck-deep in quicksand.

The realization also came to me that I was at my own infamous two-year mark. Maybe that's where a lot of that was coming from. My second year in any place is usually filled with the beginnings of "the itch." By the third year, I've chosen somewhere new. I didn't think that would happen that time, not in a place where I did truly feel good. And I did love it there. I thought. Hell, I didn't know. I kept letting stuff get to me that I probably shouldn't have. And then I started thinking too much. So I decided to choose fight over flight this time and would spend my time ignoring the outbursts, the lies and attempts to smear my reputation that were thrown around, and just keep my eyes on the prize—my next destination.

Love Can Make You Question
Friday, May 21

Dear John,

Last night's talk was so emotional. I wonder if it wasn't because of what's going on, the plans you talked about. And if, when, you come home, I find myself wanting to be there. But that means leaving my own home, and giving up my life here. A large part of me feels I'm ready for it, that I'm okay with it, because how often does this kind of happiness come along? And why give it up? I can't be a continent away from you anymore. Maybe if we were both younger, but we're not kids with our whole lives stretched out in front of us. Leaving my home and life here for your shore is not a decision I'm taking or making lightly, nor will I make it on my own. We will make the decision together.

There are so many things, and people, involved in this decision. This isn't something that could happen quickly. This is still way down the road, next year, after you get home safe. It leaves me lots of time to think, and lots of time for us to make the decision together. I couldn't be there on your shore, no longer my home, while you are half a world away in the middle of a war. I couldn't handle it. I need to be here in this land, in my home; I need my life here, my peace, to make it through this.

Could I give it up? Would I give up the dreams I had that brought me here? I told you I could, and I wasn't lying. I don't think it was just the emotionally charged conversation that made me say it. Could I be happy there? I'd miss all of this land, the footprints of my ancestors. But we have to, we must, do what we can to be happy. Would I give up my future happiness, just to not touch that other shore again? I say to myself I really wish I had my mom here to help me figure this all out, but I know what she would say. I hear her voice now, and I feel her. I am confident in what she would tell me. She taught me well. I told you I could do it, as long as I could go back across the ocean often.

That's the problem, I can't say goodbye to you. I don't want you not in my life, and not in my future. There have been too many people taken away from me. I can't bear for you to be taken away too. You have to get home safe. You have to.

A Northern Coastal Getaway–Cefalù
Just about mid-July

Nothing much had really changed in the work scene, and I had my first day off in a month. Those 12-hours, seven-days-a-week things had exhausted me to no end. I got myself into that situation by not being able to say no, thinking I couldn't take the chance as I was the foreigner needing that job. Anyway, after asking my Sicilian co-workers where I should go, they me that there were two places Italians/Sicilians and other Europeans went in Sicily for their summer vacations: the beaches of Taormina and Cefalù. What did we decide? Well, because we're nuts, Kim and I took off for a much-needed buddy-day to the beach at Cefalù for this crazy-hot, sweltering, Sicilian summer day.

An interesting and funny side note. What is it about older Sicilian men when a woman asks for their opinion about a certain place to go? All of a sudden you're getting directions to a place, complete with outlining it on the map, when you've informed them—at least five times during the conversation—that you have already been that way, already been on that highway seventeen times, and have actually passed that city many times before, and you really weren't asking for directions anyway?

"Which way are you going?" the man who I asked said.

"We'll be taking the highway west towards Enna and then going north, because we've taken that highway many times," I responded.

"Ah, well then you need to turn right out of the TLA and head for the highway signs that read Enna to the west."

"Right, we've taken that highway lots of times."

"So when you get to that highway, head towards Enna, it's a beautiful drive and a great highway," he ever-so-helpfully let me know.

. . . breathe Maria, breathe . . .

"When you get to the split of the highway . . ." he continued.

"Oh, you mean that point where you can go either left or right, east or west, and Cefalù is to the right, east, so we go right?" I responded.

"When you get to the split of the highway, you want to go right, east."

"Yes, I've been that way many times."

"It's very easy, you won't miss it, you need to go right, east, at that split, towards Cefalù, you'll see the signs, so head that way."

And so it went, on and on and on and . . . *basta*!

Cefalù was ridiculously crowded, but gorgeous. I started feeling my usual claustrophobic "get me the hell out of here" when we got to the beach itself and had to try to find half an inch of space in which to put our stuff. Getting into the water, though, calmed me as always. Now, Kim would say at this point, "Uh Maria, you didn't make it out past the rocks." Well, yeah, but those damn rocks led out to the sandy part of the sea, big rocks, little rocks, tiny rocks, ouch ouch ouch! I wanted those jelly shoes that the Italians were wearing, because that's the smart way. Normally I have no qualms whatsoever about getting thrown around or knocked over by huge waves and have a blast (and they were rolling in big and fast), but when you're knocked down onto rocks while trying to get out there to the sandy part it's not much fun anymore. We decided next time to head to the south coast and make sure to have those type of shoes! So I was able to brace myself against this huge rock and let the waves overtake me. It was cooling, refreshing and I was able to get that wonderful water feeling. I wished I could just live on it!

We found a great little beachside restaurant named *Il Gabbiano* on the coast road; about 20 types of antipasti (we were both antipasti freaks and usually just got one big plate of eggplant, zucchini, parmigiano, meats, cheeses, all sorts of fun stuff like that). Cefalù itself was pretty nice, and worth spending a day exploring; the Duomo—the old *lavatorio*, the "washing place"—was interesting (though stinky from the homeless and others using it as a toilet) and down a stone staircase reminiscent of a grotto. It was, or would have been were it not for the smell, a great little cool place to sit and relax our hot feet in the cold springs. We stopped in a few wine shops, as we were always on the lookout for some of our favorite blends of Nero d'Avola/Cabernet Sauvignon, Nero d'Avola/Merlot, and the king Nero d'Avola/Syrah. Yes, we found a few different producers and bought them all.

❧ ❧ ❧

I'd been doing a lot of thinking also about what I wanted for my future, both near and far. My immediate future was, of course, getting away from the narcissistic crap there. It should've be an easy enough decision, though it wasn't. Mostly because it was a scary-as-hell decision. If I went for what I wanted—which was to do all the assistance on my own of teaching the new arrivals about Sicilian food and culture, how to get along there, introducing them to the supermarkets and wonderful small *agriturismi*, independent of the TLA—it meant taking a leap of faith involving renting an apartment in a town close to base and making it happen. The commanders insisted it would be a great idea and they were one hundred percent behind me on it, assuring me that I was and always would be their go-to. But it meant no immediate income, at least until I got it started. And then there were the thousand what-ifs: what if it didn't work, what if it no one wanted to pay for the service, what if I ran out of money. What if what if what if.

There were so many pros to the idea. I'd be living in a nice town called Trecastagni, where I'd be able to go see things and walk all over, which was something I missed tremendously. I wouldn't be dealing with this kindergarten crap. I'd have my life back.

Then there were the cons. It was possible it wouldn't work out. Then I'd run out of money and the prospect for employment was next to nil there. I'd be back to where I started almost two years before.

I was going to be 46 in a couple months. The dreams, the desires, that I left everything for, were not attainable in my present position. They could be if I took this chance. Leaving the position, the status and respect that I'd attained with the commands was a tough thing to think about. The questions flowed through my brain, "If the individuals don't have the money to pay for the services I want to provide them, where will they get it? Where will they get what I give them, what they say they enjoy so very much about coming to the TLA? They'll go back to spending their time here sitting in front the television watching 900 channels while the beauty of Sicily awaits them. Staying in the triangle of base housing to base work to base food shopping. Never taking off for a small *agriturismo* to try the wonderful foods because no one will be arranging their weekly dinners for them. No one to draw maps, give them itineraries for seeing all that this island has to offer. Who will send them an email two weeks before they get here, to alleviate their concerns about coming to a foreign country for the first time?" I couldn't stop my thinking.

I wanted to be concerned about them, all the future new arrivals and reservists, but I had to be concerned about me too. I couldn't continue that level of stress, the working seven days a week for 12 and 14 and 16 hours straight.

It was a scary thought to take the leap.

Earthquakes and Volcanoes
Thursday, July 22

I heard the familiar ring attached to Kim's number on my cell, glanced at the clock, and my heart skipped a few beats.

In my life I've never had a phone call at 4 a.m. that was good news.

"I'm sorry to wake you, but I'm scared," she said. In the span of two seconds, many scenarios went through my head. Someone in the house, Kim hurt; Zanni (the first rescue cat) escaped and gone; Devra; fire.

Wide-awake now, I immediately asked, "What what what's happened?"

With a bit of a tremor in her voice, she said, "Either there's a poltergeist in my bed or there's an earthquake. All the car alarms are going off in the town, and my bed literally moved a few inches, the dogs are barking and everyone is outside!"

So I did what any best buddy would do: I said, "Are you alone?"

To which I received the response, "MARIA!"

I then said, "Obviously it's not because you're having fun, so . . . WAY COOL, " I yelled, "the volcano's getting ready to erupt!" Maybe it wasn't the calm, soothing, best buddy thing to do, and I was of course concerned with her safety and all that, but we'd been waiting for Etna to erupt the whole time we'd been living there.

Why did she feel the quake and I didn't? Well, she lived in Zafferana Etnea, which is halfway up Etna itself and one of my favorite towns in Sicily. I lived at the bottom of Etna, and felt nothing in my apartment. I'd been through a couple quakes before in California, and maybe I slept through it, but I don't recall quakes in California having a big boom noise before them. The boom is the precursor, the force of the volcano itself as it explodes within itself, rumbling in its precursor to eruption. Later that morning we saw thick white smoke billowing out. I'd been hearing from the locals that the eruption usually took place about three weeks or so from the quake. Personally I couldn't wait!

They were wrong. The very next day, I saw a sight I never imagined in my life. With a huge, window-rattling BOOM, Etna rumbled and exploded in a both terrifying and awesome mixture of rocks, ash, and burning lava. As I looked over the land and stared at the plume bursting out and the river of lava beginning to flow down, criss-crossing through the hills, my heart was pounding and racing from this terrifying demonstration of nature's power. Being so close to it brought about feelings that have never left me.

A Real Vacation Can Bring Clarity
Friday, October 15

The time finally came—a real, one-week vacation, destination Malta. It was quite the choice between Malta, Tunisia, and Greece. Timing-wise, Malta won. If I had had more time for the vacation, Greece would've won hands down, as I was thinking of Corfu. I prefer to go where I haven't been before and, while I had been to Greece, I had not been to Corfu. Tough decision!

I so needed this break. I felt a little bad about the timing, as one of my people who'd been there for a couple months would be leaving the day after I came home, and now wouldn't get to have his "final dinner" that I usually arranged when one is leaving. But that was okay, they knew how to make me feel better and just said, "Please don't be concerned about it—you do so much for us, and now it's your turn. Go. You deserve a break. Forget us for a week!" I really did meet some wonderful people throughout my time there.

I bought a tour-book for the islands and, as I was reading it, I thought to myself that I surely couldn't get into too much trouble if I just winged it, right? I didn't really want to "tour," but wanted to see things I hadn't; and then I wrestled with the

other me, the one who said she wanted to do nothing more than relax, swim, jacuzzi, have a couple massages.
And sleep.
And think.
. . .
. . .
. . .
. . .
And not think.
Just be.
I wanted to sit and stare at the water. At the beautiful blue of the Mediterranean. I wanted to forget everything and everyone. I remember wondering if that was a bad thing and made me a thoughtless, selfish person. I hated that I'd let my stress rise to that level; rise to the level that I'd forgotten me. I'd lost me. My attitude towards certain people in the recent past had been horrible, and that wasn't me. I was hurting people, and I abhorred that in myself. I wasn't sleeping well, was having daily headaches, and I didn't want to eat because it made me sick and food wasn't sitting well. I seemed to sleep yet I woke up exhausted as if I hadn't.

But I vowed to relax while I was away, to find myself again, somewhere in that beautiful expanse of Mediterranean water. Somewhere in there, somewhere out there, was me. And at the end of the vacation, I would go home—go back to my life there—and make amends. I would be me again.

‰ ‰ ‰

Sometimes we descend into the dark. And then we claw our way OUT, into the light.

"*It may not be too difficult to do good; it is more difficult to be good.*

But to maintain a good mental attitude and to do some service to others in the face of accusations, criticisms and obstructions is most difficult of all." (Buddhist Thought of the Day, a few days prior)

"Some persons are like letters carved on a rock; they easily give way to anger and retain their angry thoughts for a long time. Some are like letters written in sand; they give way to anger also, but the angry thoughts quickly pass away. Some men are like letters written in the water; they do not retain their passing thoughts. But the perfect ones are like letters written in the Wind; they let abuse and uncomfortable gossip pass by unnoticed. Their minds are always pure and undisturbed." (Buddhist Thought of the Day, one day prior)

I think someone or something was trying to tell me something. It'd been a rough ride the previous month or so. Malta was amazing! I took a couple small tours suggested by the hotel, which were beautiful drives around the island and over to Valetta, and stops at archaeological sites. It was a bit chaotic there, a lot of traffic and noise, but I enjoyed every minute of it. The rest of the time was spent doing basically nothing but swimming in each of the two (I have this tendency to not stay at one hotel for the full time I am anywhere, I have no idea why) hotels' many freshwater and seawater pools, going from pool to bar-at-the-pool to pool to lounge chair to bar to pool, rinse-and-repeat! The tours were interesting, but I found that I spent so much of the time staring at the sea, feeling the wind on my face, and wishing John could be with me instead of deep inside that stupid war in Iraq, with the possibility of never feeling the sea wind on his face again. I tried to think of other things and not that. Tried to think and make some decisions, but I found it difficult.

When I got back from vacation, I found that something had happened to me; that somehow my mind had decided that my patience with my work situation had come to an end. My attitude began to change—not completely, but it was starting, and that was the important thing. The passive female American worker in a foreign country? I think not! Work stress, nasty, back-stabbing coworkers, and office hell happens everywhere in the world, even in "paradise." Years of strong Sicilian female blood began to rise up and say, "Hey, not this time buddy, this ends NOW." I would defend myself, whether anyone liked it or not. I made the decision that if I lost my job because of it, then I was past caring and knew that the commanders had my back in that there was a reason why they sent their people to where I worked. And they had a choice.

After the darkness, the light always arrives.

I See Dead People
Monday, May 16

"Hey Maria, I wanna go see dead people."

"Uh Kim, I thought you bought *Sixth Sense* on DVD."

"Well I did! But that's a movie—I wanna go see dead people dammit." Kim was being quite adamant.

"Okay tes, *stai calma*. When and where?"

"Let's go to Palermo. Like soon. How about after the dinner on Friday?"

"Palermo's close. Okay. But not Friday because we won't get home until midnight and we'll be drunk, remember?"

"Oh yeah. I forgot. Geez, it's been so long since we've done the dinners. Okay, let's leave Saturday."

"You're off work Saturday, I'm not."

"Tell him to give you the day off."

It took me a minute to stop laughing at that crazy suggestion, so merely said: "Yeah that's gonna happen. I'll talk to him though."

An hour later, I called her back, reporting, "Okay, I've got Saturday afternoon off, he was in a human mood."

"Yay! I have to just wait for the landlord to come to get the rent and we can go. I should be able to pick you up by about 2:00."

I'm not sure why I bothered pleading for the afternoon off, since an SMS finally arrived at 4:00 p.m. with the pronouncement, *"Landlord just left, leaving house in 10 minutes."* Her landlord never showed up on time. But it didn't matter—it was time for a buddy trip! The sun was shining, it was warm, and had been far too long since we'd done this; we were so ready!

With the Eagles playing on the CD player, as all road trips started off with this CD, we spent the first hour relaxing and discussing the last evening's events. It had been a dinner just like it used to be in the beginning—a fantastic group and nothing but laughter. People who worked together all day long split up and met others. This was something I strove for when I organized those dinners. Just sharing fresh, delicious food and wine. We usually always took *before* and *after* photos for blackma— I mean, because they're just too funny! The changes that came over everyone, with ranks not mattering for these few hours, were fun to see.

By the time we reached Palermo, the sun was beginning to set as we made excellent time; after going in 17 circles down 62 one-way streets in the heart of Palermo trying to find the hotel, the *Ai Cavalieri* finally appeared. Though a *Best Western*, it didn't seem like it; very elegant, prices were good, staff very friendly and attentive. It had been a bit of a stressful time the last few months for both of us so we splurged and got a suite with a jacuzzi tub in it. A bit spendy, but worth it! Actually the shower massage was even better than the jacuzzi tub—it had one spray setting on it that had me yelling out: "I want one of these!" I never was able to find one.

Although we had initially arrived in Palermo at 6:40 p.m., by the time we made 653 circles and arrived at the hotel it was 8:00 p.m. and all we could think of was food. We were tired and not up for much, so stopped into a Chinese restaurant for a quick plate. We had our plans in place for typical *Palermitane* dishes such as *pasta con le sarde* (pasta with sardines, fennel, pine nuts, raisin), as well as couscous and *baccafiggu* (Sicilian) for the vegetarian the next day. For this overnight trip to a city as huge as Palermo, we'd decided on three easily-seen things: the botanical gardens, the Norman palazzo, and, of course, the dead people.

The botanical gardens were quite interesting, beautiful, and worth spending a little time wandering in, admiring all the greenery, statues, trees, taking the obligatory "photo inside the tree hut" thing. There was a pretty little ground aquarium with different colored stones in a large circle. Kim upset the entire ecological system (although she vehemently denies it).

The conversation went like this:

"Look, there's a little tiny fish-bug-thing on the leaf. He's stuck."

"I'm sure he'll figure out how to get off."

"He's stuck."

"And? Oh hell, what are you doing . . . " I said as Kim ducked under the fence and tipped over the leaf.

"See? He's now swimming happily, happy to be free!"

"Hmm."

"What?"

"So what if you've now just upset the whole ecological system? What if he was laying something on the leaf?"

"No, I freed him!"

"Or he was meant to be there and some dragonfly-type insect is now going to die because that was his lunch and then some frog was going to eat the dragonfly and now can't?"

"Nope, I did a good thing 'cause now he's free!"

"While upsetting the entire ecological system! And now the fish and bug world is forever topsy-turvy!"

At this point people were looking at us because we were laughing so hard, coughing from gasping for breath. It felt so good, because we hadn't been able to do this kind of thing for so long! After leaving the gardens, we wandered back to the car and decided we'd get to the Norman palazzo, lunch, and leave the catacombs for last.

Being Sunday, the palazzo was closed, so our time there was spent just walking around it and ending up at the cathedral, which we immediately departed after saying, "Oh look, another church," went in, looked around in a 180, and left. That was never our thing, we had no real interest in seeing churches. Off we went to walk around and have lunch, while waiting for the catacombs to re-open. Sunday afternoon is not the time to wander the non-center neighborhoods trying to find couscous and fish, or even a trattoria that was open. But we were nothing if not stubborn and determined! It took about an hour, but we finally stumbled upon a small place, crowded with Sicilians, and enjoyed a cheap, filling, high-quality meal.

Now, it was time for dead people—I mean, the catacombs. The eagerly anticipated catacombs. I'd heard far too many times from so many people things like, "It was so creepy I couldn't stay!" or, "Oh my god, it's just oooh ick yuck." When we walked in, I felt an immediate sense of respect at everything I saw, and couldn't believe how many people were just basically running through it, glancing at one or two of the bodies, and heading straight for only the famous "little girl".

The background on the monastery's embalmed mummies is pretty cool. Back in the 16th century the monks ran out of room in their cemetery and began to excavate crypts, mummifying the bodies of those who died after, mostly just their own friars. Some were embalmed; others sealed into glass cabinets; but all were left in their everyday clothing and even with their penance ropes. As the years went by, it became almost a status symbol to be "buried" there, and some of the richer and more important people would put it in their wills that they be mummified and placed there. Some even had the audacity to put in their wills that their bodies were to be "taken care of", including changing the clothing regularly.

The friars would make sure the donation payments were made in an interesting manner: as long as you paid, the body stayed. If your relative no longer sent money, your body was put aside on a shelf until they resumed payments.

The most famous, and last, interment is known as "the little girl", Rosalia Lombardo. Mummified in the early 1920s when she died at two years old, she is the most perfectly preserved body there, performed with a new and special embalming procedure. Hers is most famous for how remarkably alive she looks, as if simply sleeping. Her body has frightened many people.

There were 8,000 corpses and 1,252 mummies at last count in 2011. If you wanted interment there, you had to be cautious how you lived your life: your placement was determined by men, women, virgins, children, priests, monks, and professionals.

While I found "the little girl" to be incredibly interesting, we were more amazed at the other bodies and things such as how the embalming stopped hair growth. Or would that be hair loss? You could see moustache whiskers! It was interesting to see entire families, and to speculate by the year what the reasoning was for an entire family being wiped out. Did they all die at the same time? Or did they just have all the coffins from the family and put them up together? Speculation. The priests' section revealed the wide variety of clothing they were buried in. Some in full colorful robes, others simplistically basic. The cardinal in his full finery. The care the women were given in burial, with knees seemingly bent modestly. Some with such peaceful looks to their faces in death. Had their eyes met a loved one's as they took their final breath?

All in all, it was quite an interesting little trip for being just one day and night. I really wanted to take a few days at some point and go back to wander the streets. During the drive, the contrasts were startling, one moment upper-class, then immediately older and very mixed, then residential. The city was huge. While it was very new in many parts, it was, at the same time, so very culturally, archeologically and artistically rich.

We got on the autostrada to begin the quiet trip home, tired but content with what we had managed to do for our little one-day trip. It was much-needed buddy time, and much-needed relaxation time too.

Crazy Nights
Saturday, May 28

After spending a wonderful, laughter-filled evening at a fantastic, newly discovered *agriturismo*, I mentioned to my driver (a TLA co-worker) on the ride home that there was one sound that made me smile every time: the sound of all the voices in the van jabbering and laughing. It was loud, it was noisy, but it always made me smile, because it meant everyone was having a wonderful time. And that was my goal at every dinner. The reason why I made myself nuts planning and organizing them.

It was the laughter. The playtime. And that look in their eyes when they gave me a strong hug and said, "Thank you so much for making my last night here so memorable."

The Romance Fades; Reality Rears its Ugly Head
Late 2005

The darkness descends again, but this time it brought light with it. Bear with me for a moment here.

The questions kept raging through my mind, what the hell was I doing, what had I done? I was playing with "halt" (hungry, angry, lonely, tired) more than I wanted and was three out of four most often, with a full four out of four the remaining times. I gave up a lot to go to Sicily, and there was just so much conflict within me, in me, around me, surrounding me, smacking me constantly over my head. I wished with all of me that I could just crawl back into the wonderful existence I had in Florence; Lynda and I were poor as church mice, but we were happy, healthy, and alive. How many times we walked from the apartment and through the city, along the great river. We would simply walk and talk, about our lives, about this huge decision we had made, and what we had dreamed would be the outcome, the result. How many times we had stopped and gazed at the river, at the lights of Ponte Vecchio, at the grand Duomo rising high above the skyline, the stars in the sky. What happened to those dreams?

In my new life there, I discovered that the realities of life were very different. It was no longer the Italy of my youth. The realities of life there while not on vacation were the same realities of life everywhere. Most of the non-retired, non-wealthy expats (those who hadn't sold a house and used the proceeds to buy and renovate a villa) had to work 14, 15 hours at three jobs, sharing apartments with two, three, four other people to afford the rent and bills. If I were one of those people who was retired with, say, a pensioned income steadily coming in, and the proceeds from the sale of a house, then it probably would be as if I were on vacation. Or if I were there under one of the huge company/government work contracts like the embassy or FAO, or any of the others. Then I would be free to enjoy that quaint little existence, taking walks, sitting in the town café for hours on end, spending my time wandering markets. If one can do that, then more power to them. That's a wonderful thing to be able to do! Heck, there's a part of me that in a way envies that ability; maybe that's why I used to play one dollar on the lottery every week.

However, only a very small percentage of the people both in Sicily and in other expat communities across the world are able to do that. Not many others can. In the preface to this book, I promised that I was going to share the realities of life which occur when you scramble to make a living and afford rent in a large and expensive city. I promised that this wasn't going to be anything about being in a fabled paradise.

And so, I feel obliged to share with you the honest realities about this country that is in my blood, my heart, and which I have always loved. As I was of the societal membership that needs to work at a job in order to have the money to pay the multitude of bills, deal with governmental bureaucracy, shop when all the other working people shop, trying to time the traffic, and dealing with the non-stop, every-other-week transportation strikes, I viewed this country in a very different light. The little outdoor markets were usually only open while I and most other people were at work, so we shopped at the supermarkets. Yes, the large supermarkets. Why? Because that's all the time we had. We stood in the lines and dealt with it because we could get all we needed there, in one place. It was still very fresh, the fruits and vegetables brought in daily, the meat and fish fresh. We shopped for a few days or a week at a time, buying Italian-produced canned tomatoes for instance, because we knew that they were good and we could pop open that can and make a beautiful sauce for our pasta that was just as good as if we had had the time to go shop for tomatoes at the market. Economics are economics—it is cost-effective to do this, especially if there's a sale. The use of microwaves is becoming more frequent, pre-packaged foods being consumed, carts full of frozen foods.

Time. Economics. Convenience. Necessity.

Just like anywhere, we dealt with cultural differences in the workplace, with employers who were like employers anywhere else. Some good to work for, others just general tyrants who wanted everything their way, and who wouldn't listen to a suggestion if their businesses depended on it. I'm sure we've all run into those. Yet, another important factor in this equation, is that the possibility didn't exist to just go from job to job. They were not plentiful nor easy to come by. Unemployment was crazy-high, so we stayed where we were. Instead of telling our employer to "take this job and . . . ," we took it, so that we had the means to live, to survive in a foreign country that we'd chosen to call home. And that within us we loved, for it was deeply entrenched in our hearts.

I spent a long time there recently dealing with these cultural differences in the workplace. Our clientele was 95% American, so I could not be "Sicilian" when dealing with them. On the other hand, I could not be "American" when dealing with my Sicilian employer. Someone once told me that I used my duality to my advantage, that I was Sicilian when it suited me and American when it suited me. When that was first said to me, I took a bit of offense. But perhaps it was true. I used my "Sicilian-ness," my lineage, when I needed it. When I needed help from a *paisano*; when I was out and about in town or helping someone. When did the other part of me come out? It's hard to tell exactly, but it wasn't a part of me that I used to my advantage, as I did with the Sicilian. It wasn't something that I was even really aware of. But I was still American, my thoughts many times American, as were my seeming sensibilities when problems and conflicts between the two arose. At the same time, I was Sicilian, my thoughts many times Sicilian. I was raised in two worlds, ever walking back and forth along a swinging bridge, and it had been swinging more and more as the days passed.

It's clear by now to anyone reading this, that what started out as promising had become a match made in hell. The amount of stress I went through with the constant berating, put-downs, having things thrown instead of handed to me, the yelling—this working situation was entirely foreign to me. I was used to being self-sufficient, secure in my intelligence. A firm decision was desperately needed.

When I had decided to leave it all six years previous, I wanted to do just that. Leave it all. Go back to my roots. Go back to what I knew so very many years ago. To immerse myself in the language, the customs, this world. I was like so many others who fell in love with this country when I lived there, and that love came back to me when I visited for the school reunion. It all seemed so quaint, so opposite to my life at that time.

I didn't want to live the life and lifestyle that I had been living for the last 25 years. During those years, I lived a conflicting life in my mind—I had changed and returned to the States as a different person, with different thoughts and attitudes and views. I've mentioned before that when I returned to the States back in 1979, I never felt as though I fit; could never find my niche. Everything was so different.

So I decided to go back. To where it had always felt so right, so comfortable. And I found myself once again confused. Not sure where I fit. Again living a dual life, walking the tightrope swinging bridge. Is it any wonder there was confusion? Is there any question why so often I felt so lost?

I won't go on too much more about this darkness, as I think you get what I'm saying. The frustration that was interfering with my life. Interfering with my dreams, my wants, my desires. Questioning who I was. I faltered in my language, confused as to which to speak and things came out a jumble sometimes (just like any bilingual person). My body was never sure what was going on as I spent time with the guests, eating the American food bought in the commissary. Long-forgotten tastes came to the surface. Desires. Memories.

So the decision to be made was whether, or even how, I could live in both worlds, and reconcile both to stand side-by-side, to live within me in harmony.

Il Mio Sconosciuto
. . . or how an otherwise dull evening became a Mona Lisa smile

After all the darkness, there came a piece of the light that shone through. A little story of a happy little memory.

As I sat at my table on the ship coming back to Sicily after spending a few days away, out of the corner of my eye I noticed someone coming my way, looking for a space to sit to eat. As I felt his presence, I glanced up and our eyes met, before I quickly looked away. A minute or so later I glanced up again, only to find him doing the same. This time I smiled before looking away, and the smile was returned. There was something in those eyes, a sense of recognition. I questioned myself internally, *Have we met before? Passed each other somewhere? No, I think not. You are unknown to me, you are my* sconosciuto *(stranger, unknown).* As we continued eating, his phone rang and he began talking. I thought to myself, *this could be fortunate*—I was sure I heard the Sicilian dialect, replete with slang.

It was nearly time for the ship to take sail so off I went to stand on deck. Out of the corner of my eye, I was pleased to see my *sconosciuto* was right behind me, though still not having spoken even a word to me. As I stood alternately watching the take-off ritual and the sun beginning to set over the city of Naples, I already knew he was standing beside me. We two *sconosciuti* turned to each other and smiled, again feeling a sense of . . . *conoscimento*, knowing. Perhaps it's possible, during all my travels, I suppose. I heard him softly ask if I spoke Italian; I've been told I look Italian, with my Sicilian blood, but I guess not to everyone. Of course I answered yes, and he responded with, "I'm so happy, because I heard you speaking English on your cellphone, so I wasn't sure I'd be able to talk to you."

When he asked my name, I almost didn't want to say. What fun it would be to keep it a shipboard moment, a sense of the romantic to go along with the hot, crowded city becoming glittery, shiny and pretty in the sunset. "Maria," I replied, "and yours?" With a grin, he said, "Max." I laughed and questioned how that could possibly be Italian. With the cutest of grins, he teasingly said, "Okay, my name is Massimo, is that not Max in English?" Giving him points for that try, our conversation continued as I asked if he was Sicilian, judging from his accent. With a proud puff of the chest, he declared, "Absolutely not! Born and raised in Napoli!" Although I was tired, I accepted his invitation for coffee. I couldn't resist those eyes. There was something about him, and I wanted to continue the conversation, the release I was feeling from laughing and enjoying myself, knowing what was to come the next day back at the office. We talked of life, of the world, of the importance of being a good person. He told me stories of life as an Italian over-the-road transport driver.

Later, he and I played like carefree children on the deck of the ship in the rain, listening to thunder and watching lightning over the churning sea, doing gymnastics on the railing and getting soaked from the rain while playing "I'm the king of the world", laughing and just having fun. Well into the night we stayed on deck talking and listening to the water rushing by as we sailed through it; while it seemed the rest of the ship was asleep, there was just us. This night was made for something like this, it was ours alone. As time moved on, we didn't know it.

Was it the romance of the journey, the commanding nature of the stormy sea, the booms of thunder and cracks of lighting; or was it simply the thrill of knowing we would be only a single part of this moment, there would be no tomorrow for us? In that knowledge, that one single moment, we were drawn to each other, succeeding in making a pocket of warm air where we stood. His breath was warm as he whispered in my ear, "Close your eyes and just listen, listen to the wind, the thunder, the beat of my heart." The lightning was not in the sky, for its electricity was there, charging the small space of warmth we had found and made.

Though the wind howled, I heard his breathing.

Though we did not quite touch, I felt his skin.

In an instant the warmth was almost too much.

I opened my eyes to find him watching me; those eyes had become the color of the stormy night sea.

There was only now.

Words were unnecessary.

We closed that space and sealed the pocket of warmth. His kindness, gentleness and compliments helped ease a little of my stress, feeding my ego and making me feel good about myself again. It had been too long since I had let go and played, just simply enjoyed being alive, without thinking about anything. There had been too much pain; I needed this. When he told me he admired me for what I was doing in my life, for taking that chance, I felt my heart swell. We talked about this book, and when he asked if this night, this *bella serata fra due sconosciuti*, would be included, I knew it would be. How could it not, this beautiful night between two strangers?

Little slices of life. Little things given to us that help us through when we're feeling bad, when we're feeling afraid, when we're feeling stressed about what's to come in just a few hours.

Will I ever forget those blue eyes? That smile? No way. Will I ever forget how I felt when he said my eyes laughed too, that I gave him a sense of hope for the future at his young age?

When I remember those eyes and that smile, it helps calm me.

I'm the king of the world.

Philosophical Reality Intrudes

While having a long conversation with one of our visitors once, I was reminded of why I had left it all behind. The differences in thoughts and life-views that I experienced from when I left Italy at 19 throughout the remainder of time until I returned, from what I had learned in my time since, looking at the world through adult eyes.

We are sheltered always by the realities of what is going on in our world. The highest leaders allow for the masses to hear only what they wish for them to know. What they need for their justification. For me, each day was filled with listening to those who were put in harm's way. My nights were filled with longing for one who is in harm's way every minute. Those who were giving up their lives, their homes, their loves, as a result of what their leaders dictated. I listened to their stories with both sides of me, and saw their eyes shadowed with the pain of what they'd seen, done, and been through. I bid them goodbye, telling them to please stay safe and to return. Some did—and some didn't. I listened during this conversation for many hours to one who was young in age, but equal to me and then some in what he had witnessed and been a part of. I listened as he spoke of the horrific realities of our present world, searching for body parts from a downed airliner, and I tried to listen with both sides of me, even objectively. He spoke of the near future-consequences that are kept out of the media and not included in the "reports" of the leaders. We are kept sheltered and safe and feelings justified because of what is untold.

Words of songs take on new meanings. We shared our time listening and singing along with Simon and Garfunkel, Jim Croce, Irish jigs and Nova Scotian traditionals. We spoke of and toasted to the frailty of life; of doing what is necessary to snatch, to grab and hold on tight, to everything that makes us smile, gives us comfort, helps us continue on in this life and to maintain our dreams. To never, ever, let go of our hope and dreams. We exchanged cultures and gave of ourselves. We learned from each other. And that's what it's about. Acceptance and knowledge and learning, forever learning. What started for me in six years of international schooling surrounded by 10-20 cultures all those many long years ago, continued to that day and for the rest of my life.

It was times like those that reminded me that if I continued to remember what I'd learned, if I continued to remind myself that I am in fact of two worlds, then maybe I could find a middle ground. I could find a way to shorten that bridge, and stop running from one end to the other. I could make it stop swinging, and that would allow me to continually cross over with ease.

Hell, sometimes I thought I should've just gone with my initial idea of selling squeaky motorized rubber duckies in Duomo square. But then I wouldn't have had the experiences I did, the good among the bad.

There's Always a Why

I suppose after reading the last few chapters you might be asking why. Why did you do this? Why did you go through all of this, when you could just as easily have taken off? You talked about your psycho boss and working for someone you personally disliked, despised even, who made you feel small and insignificant and made you question your very worth, and how your life then became one big question. Why didn't you put on your big-girl panties, pull yourself up by the proverbial bootstraps and simply leave?

Why indeed.

Do you remember the first time you visited somewhere new? A new culture, with new foods, new sights, new sounds? I do. The wonder of it all, as your eyes took in the beauty of the land, the awe-inspiring sculptures, the crumble of the ruins, as your mind struggled to reconcile our bright, fancy, technological world, with the world of so very long ago.

Do you remember how you felt? As excited as a child, eyes open wide. I must remember it all, you think, because I don't know when I will ever get here again.

Whenever I got so tired, when I thought I couldn't take it anymore, in through my door walked a weary traveler, a little frightened underneath the exhaustion of moving, packing up, leaving their world behind, and 18 hours or more of flying, unsure how they were going to communicate even to check in to the hotel. They were stepping over the threshold into their new life and the fear was almost palpable. I saw the change in their eyes as I spoke in their own language and welcomed them to their new home with a smile and peaceful calm. Their resulting smiles lifted me up. They didn't feel so afraid, nor so far from home anymore. I told them I would help them to adjust and to not be afraid.

Why did I do this? Well, I vowed to take them on a little journey and show them the wondrous things they had to look forward to in their new home.

It was the dinners I took them to. Watching their eyes light up, and the resulting smiles as they tasted all these new things. Watching them relax as the wine flowed. They were outside their gates and barbed-wire fences, and in that moment, for that evening at least, they had no rank of which to be concerned. They were beginning to understand that they just might be okay in this new life for the next few years, learning these new things.

It was their laughter that was music to me, and made all of it worthwhile. It was when they came to me to clear up some misinformation they were given about the culture. I took them to the grocery stores, to the market, to the bar for a coffee. As we interacted with the locals, I saw the beginning of an understanding in them, that all of those warnings had to be taken with the proverbial grain of salt. Italians and Sicilians are just like people anywhere else. They smile at you when you pass them on the street, they are not stealing from you at every turn as you were warned. I watched my charges begin to relax as they were introduced to that world. To the world I had made my home.

How many memories I have of all of the people who came through my door. How could I possibly begin to describe all the dinners, the places I took them to, introducing them to this culture through its food and its ritual of dining. I purposely always chose out-of-the-way places, the *agriturismi* and family farms, so that they could experience, many for the first time in their lives, the way it is done there. The looks on their faces as they ate true, fresh, sometimes still warm, ricotta—no additives, no preservatives, not the part-skim-low-moisture-yada-yada stuff that isn't anywhere near what it is truly supposed to be; the plate after plate of antipasti that contained no deep-fried cheese or potato skins, but contained vegetables picked fresh that morning right there, marinated or grilled or simple; the two different types of fresh pasta, different from restaurant to restaurant; the meat dishes, sometimes specialties, or sometimes a mixture of beautiful Sicilian sausage, steak, veal, pork; and the desserts, oh the desserts, a sinfully lush, sweet ricotta blended to creaminess placed inside a pastry shell that brought audible sighs of pure delight upon tasting, or typical Sicilian sweets, or fruit. And let's not forget the endless local wines, bottle after bottle, toasts made to new friendships and old friends returned, inhibitions and fears laid aside as this introduction continued.

They came into my life, sometimes for only a couple of weeks, while others came for a couple months. And one, Kim, even came into my life and stayed forever as my best buddy. Some were new to me, while others returned once or twice a year, always with a huge smile as they walked through the door, asking: "Do you remember me?" My response always being, "Of course I do! How could I possibly forget you?" Invariably their second question was always, "Which restaurant are you going to take us to this week? I've been looking forward to it since I was told I was coming back! Can we go to X? Oh wait, no, how about Y? Oh wait, I remember that dessert at Z!"

And I would smile, let go and laugh, and remember why I did it. When they left, they told me I had given them a gift they would never forget, a memory they would take home with them. But I wondered—did they realize what a gift they gave me?

It was their laughter that came back to me when I looked at the pictures from the dinners, at the before and after shots. I could always hear the voices, the laughter, the clinking of the glasses, *salutè! salutè!*

It was the nights spent exploring the city with new friends as we, fortified from food and repetitive *digestivi* (after-dinner liquors, *amaretto*, *Sambuca*, etc.) from various bars throughout our search of the nooks and crannies of a city built, destroyed by lava, and rebuilt from the rubble.

It was the barbecues held on various apartment balconies, time spent relaxing with old and new friends, trying various varieties of wine, sharing our lives. I watched them gaze out at the landscape, the mountains, sea and lights of various villages; I saw the long, slow intake of breath and watched their eyes close, breathing in the night air, the silence and peace of the endless ages of times before them. What was it about those Sicilian views that opened the mind and heart, revealing the depths within us, revealing things we never otherwise would have?

It was times like those, the life I led there, that led me to meet Kim. My rock, my balance, my yang.

It was the smiles, and the heartfelt thank yous I received when they left the little TLA nest I gave them. They were ready to face their new adventure, and I was then ready to continue on. They gave me that.

They were my why.

Desperate Times Call For...
Wednesday, June 8, 2005

The time came finally that I made the decision. Found the confidence and strength to rise above it all, find my dream again and, mostly, find myself. Gathering all my fortitude, I gave my notice, bought train tickets to Rome for a week to hopefully take care of my citizenship papers, and spend some much-needed relaxation time with Lynda. I needed to get away from there for a while, and let my mind settle. My meditational breathing routine hadn't worked for a few nights since giving notice—I couldn't seem to calm my brain enough to concentrate or even get to as high as a count of three before my mind flew off in ten different directions. I was sure that leaving for a few days would help, though, getting out of the situation.

When I returned, I would live in the same apartment for some months and start work on this book. The rent was dirt cheap, and I'd saved up enough money to live there comfortably for at least a year. I gave myself a year to relax, enjoy Sicily, and see if I could bring this mission to fruition!

...Desperate Measures
Wednesday, July 27

A month and a half later my routine began to calm and, though I was doing a lot of staring at blank pages and spitting out worthless drivel, with Kim's help I began to relax. When questioning how I was doing or feeling, I slowly let go of the anger and hurt. There was so much anger. On the last day, I had refused to rise to the bait, but the words hurt nonetheless. Standing next to the bar in the lunch area of the office, which he had locked to prevent anyone disturbing us, I tried to remain calm as the boss sat on a barstool and demanded I stand and listen to him.

"Why did you bother coming back after your little trip to Rome, that you said was urgent for paperwork? Not that I believe that's why you went," he began with a sneer.

"I told you I would be back in a few days and would stay two weeks to train my replacement," I calmly replied.

"You shouldn't have come back. I don't fucking need you here, because Anna knows how to do everything. And even better than you." Anna was his girlfriend, a German woman who spoke no English in a business requiring fluent English.

A bit taken aback, but not expecting anything different, to be honest, I replied, "I gave you my word, and I always keep my word." I bit my tongue to prevent my anger and temper as I added to myself: "Unlike someone in this room."

I could do nothing more than stare in shock as he got off the barstool, picked it up and slammed it down, coming towards me, shaking his fist. I began backing away from him.

"Get the hell out of here and don't ever come back! Don't ever step foot on this property again, and do not ever speak to anyone associated with this office again. You will never again be allowed to get a ride from anyone here in my vans." As he pointed at the door, backing me towards it, some more choice words came out.

I couldn't speak to say anything more than, "You are wrong in what you're saying, and have no right or reason to be saying this. You. Have. No. Reason."

As I left and was out of his line of sight, I began shaking and crying from the intensity and fear—Was I at fault in this, I wondered? Perhaps a bit, if I'm to be honest about it. It always takes two. But as the days passed, I found I was able to breathe a little, and the cobwebs were beginning to clear. I was able to sit down one day, put a CD into the player, put the headphones on, bring up a blank page—but instead of just simply staring at it, my fingers began to form some intelligible words on the page. And I began to write. And write. It just started coming out of me. And I started to smile again. It felt so damn good! I had my mind back, and finally I began to feel like me again.

My "favorite commander" stayed in touch with me, making sure all was well and seeing if there was some way we could find to hold the dinners again. It made me sad, to be honest, whenever he said incoming people were always asking about the dinners and if we were having them. *Perhaps we'll find a way*, I thought.

On the playtime side, Kim was just about finished with the last paralegal class of hers (Legalman First Class, way to go!), which meant we finally got to spend some time together. It was nice, because both of us really, really needed our buddy time. We got some beach time in, swimming in the sea; hung out countless times at her house up on the side of Etna relaxing and just "being"; played with the cats and kittens; watched movies; ate and drank wine; kicked back on the balcony staring out at the sea and the erupting volcano. I guess I was doing what so many made the move to do, but on a more supremely moderate, smaller scale and for a limited time.

I knew I'd need to make a decision at some point soon, because the responsible part of me kept reminding myself that I needed to watch the saved money that I had and to be careful with it—I hate it when that responsible part of me rears her little head!

THE ITCH BEGINS . . . AGAIN
Thursday, August 11

A deserted August and empty TLA introduced me to a few contractors staying there long-term who became dear friends, and spending so much time with them started that same old desire in me. Gave me that familiar itch. Hearing them talk about their lives in their country, describing their cities, and telling me all about what life was really like there. No, not really what life was like, but describing the real culture. It made me want to see it, to be a part of it. Because it was something new. That was obvious.

At that point, I could honestly say I was tired of the life there in Sicily. It wasn't fun anymore. Not exciting. Is that strange to think? So many people dream of going there, whether for ancestral purposes or because of thoughts put in their heads of the life portrayed in films and books. It has its charms, indeed. Does it ever! But did I want to stay there forever? Or simply make it a "home base"? I knew that wasn't a feasible idea because I didn't have the finances to simply come and go traveling around, and keeping up rent to have somewhere to stay during trips. So it said to me that it was time to go. Time to find somewhere new, a different place to call home, at least for a while.

I had stopped caring about, or being concerned with, what people were saying about me, and it was so freeing! It opened up new paths, new ideas, new dreams and goals. I learned long ago, at the end of 1994 with my mom, that it all truly can end in the blink of an eye—which meant I was no longer willing to sit and be bored, or do nothing, waiting for "someday". The time was now. My mind raced, begging me to take a healthy drink of life again. To feed my soul. To take charge. When that responsible part of my brain reared its head and made me consider the whole financial aspect of it all, I stopped and reminded myself that even with the financial fears at the beginning of this journey, I had still made it. Then, after a time, with only 200 euros left, I did find something, and I survived. I survived the fears. I survived the tears. And I was so much stronger.

Somewhere Down the Road

Oh my love,

Sometimes goodbyes are not forever.

Sometimes I think about you and wish that it had turned out differently. When I see beauty around me. When I see a painting that widens my eyes, tilts my head, and makes me smile from the feelings it arouses. But mostly when I see a sculpture. And I remember. It's those times when I miss you, and miss watching the beauty you create. I remember watching in awe your hands, as your fingers felt and shaped the clay.

The same hands that touched me, and brought to life passions I never knew existed.

I can feel even now the coolness of the night air and the slight breeze as you walked me home that first night, a walk I had made hundreds of times alone even in the dark. You said you wanted to keep away any bad night things.

I can see even now the look in your eyes as I looked back at you after parting at the gate. Walking the three steps back to you was not even a thought, nor anything I consciously did. I remember your shy smile at that moment. And I remember the feel of you, knowing that this was the moment our lives would change.

The memory of it even now closes my eyes and brings a smile.

Gazing out at the stars in the sky over the hills and sea, you said you wished you could stay forever. You wanted to paint Etna with the light reflected from the moon. I wanted to see it through your creative eyes. I remember wishing at that moment to never have to leave the safety and warmth of your arms.

I can hear your voice as you said you knew beauty because you looked in my eyes. I can still hear your whispered words of love as your sculptor's hands gently treated me like a soft piece of clay, and the fiery passion in your artist's eyes.

I can see even now the look in your eyes when you left. That cocky little grin that made me smile through the tears. The wink as you slung your bag over your shoulder. The intensity of your words, I will come back.

Did we somehow know, even then, the destiny of us? That we truly did have the right love, but at the wrong time?

It must be the air tonight, the smell on the gentle breeze, that brought this back to me, though so much time has passed. Sometimes these thoughts of you taunt me, and so I play with the memories and of what might have been.

But the memories of you are not a bad thing, because memories that bring smiles can't be wrong.

Different Air

With plans formulating themselves in my mind, I spent two weeks at Kim's house in Zafferana, taking care of her cats and house while she was in the States on vacation. It couldn't have come at a better time. The escape, the grounding, the ability to go away and think. Just think in the peace and quiet of kitty purrs and a rumbling volcano.

How beautiful it was. The end-of-summer weather just beginning to change up there on the mountain. The late afternoon stormy rain cleansing the streets. And the cats. I fell in love with two of the new babies, and she knew damn well that I would! Every day I would walk up the short, steep hill into town, just wandering the streets, stopping into stores to window shop, and simply breathing in the air. The air was different there, and it made me realize something.

I've written about the realizations that I came to, about not being happy in Italy anymore. But it occurred to me that I was, in fact, happy for the most part while in Zafferana. That was precisely the type of town I could live in, and probably what I was looking for when I went back to Italy initially. It took me a while to realize what it was, and it was simple. I wasn't in Motta. I wasn't in my apartment overlooking the TLA and the office where I worked, seeing them. I don't think I realized what an impact being in that position had on me. It made it entirely too difficult to get past the feelings, past the anger, when it was still so much a part of my life because of where I lived and what I could see.

Did I still want to leave Italy? Yes. Would I miss it? I suppose, if I'm to be honest about it, I would in a way. But I was ready for a change. Ready for something new.

CHAPTER 13

CITIZENSHIP HAPPENS AND MY WORLD OPENS

Thursday, March 9

With the decision made and tickets to my new destination bought, it of course seemed strange that I began to experience a lot of wonderful things in the final two and three weeks before I left, all creating and giving me such great memories of my time in Sicily. Fortunately, my neighbor, Nino, was at a spot in his professional career which meant he was home for a few weeks; we'd never really communicated with each other but, during this time, he ended up giving me the last memories I have of life in Sicily, through friendship, help, food and wine. I owe the completion of my final paperwork to Nino, as he wrangled answers out of the small-town bureaucrats.

I also owe the completion of my Shakespearean play, begun back in 2001, to Nino, as together we chased all over the town, back and forth between the police and the comune, playing tourists as we waited for people to do things. Getting back to the apartments, he decided to show off his cooking skills with a basic plain pasta pomodoro and a platter of cheese. What a wonderful time we had, drinking an entire bottle of wine as we talked and talked. I saw a new side of the culture, one not usually seen, as he told me of his marital situation, going through a divorce, having two grown daughters. Hearing his tale, seeing it through the eyes of a Sicilian man, was a lesson in and of itself. The Italian culture, and even more so the Sicilian culture, is so very different and I really enjoyed learning about it. In vino veritas we talked of life; of him growing up without a father (who had died when he was just three) and his mother working so very hard to raise five children on her own; of what is real and true and important in life.

This was life; what it's all about. Not working for money, for reputations, for this, that and the other thing. It's sitting at a table drinking wine, eating a simple pasta dish, cheese and just talking and laughing. There was nothing between us except friendship and a love of good wine. Just two people of the same age who had had good and bad in their lives, sharing and understanding cultures.

I wonder if the stars had lined up exactly right or something, for that to have happened when it did. Karma. The previous couple weeks I'd been fighting panic attacks about what I was doing and the decision I'd made. Fighting major fear. As I sat there realizing that in a week and a half I'd be taking all of my things to Kim's and would be at her house until I left for my next destination, I thought it was a very good thing that my last few weeks in Sicily would be spent in Zafferana, away from Motta, away from the TLA, away from everyone and everything I had known over the last three years. The best and truly only way that first little adventure should end. But one thing I was also glad about was that, during those last final weeks, I was spending time with a Sicilian friend who was not a part of that other life. In those last days there, in the shadow of the source of the pain, it made a wonderful set of memories.

And that's what it's all about.

Well, that and the fact that finally the person at the comune working on my file had found the initial "certificate of citizenship" issued by Rome which, by the way, was in the folder the entire time but she "didn't see it". I was issued my Italian identity card, clearly stating that I was, in fact, an Italian citizen. I couldn't have accomplished it without the help of Nino, who basically just stared her down and demanded she do her job! In those exact words. The only thing remaining, which wasn't even a necessity but I wanted it anyway, was to get my little red passport.

With that identity card in hand, I truly had a world at my disposal: twenty-seven of them to be exact!

Part Three

CHAPTER 14

PREAMBLE TO A NEW LIFE—
THE FINAL GOODBYE: TEARS, FEARS, LOVE, AND MOST OF ALL, HOPE

March, 2006

Kim had insisted that it was only fitting that I spend the remainder of my time with her up in Zafferana, as she herself prepared to leave for her new duty station in Virginia, one week after I was leaving. I was so very worried about what it would do to us, to our friendship, but it turned out okay in the end. It was hard to leave my apartment—you wouldn't think it would've been but my outlook had changed so much. I spent the last afternoon with Nino, who plied me with shot after shot of *"Salute!"* and *"To the future!"* under the guise of "Hey, you will need this for fortification!" I was already packed and just waiting for Kim to get off work, so I wasn't sure exactly what fortification I'd be needing, but it was very sweet of him nonetheless. Poor Kim, though—she absolutely despises the smell of anise, and my shot of choice was, of course, sambuca. By the time she got there, I was boo-hoo'ing and all emotional and she could barely stand to hug me because I was breathing out all that anise smell with each crying breath. But that's what best buds do; they make a couple gagging noises, say "You had to choose sambuca?" hold you at arms' length, give you a bunch of Kleenex, and throw you into their truck. It seemed like the parking lot of the apartments were very crowded for some reason; I know it took barely a few minutes for word to get back that I was leaving.

So off we went down the autostrada to Kim's house, music on and me blubbering still. No, I am not some crazy crying emotional female—it was all the wine and shots at Nino's! Thank goodness for the long drive as it gave us a chance to talk and for her to get out of me how worried I really was. My friendship with Kim is, and has always been since, just about the most important relationship in my life, and I would've gladly slept in the street if it meant saving and ensuring that living together for two months was not going to hurt it. We are both alike and opposite in many ways, and this is probably why we get along so well. However, living together has its ups and downs, and when two people are going through their own emotional difficulties, times can get heated, misunderstandings can happen. But we've always found a way to come through them with no permanent damage—a few dents and bruises, but intact.

I found I couldn't get the feeling back, that feeling I had three years before when I stepped off the plane, even being in Zafferana. I tried so hard too, wandering around the town, stopping and staring out at the sea and the incredible beauty of Mt. Etna, its forest and lush green land. I tried so hard. It just wouldn't come. This was my land, my ancestral home, and the home that welcomed me and gave me many beautiful things. I wanted so badly to get it back, the feeling, the love. But dammit, it just wouldn't come. All I wanted was—out.

Our last night on the same land was spent with a memory to last a lifetime. Kim had surprised me by snagging tickets to see my all-time favorite band, the Eagles, in concert in Rome; what phenomenally better way to part could she and I possibly have? So with all my three suitcases plus backpack in tow, off we went to Rome. We were staying with Lynda, which was so nice as it was about time the two of them met.

The concert was absolutely incredible. We had standing spaces and we were so very close to the stage. Kim was happy that she was so close to Henley, and I was ecstatic to be that close to Frey. She forgot her camera but I had mine—she was a bit disappointed to see the photos, probably because there were only one or two of Henley but about 30 or 40 of Frey.

Later that night as we were drifting off to sleep, it felt good to just be with her and talk softly of taking care and it didn't matter that we'd be 6,000 miles of ocean apart. That it would be okay. We were best buds, and no amount of ocean could ever change that. But we'd been constantly together for three years, and I felt like I was truly losing a piece of me. And I wasn't entirely sure I could make such a huge upcoming move knowing she wasn't right there for me to just simply send a text or make a quick phone call. I didn't want to let go of her hand as we talked—the hand that had held mine many times in a show of comfort, in a giving of strength, in a giving of calm. Buddies. It was good in a way that her alarm did not go off and she woke up late with just enough time to dress and get to the train. After the absolute shortest, quick, final hug, she was gone. Even now as I write this, a few tears are escaping. I got back into bed and cried, knowing I wasn't going to see her any time soon. I think at that moment I realized I was alone in what I was doing. I already missed her, so very much.

As Lynda and I walked around the market area of *Porta Portese* on the way to get my plane tickets, I knew it was time to go. I had no feelings for this city anymore; the love was gone. I couldn't find my city, the one I had dearly loved for so many years, over half my life.

Another teary goodbye 10 hours later, this time with Lynda, I was in the hired car bound for the airport, plane ticket in hand. I felt raw inside, even though in many ways I was also so excited. First Kim, then Lynda, then Italy itself.

◈ ◈ ◈

Thus ended my years back in what I thought to be, and always felt to be, my home. I was sad; sad that my time ended like that, and sad that part of me still feels that way. But talking to two wonderful people, a young married couple from outside my new city who were sitting next to me, lit the fire in me, and gave my sadness a place to rest and co-exist with my excitement.

I was able to relax a little, to the extent that as the engines throttled down to prepare for landing and I was looking out the window at the beauty of the land, I started to smile. As the wheels touched down, the enormity of it hit me; gone from Italy, gone from my first dream. Gone from Kim. Everyone I knew. As the tears started yet again, through it all I felt the smallest, tiniest, of stirrings, of the beginning of a smile.

The road had whispered my name yet again.

CHAPTER 15

STORIES FROM A TRULY NEW LIFE— IN ALL WAYS

WELCOME TO ENGLAND!
Fancy a Spot of Tea?

Dear England,
Thank you for calming and quieting this beaten and battered soul. You've welcomed me with open arms and given me back some of the things I'd lost and so desperately needed.

You are still so very new to me, but your gentleness amazes me and slowly but surely has helped me to begin to smile again.

I'd heard so much about you, good and bad, but so far I've found that mostly the good has touched me.

Is it your cleanliness, compared to what I'd seen in my other home? To smell the air after your gentle rains, the freshness courses through my blood and my very soul. Is it your green grass, the rolling hills, the sheer beauty of your landscape, the rocky shores? Or is the pulsing, pounding sound of your coastal waters meeting your shores that is matching the nearly lost but slow renewal of the beating of my heart?

I had almost forgotten what it was like to feel the joy and see the beauty of what was around me.

I am beginning to feel alive again.

I am beginning to feel again.

Slowly you have helped me to regain my love of discovery, my excitement of all things new to these eyes.

I'm not completely there yet—but we're getting there.

ั∾ ั∾ ั∾

So as you can see, I chose England as my next destination, landing specifically in London. I hadn't seen England since 1972; it didn't seem to have changed much. After checking in to my little bed-and-breakfast in the Victoria area, I went walking to get acclimated a bit. I stayed near to the hotel as everything was so new, and my emotions were still so very raw—I couldn't really think much, my brain was in a fog.

Knowing that the first order of business was work, I got talking to the receptionist to see if she might know of something I could do or where to find some work. I'd previously looked into going back into legal secretarial work, but the firms wanted knowledge of British law, and that was going to be a pretty big sticking point, meaning that field was probably well behind me at that point. She told me there was a small bed-and-breakfast (B&B) possibly looking for some reception help, and off I went. Though the outside was a bit seedy, I gave it a chance and went in to talk to the owner. He had already found someone, but knew of another B&B across the street named *Surtees Hotel* that needed someone. Off I went again, met the owner inside, and ten minutes later I had a job as receptionist . . . working the night shift from 7:00 p.m.–7:00 a.m. As horrible as that sounded, I needed the work because, even in the 24 hours I'd already been there, I saw how expensive the city was, meaning there was no way I could sit back and relax even for a little while.

London is a beautiful, crazy city, vibrant, full of life, so very international, so many different languages spoken everywhere. It seemed to have a well-oiled chaos. There was a method to the chaos that encompassed so many cultures, and I loved every minute when I was out and about. In the one-kilometer radius of the hotel were restaurants from eight different countries. I was in food heaven. Since so very much has historically been written about the city itself and everything to see there, I won't go into it that much. But it should be said that this is a city where the regular street police do not carry guns—and for someone raised in both the US and Italy, it was startling to say the least. I actually didn't believe it at first, and a couple co-workers and I stood outside at 2:00 a.m. once and stopped an officer going by so that I could ask him myself.

The treasures this city holds are enough to give you eye- and soul-candy for as many days as you want. However, for someone needing four distinct seasons, this wasn't going to cut it for me. And let's face it, because of the internationality and the financial and business aspect of it, London is an exceptionally expensive city in which to live. If I hadn't been given a room as part of my pay, I wouldn't have been able to stay as long as I did. Working in a small B&B gave me just enough to survive to buy food and take an occasional super-cheap day-trip every few months—but it was not enough to have my own apartment or really even to rent a room.

And I needed some sun!

But damn, this is a gloriously beautiful, welcoming, friendly, amazing city and country. I was determined to enjoy every single minute of however much time I was there.

Winnie the Pooh and Tigger too!

If you're a fan of Winnie and the gang, and you go to England and have a little extra time, you must get to Hartsfield, just outside of London, where you'll find Pooh Country, Pooh Corner, Poohsticks Bridge, and the 100-acre wood.

Yes, it's real.

Well, except that it's actually 500 acres, but does that even matter? There's something magical about going to this tiny hamlet, where you'll find all of this. Pooh Corner is the name of the store where Christopher's nanny would take him to get sweets. The store is chock-full of memorabilia and you'll find you'll be smiling a lot in here and will probably say *awww* quite frequently! However, what you won't find (at least you'll find only very little of, thank goodness) is the Disney version of the Pooh characters. The real version, A.A. Milne's drawings, only very slightly resemble Disney's version. (Why Disney ever decided to change the originals and make them so very different is beyond me. The originals are fantastic.) There are collectibles of every kind—from card sets to stuffed animals to serving-ware to books to just about everything, including bags of the same sweets that Christopher would eat. The store has a little tea area off the side, where you can enjoy a nice cup of tea served in character cups. There's also a website, at *www.pooh-corner.org*.

In the store are maps to the surrounding area, the 100-acre wood contained in Ashdown Forest. Here is where you take off along trails and, according to the map, you'll be able to trace the footsteps of Winnie and the gang. Place-markers will show you where the characters lived, Piglet, Eeyore, and all the rest. You'll also find Poohsticks Bridge—thousands of tourists have picked the place clean of sticks, so make sure you pick up a few along the way so you can play your own game on the bridge.

There is something magical about wandering the area, letting your imagination go and seeing all the characters playing out all the stories you've read and heard. I found I kept singing, *"You'd be surprised there's so much to be done, count all the bees in the hive, chase all the clouds from the sky, back to the days of Christopher Robin and Pooh"* and kept seeing it all happening around me.

It's a recapture, I think, of innocence, of wide-eyed wonder: a bear with a honey jar stuck on his nose, a bouncing tiger, the floppy ears of a donkey, a wise owl, a rabbit. Maybe that's why you leave the area feeling a bit more relaxed, a bit less stressed, and with a smile.

Go. It only takes a few hours to rediscover the joy.

Go. And remember.

Oh Baby, Men in Kilts

A much-deserved couple days off in a row took me to Edinburgh. A place I've wanted to go for quite some time now. Men in kilts. Oh yeah, baby! I wish I could've timed it to when there was some Highlands festival or something. Or even a little festival where there would be kilted men. Doing kilted men stuff. Like they do at the Games, you know, swinging some huge log or something around, the wind kicking up as they twirl.

I took the train up. Though flying may seem to be time-saving way to get there, in reality it's only about four hours from London to Edinburgh and, by the time you factor in getting to an airport, checking in, security and flying time, it actually takes just about as much time to fly as it does to take the train. The prices are about the same; besides, taking the train is good. Less of a carbon footprint. More to see. And that's a good thing. And I love trains, my second-most favorite mode of travel.

I'd made reservations to stay at a wonderful B&B named *Clan Campbell Hotel*. Totally recommended; loved it! I had decided many months previous that I would stay there if I went to Edinburgh because the owner (well, former owner since he gave it over to his son to run) had stayed at our B&B and we spent hours talking about the hotel business. When he described his place, I just knew I'd stay there when I visited.

I only had a day and a half, two nights, but it was enough time to give me a nice little break and a taste of the city. I just played it by ear and saw what happened; that's how I travel-roll! It also gave me a little chance to see what the city is like, since Edinburgh had actually been a small niggling little thought in my mind as somewhere it might be fun to go for a year. Time would tell.

∽ ∽ ∽

I fell in love. It was just a slight attraction before arrival, but pulling in the station, it became a full-blown love affair. I was madly, nay, passionately, in love. My heart, fickle is thy name! Perhaps this is why I cannot seem to tame this heart of mine. It is too wild. My eyes are too easily turned when I gaze upon such exquisiteness. My heart sung with such joy when I gazed upon the beauty of the hills, the land, the meandering streets.

While on the train, I met a wonderful older woman, born and raised in Stirling, Scotland. We chatted our way from Newcastle to Edinburgh, me asking her a hundred questions about Scotland and everything we passed. I love solo female travelers who are so sure of themselves, so incredibly knowledgeable, so intelligent. She watched me with a smile as I stared in awe at the landscape, my eyes wide with childlike wonder at the beauty I saw before me. The slow and subtle changes, as each hill seemed sharper, the grass a deeper green, the shifting and changing colors of nature defying everything I imagined. As we rounded a bend, I got my first glimpse of the Scottish coast. I put my hands on the window, I wanted out! I wanted to walk along that coastline, go climb along the rocks. She laughed and said, "Oh but that's nothing! Wait until one day you see the Highlands and the northern Scottish coast."

As we passed Berwick-upon-Tweed (that town just cried out to be explored; another time) the landscape changes were not so subtle now. I felt I was in a different world. The light outside changed and I looked behind me through the window to see why. In a moment there loomed before me a forest, huge and thick with tall pines. It was at once dark and gloomy and forbidding, while at the same time it hinted of glimpses of light and coolness and an invitation. What mysteries lay in its depths? What secrets did it hold? I wanted to know. I wanted to explore its lush world, to be held within. It stirred in me a desire, quickening my pulse and the beat of my heart.

It wasn't to be the last time that happened on that whirlwind trip.

Something was brewing.

Magic was stirring.

❦ ❦ ❦

My lust began as the train pulled in, and I got my first glimpse of Edinburgh Castle and the Princes Street Gardens, seen from the tracks. The air smelled different here, fresh from earlier rain. The streets glistened as I exited on Market Street instead of Princes Street. As I came up the stairs onto the street, to my left I saw a huge mountain rising up. What was that? Just sitting there in the middle of the city!

I had a feeling I had exited the wrong way and so went up the hill and around the corner. There in front of me were the beautiful Princes Street Gardens, with the castle high up on said huge mountain sitting in the middle of the city. What a glorious first five minutes I had! First the mountainous peak and then this. I knew I had to get back here and explore.

Though we were nearly five hours late, I had kept the hotel informed so there was no check-in issue. On arrival, I was immediately rewarded after a long, tiring journey with superb, four-star comfort in a three-star little hotel B&B. After a quick drop-off of my bag and a splash of water on my face, I headed down to talk to the owner, John, about his recommendations for the night and for dinner. It was going to be a short night because I had worked the night before and at this point had been up for 25 hours. I also knew that was okay, because I had the entire next day, and the weather forecast was for sun. Oh yeah, I was ready!

My first Edinburgh wandering took me up Dublin Street, through St. Andrew's Square, and over to Princes Street, where I attempted to go into the Gardens. I say attempted because my timing sucked and the guard stopped me, saying the gardens were closing. I asked him what the mountainous peak was, and was told it was called Arthur's Seat, an extinct volcano. I wanted to keep talking to him because I was diggin' on the Scottish accent, so I got him talking about it being extinct and how I needn't worry about it shaking underneath my feet. I just started laughing and he looked at me a bit askance, so I explained, "Sorry, I didn't mean to laugh, but it's just what you said about me not needing to worry. See, I lived on the side of an active volcano and got woken up often by the shaking and went to sleep with the line of lava out my window."

I skipped walking Princes Street because, as most anyone

who knows me knows, I am not a shopper. Oh, I am so not a shopper. Have I mentioned I really hate shopping? I can't even go shoe shopping because, after trying on three pairs, I just end up annoyingly saying to the salesperson, "Just give me something, anything, I don't care!" I do the same thing with clothes too. Five minutes and it's stick a fork in me 'cause I'm done.

I made my way down around the train station and the bridge, so that I could stare out at Arthur's Seat. I could see the path and saw little tiny specks moving up and down it. It reminded me of the path going up the volcano on the island of Vulcano off the northern coast of Sicily. I'm not that ambitious, so didn't climb it, but decided to go to it the next day.

I was running on empty at this point and made my way back, walking down Leith Street and looking in windows and at the scenery around me. Even as tired as I was, I knew there was something about this place, this city. I realized that I was breathing air that was cool and that held . . . something—there was a magic beginning to swirl around me, playing and teasing me.

It was giving me a hint of what was to come.

Back at the hotel, I treated myself to a glass of wonderful red wine, relaxing on the comfortable couch, and just chatting away to John, the owner of the B&B, son of the previous owner who had stayed at the London B&B where I worked. He was so very welcoming, asking me how dinner had been, and what I had been up to afterwards, and what I had seen and done. It was the same thing I always tried to do with the guests in London, and was happy to see it done here too.

What a great way to end this day, and introduction to this city.

I felt like a child at Christmas. All I wanted to do now was sleep, so that the morning would come faster, and I could get out there and see what all that was there. I didn't want that teasing anymore.

I felt like I had opened a door leading to a mysterious room, where there was a sign saying, "Enter if you dare."

If you dare to experience this world, dare to close your eyes and breathe. Allow the magic, but be careful—it's a sneaky one, that will catch hold of you.

I did dare.

⁂

The next day found me wandering all around Edinburgh, taking the sightseeing hop-on hop-off bus, as I knew it would take me to all the famous sites, and I could do it all on one ticket. I really love those buses and find it a great way to get an initial feel for a city, what is has to offer, how far apart things are. I always try to take them, and have taken all of the lines in London a couple times.

On leaving Edinburgh, I knew that I would always love this city. There truly is just something magical about it; whether it's just the accent, the history, the stories and legends, I just don't know. But it is somewhere I want to return to when I have much more time to explore.

Were Robin Hood's Men Really Merry?
Probably Because They Never Went to Notts Jail!

For that year's birthday trip, I chose Nottingham because, well, Robin Hood. Also, I love archery, and who wouldn't want to play in Robin Hood land? I had decided that birthdays are meant for spoiling yourself, and after much research chose the *Crowne Plaza* for its offerings. After having worked my regular night shift and not sleeping, I went to the train station and took off on the 8:30 a.m. train for my little birthday getaway.

I love the trains in England. They're fast, clean, and quite comfortable. I've yet to encounter someone working on the trains who wasn't polite. For just a pound extra, I got first-class seating and thought that was the right way to start my *spoil me* day. I was really looking forward to it, as I hadn't really done one of these for a long time. Although I suppose getting a massage every couple weeks is spoiling myself, but I call that therapeutic.

After an uneventful train ride, we pulled into Nottingham. It was nearly four hours to check-in time, but the hotel let me drop off my backpack in their secure area, and I went back outside, hitting up a couple of the police officers patrolling the general area for suggestions of what to see for the next four hours. First order of business, they informed me, was the castle, situated up a little hill and looking quite imposing in its own right. Off I went, armed with my directions, choosing on instinct a side street that rewarded me for my *let's see if this leads there too* thought. The architecture on the buildings, shops and apartments alike had me picturing myself back in the stories of the age of Robin Hood and his merry band roaming around.

In front of the castle is the famous Robin Hood sculpture, along with two others of Robin, Lil' John, Tuck, and Maid Marian, all beautifully done. Along the walls are plaques depicting various scenes, such as Robin shooting his last arrow upon his death, among others. Wind your way around the paths and you get to the castle grounds entrance (with its requisite souvenir shop), and then enter the grounds. Absolutely beautiful. There are various flower sculptures of Robin and Marian, plus a memorial to fallen servicemen surrounded by gorgeous flowers. The grounds are large and you just get this really peaceful feeling standing there, looking up at the castle. As I got closer, I was entranced by the sound of a waterfall; knowing me and water, I had to find it. I followed the sound and there it was, a little waterfall coming down a stair of rocks. Nice.

Following the path up to the castle, you're rewarded by an incredible view over the city of Nottingham. It was a bit misty and cloudy, so the view wasn't as clear, but it was still worth it. I could see all the hills and trees and oh so far! I wandered around in the castle for a while, looking at all the exhibits. One could easily spend a couple hours in here. I didn't, though, as I still wanted to see one more thing that morning before getting to the hotel and pampering myself with the pool and jacuzzi; besides, I was starting to feel the fact that I'd been awake since 5:00 p.m. the previous day. I wandered through at a good pace, bought a couple cute souvenirs and made my way back down and out to go to the "oldest pub and inn in England," and the Story of Nottingham Museum.

This museum was really cool; very small and not on the beaten path but right by the oldest pub location. It was like wandering around in a very small home, but its articles gave a very good depiction of life so very many years ago in Notts; attached and under were wonderful caves that had been discovered and used later for air raid shelters. Being down in the caves was cool and quiet. Just sitting in the rock formations there was fascinating—I was able to imagine what it must have been like, both when the caves were used for whatever they were used for, and also what it must have been like to sit in there as bombs were falling all around you. What stories of the lives, the hopes and dreams of the people tucked away hiding and taking shelter here falling away as your world was literally crumbling around you. If you sit quietly, looking around, you can almost hear the voices.

The caves were okay, fast little tour of two rooms of an old tannery, one of another air raid shelter, and a very short path of a couple holes in the wall. I give the guide an "A" as he was smiley and very interactive, which was great for the children on the tour. He was knowledgeable and made it fun for them.

I found my way back to the hotel, as by that time it was 2:00 p.m. I was tired and hungry but wanted to get a swim and jacuzzi in. I had chosen this Crowne Plaza for its reputation and offerings for my pampering, spoiling birthday getaway. Though I had some issues with the hotel, there were good things too. This isn't a hotel review, so I'll get back to my fun! Though not great, their offerings were really nice and I enjoyed myself with swimming and hanging in the jacuzzi for a few hours. One kind of funny (sad?) thing—I asked the receptionist for a dinner recommendation with good quality and price, and was told, "Go to the area by the cinema where there is Pizza Hut." Busting out laughing, I gave a hearty "Cheers!" and went off on my own, finding a cute little Sicilian place with decent food, which was inexpensive and fast.

※ ※ ※

My plans for the day were simple, the Galleries of Justice and the caves. I thought it would be really interesting to see what justice and the courts were like back then, and it ended up being absolutely, completely, totally worth the time and money! If ever you're in Nottingham, *do not miss this place*. Part of the allure of the galleries is the interaction and surprises, so I am not going to say any more about it because it would ruin it for you—suffice to say, I had a blast! One thing's for sure, justice back then is light years away from now.

All in all, I'd say it was a good trip, a nice little getaway, and a nice night and day off.

Zen in the Peace Pagoda

Not too long after, I'd found myself deep in a funk, and one day, though I didn't really feel like going out walking during my hours off, I forced myself to ignore my brain telling me I was tired. Walking in the general direction of Battersea Park, I wanted to see the Peace Pagoda. I wanted to *zen*. I wanted that feeling I get when I'm in that space in me.

Instead of taking my usual route, I ended up making a turn that would lead towards Sloane Street, where I saw a sign for Chelsea Physic Garden and thought that might be nice for a stroll. After making my initial turn, I happened upon Chelsea Pensioners Hospital, a huge place with an old cemetery. Looking at a few of them, I was barely able to make out the words due to age—one was from 1703, another from 1690; on one was the writing, "In the memory of (whomever), sixpennyman of the hospital." Sixpennyman? Having no clue what that was, I was so intrigued that I had to find a way to find out.

Just up ahead was the entrance to the hospital and a sign with 'Museum'. I couldn't help it, my feet just turned. I wanted to know about the sixpennyman thing, so I ducked my head into a little office, asked the guy (who was in an old military uniform, which I thought was just nifty) where the museum was, and then asked my sixpennyman question. His eyes lit up as he said, "Take a seat and I'll tell you a story." I then sat down to a wonderful story about three women who dressed as men so they could serve in the military and go to battle. (I have no idea where he was from, but his accent was so strong it was difficult to follow.) But the gist of it was the sixpenny had to do with what they were paid compared to others, once it was discovered they were women. Obviously some things never seem to change.

As I was walking down the road toward the Garden, I was overcome by the beauty of the architecture of the buildings. Victorian, and with the fantastic balconies and curved roofs that looked like spires. I was walking with my head tilted up constantly. I loved the simplicity, and the peacefulness it inspired just looking at them. I kept thinking that I'd love to live in one of those. A few minutes and roads later, I crossed Chelsea Bridge and there it was, directly in front of me. Walking through the gardens and paths leading to and around the pagoda, enjoying the nature, I spent much-needed time sitting at the pagoda for some spirit-healing meditation in the peace and quiet. My brain always ends up knowing what my soul needs, if I only take the time to listen to it.

Sitting later at a small Italian café, listening to the language and eating the food I had eaten for so many years, it gave me pause to consider on this move I'd made. The language and food weren't pulling at me or tugging at my heart; I realized I was very happy there and had made the right choice. I was in the midst of some of the most beautiful architecture I'd ever seen in a city that is, for the most part, remarkably clean considering the amount of people living here; the city with an incredible vitality, a joy to it, full of life and energy. I had the best of it all there. Everywhere I went, different cultures intermingled and interspersed, and my need for internationality in all parts of my life was easily fulfilled. One road was all Moroccan, another Oriental; turn a corner and it was African, Turkish, Asian; on and on it went. I could experience the differences in the cultures and their foods and knick-knacks. I could go to a market and there would be booths and stalls full of every ethnicity. I could go to the outdoor street-food market and return with one item of Moroccan food, one of something from Ghana, one from Turkey.

It was, all in all, a good day, and helped to remind me that even though my eyes didn't shine right then, I did know that I was in the midst of a wonderful place.

We can have it all. If we just look for it.

Give Me Back My Crystal Ball
July 2008

Writing has always been a form of therapy, so to speak, for me, and the only way I was ever able to convey what was inside. My thoughts and feelings. It's always been my method of making decisions, of working things out.

I hadn't written since leaving Sicily, and I had missed it. Missed writing. Years and years ago, one of the writing assignments given in English class was "Describe what you see in the mirror." I was 14 or 15 at the time, and pretty hard on myself, due to low self-esteem. But we were supposed to be honest and the assignment was about writing descriptions. I remember the comments on the paper that the teacher, Mr. Brophy, wrote and I think I always will. He complimented my descriptions, but said I was being too hard on myself, and to stop putting so much emphasis on what I thought *other* people saw.

Why'd I bring this up? Well, I think it's because of the funk I'd been in the last week or so. I would look in the mirror and be even harder than ever on myself because of the changes I saw. The changes from when I had arrived in Europe nearly three years before. My body had changed, my face had changed. I'd only just gotten over a horrid cold I had for two weeks, and I looked like death warmed over. It was a cold for goodness' sake. I didn't used to have the dark circles under my eyes, and there was a dullness to my eyes. I'd been told all my life that they were my best physical feature, and that they were beautiful. I blush even now at some of the comments I've received when some have looked into my eyes at various times. I've never taken compliments well, and would always look away and close my eyes.

But at that time, the shine seemed to be gone. There was no life in them anymore.

I knew my work schedule had much to do with it, and my quality of sleep and life (or lack thereof). Though it would change soon, as that's a decision I had made. I wanted to look in the mirror again, and wink at myself when I saw those eyes.

Soon the funk would be over, as it never lasts too long, so I couldn't allow it to take hold, or at least too deep of a hold. There was too much life still out there, too much still to see, and far too much left to experience.

Always forward.

The Real, Honest-to-Goodness Holiday!
Still September 2008

Yep, I finally took one, after so long. I chose a cruise along the eastern Mediterranean that left from Venice, stopped at ports in Italy, Greece, Turkey and Croatia, before returning to Venice. Those who already know me wouldn't be surprised at that because they know it's my preferred mode of travel. Being on the open sea, feeling the gentle sway of the waves under my feet, sleeping to the oh-so-gentle rocking of the sea as the ship travels. My sleep is undisturbed on those nights, and my brain is put to rest. Although I loved the ports and cities I would see on any cruise I took, you could usually find me kicked back on a deck chair outside, gazing out at the open water, watching the various shorelines sliding by. I am at peace then, with the smell of the ocean or sea, the cool air coming off the water, with no sound coming to me except the water rushing by.

It is bliss, pure and simple. And I can breathe.

I skipped through Venice on the way to the ship, as I had no desire to see anything, just get myself to the ship. As soon as my feet hit the gangway to board, I could feel it all slipping away—the exhaustion, frustration, problems, pushed somewhere deep into my mind, to be dealt with upon my return. Excitement took hold in its place. I was ready for this. I skipped the first port of Bari, and stayed on ship, not wanting to go ashore. I had chosen this cruise based on three of its ports of call, two in Turkey and one in Croatia. I had wanted for so long to see Turkey, and this was my chance. It was on my list.

Katakolon, Greece. Somewhere in my brain were the memories of the 1972 school trip taken to the Peloponnese, hitting the sites of Olympia and a few others, all corresponding to things learned in our Greek mythology English class. So instead of going on one of the excursions, I chose to wander the little port town, and made my way to the beach, walking and walking along the water and around the little streets. It's where I wanted to be; my preference was to just see the life there. It was a typical port town, with many souvenir shops, a few small cafés, a couple restaurants, and that's how I spent my time. I chose a small café and sat down with a souvlaki. As food hadn't been sitting well with me for a little while, and I'd lost my desire, I ate a bit and shared the rest with a little abandoned, skinny, obviously more hungry and needy of the meal than I, kitten. I so enjoyed sitting in the sunshine feeding it, until it left, its hunger sated for the moment.

Later, my thoughts turned to the much-anticipated Turkey, as the shorelines of various Greek islands slid by, all beautiful in their own right. Of course I would have loved to have been able to wander those lands, but that will be another trip. The following two days were docks in Izmir and Istanbul, which lived up to all I'd heard about Turkey. I quickly fell in lust with the land, her people, the welcoming smiles. While Izmir was a small city, Istanbul was, well, Istanbul. A huge city, teeming with life, bursting at the seams. It was so many adjectives—hot, dusty, crowded, chaotic, gleaming, bustling, relaxed, friendly. It was full of life. And I loved every minute of it.

I discovered a little place next to Topkapi Palace called *The Jet Lag Café*, and without a second thought walked in and felt the little welcoming breeze in this suffocating heat coming from its courtyard in back. I knew I wanted nothing more than to plop myself down on one of the sofas lining the wall, and sink back into the myriad of big, comfy, fluffy, soft pillows all over them. I had to try a Turkish coffee (and quickly learned why I was not to stir it, as I drank a mouthful of coffee grounds that had gotten stirred up after settling to the bottom!) and, with the help of the indulgent employees, learned how to smoke a shisha (orange, and their choice). On the walls were two huge drawings, one of a man decked out in Turkish finery sitting on one of the sofas, and one of a woman doing the same. Both were lounging back, shisha in hand, and looking oh-so-relaxed. I decided that was my blueprint of what I was to do, so indeed I did. It was wonderful, and I knew that if I were to ever come back to Istanbul, this would be one of my first stops, and that I would tell others of it. So I'm telling you—get thee to *The Jet Lag Café* in Istanbul!

The Blue Mosque was amazing, absolutely gorgeous. I'm no stranger to Muslim culture (after the couple years of working daily with a devout Moroccan Muslim boss at the B&B in London), and knew how to dress when going on the excursion. I was surprised at how many people still had to find coverings to put over their shoulders and legs upon arrival, even though it was known beforehand and put down in detail in the excursion description brochure, and, let's face it, those aspects of Muslim cultural ways are not a secret.

I left the excursion after a few minutes in the "carpet store" and began doing my own thing, stopping of course at the Grand Bazaar and finding a little café where the people were incredibly friendly and welcoming. A cool discovery; while I'm certainly not very good at it, I am at least a little bit okay at the whole bargaining thing, getting a beautiful, small prayer rug as a gift for my boss at an absolute fraction of the first requested price. All by myself! (For that price, the rug was obviously nothing fancy or of the best quality, but I did see him using it a few times back in London.) I know many readers are probably rolling their eyes right about now, but seriously, I suck at bargaining—I try once and then am like, "Okay, whatever you say." The rest of my day was spent just walking around the city and enjoying the sights all around me.

I was sad to watch this land slip out of my sight along the water, but as I gazed at the disappearing city, I knew I'd be back. Inside I was saying, "Oh yes, I will; I hear that small thought playing!"

I loved every moment of the next two nights and days spent on the sea, with Dubrovnik being the next stop. I'd always heard so much about Croatia, its culture and people, its food and wine, and was really looking forward to it. A storm prevented docking for a bit, and tenders couldn't go because of the roughness of the sea. I loved the crashing waves and spraying water, with the inability to walk a straight line! It was exhilarating to me. Our time in Dubrovnik was very limited because of the lost time, but no matter—I walked around a bit in the town, walked the walls, spent a little time in a café having a coffee.

Back on the ship, I knew my time was coming to a close.

Soon, very soon, my peace would come to an end, and real life would intrude in a few days' time.

Little did I know that it would be so much sooner than I thought.

An Unknown Glimpse into My Future
Saturday, September 20

What was I talking about there? Well, stick with me here for this long, strange chapter, as there's a method to my madness! Please forgive me for some of it, and don't give up on me!

After about four days on the ship, I noticed a relatively small mark on my ankle, which looked like possibly the start of a rash. Just a small red mark. I thought perhaps it was a bit of a burn, since I'd been laying on the deck.

The next day I noticed it got a little bigger, but as there was no pain or itching, I still didn't think too much of it. I was, however, a little curious and, while wandering around the deck, I noticed something I hadn't really before. In the, supposedly, adults-only pool and jacuzzi, were people putting their kids in the jacuzzi. What's wrong with that, you ask?

They were in diapers.

Yes, babies in diapers in the pool and jacuzzi.

Now, those parents may not mind swimming and sitting in a jacuzzi surrounded by their children's pee and poop, but I, for one, do. I contacted security—because I really wanted to swim and take advantage of the jacuzzi—and as two came over and watched, they just simply said, "Oh, yes, that's not good," and did nothing. I spoke to the ship management (my equivalent, hotel manager) and he was appalled and said he would absolutely do something about it. The cruise-line, Costa, is known for catering to families and their ships are normally filled to the brim with children. That's great for families and those who don't mind, but it's just not my cup of tea, and I have never chosen Costa again for my own preferences.

The reason I brought this story up is that during the day, I watched the redness spread a little and begin on my other ankle also; I still kept thinking it may have been the pool and jacuzzi, or maybe I'd been bitten while walking among Turkish ruins? I looked carefully at the spot, and saw no punctures.

The following morning, while getting dressed to disembark in Venice, I noticed pain had begun in that ankle, along with some burning feeling. I looked and saw the rash had grown from the small spot, and was beginning to spread around my ankle and travel up my shin. As I waited in the lounge to disembark, the burning and pain began to get worse, and contacting Costa's reception, I was told I could not see the ship's doctor at that point as he was already long gone and I'd just have to do something about it in Venice. The first order of business off the ship therefore was to go to the nearest hospital emergency room.

While standing waiting for the transfer bus, I found it difficult to even stand, so was really happy when the Costa ("frequent") transfer bus finally arrived about 45 minutes later. I still had two days of my holiday left, and my original plans were to get on a train and go somewhere.

That plan came to a grinding halt as I limped to the train station, up and down the bridge stairs with my suitcase, and sat on the stairs with tears running down my face from the pain. I couldn't walk without pain. I pulled up my pant leg and couldn't believe it—in the hour since disembarking, the rash had spread all the way around my ankle, was now deep red and covered half my shin as well. It was burning to the touch and my foot and ankle were swollen twice their size. I stopped a couple police officers and, through my tears, asked where the nearest hospital was. They offered to get me a water taxi to the hospital, but the price was unaffordably tourist-high, and so I limped my way to the train station.

Please try to understand my mood. With the many things that followed, I knew I was nowhere near ready to return to this country. I was not only mad, but sad. At the Mestre station, I stopped a station security person, showed my leg and he immediately called an ambulance. I was crazy scared at this point as it had kept spreading; but I thought to myself, okay the ambulance has been called, everything's going to get better and be fine. This was the first—and would turn out to be nowhere near the last—time I'd ever been put into an ambulance in Italy. One attendant ask in English, "What's your problem?", and then I was forced to listen to the two attendants begin to make rude, snide comments about my weight in Italian, thinking I didn't speak the language. Pulling the seatbelt around me, one said (in English), "The ambulance is going to ride slow, I'm not sure we'll even make it because you're so fat. Your problem is you're fat and your leg and foot can't hold you, I doubt the seatbelt will go around you so you're just going to have to hold on." In Italian, the attendants laughed and said to each other, "She's so fat her leg and foot can't hold her, that's why it's swollen." I was too scared about this happening and didn't say a word as I pulled the belt around me and clicked it in place, merely staring her down.

The rest of the day was spent sitting and waiting in the hospital ER, finally getting my leg elevated, watching the redness continue to spread as the hours of waiting to be seen went by. In the sixth hour, I was taken in to see the doctor, who said she had no idea what was going on and ordered blood tests. Sent back out to the waiting room and three hours later the tests came back; she reported there was nothing indicated in the tests, and she had no clue whatsoever what was wrong. That wouldn't be the last time I heard that over the next eight or nine years. Handing me a prescription for four days of antibiotics, "just in case it's an infection", she advised that I get on the first plane back to England and to a hospital to get it looked at. It was 1:30 a.m. I was discharged and limped my way out the door on the outskirts of Mestre with no transportation, no hotel room. I was supposed to get the first plane out, but I couldn't walk.

Checking my cash, I found I had 10 euros. There was no ATM or payphone anywhere in the hospital or vicinity, and I'd had the desk call me a taxi. When it got there, he informed me that because it was 1:30 a.m., the price would be double, 20 euros to the closest hotel and he did not take cards. My karma must have been running high, because a person waiting for another taxi watched, listened, and gave the driver 20 euros, saying to me, "Someday you'll come across someone else, and you'll help them." With tears in my eyes, I thanked him profusely.

Pay it forward. Yes.

I left the Novotel hotel the next morning, stopped at a pharmacy and downed some antibiotics and aspirin for the pain. The small airport had a first-aid station, so I spoke to them to make sure flying was okay and if there was anything I needed to do. Upon hearing the Mestre story, they shook their heads and said, "Typical of that hospital, let me see the ankle." They put some salve on it to get the swelling down, and said I was okay to fly but to keep my shoe off because of the pressure in the cabin.

After a relatively uneventful flight back seated in the first row next to someone else with a bum foot, I arrived home to London, where I immediately called the hotel and had my colleague pick me up. At the clinic the next morning, the doctors said they really weren't sure what was wrong (a couple were called to look at it because it was puzzling them with the way it came about, starting as a small dot and spreading as far as it did), didn't think it was anything 'too serious,' said to continue the antibiotics and, if it didn't get better, to go to the hospital.

It got better, although two months later there was still a very light, slight redness, and the pain lasted another couple weeks, but wasn't anywhere near the level of before.

I forced myself to look at the whole trip as mostly a win, as I saw some amazingly beautiful places. What I didn't realize was that what started as one small little red dot would change my life forever.

I hate it when real life intrudes like that.

October 2008

Lynda got in touch with me about a job in Rome, where she had moved to a year prior, and I of course started to think about it; basically working out in my head whether I wanted to give it another shot. I knew that all of the population of Italy and all of the country itself were not represented by the two people in that one small town in Sicily. Nor were they the attendants in that ambulance. I knew that. I understood that. But I knew it just wasn't time—I thought there was still just too much for me to see, too many new places to explore, too many new cultures to experience. Too many new memories to be made.

Always forward. Never back.

So about the same time Lynda got in touch, I received a call from Kim, aka "tes," short for *tesoro* and which means "treasure" in Italian. With a deep sigh and a troubled voice, she said, "Tes, I have some bad news. Well, not really bad, so much as news that's freaking me out." That is not something you want to hear when you're 5,000 miles from your best bud. As the possibilities were racing through my head, I tried to stay as calm as possible.

"Talk to me," I said.

"I know you said you would never return to the States—" she began.

"Oh hell Tes," I jumped in. "Just say the word and I'm on the next flight, you know that."

"I'm being deployed for a year and a half to Bahrain," she said. I guess it shouldn't have been that surprising to hear.

"Just tell me when I need to be there, and you know I'll take care of the cats and your house." No other words were necessary.

❧ ❧ ❧

That was unexpected. Not that she would be deployed again before her retirement, but I guess it just wasn't something that entered our minds—she was a service member and had animals and a house.

When I left America initially back in September of 2002, I swore I'd never return. I didn't want to. It wasn't mine anymore, and wasn't where I felt best or where I felt I belonged. It was my birth country, but was no longer home.

But when your best friend needs you, there is no question or hesitation, is there? As it had been when my mom was diagnosed that day out of the blue, I knew that nothing else mattered. I would, with no hesitation, give up the life I'd created for myself, and go to her.

And besides, it was only for a year and a half. And Reese's peanut butter cups were there . . . and Fritos. Priorities and things you miss. Great foods in each country aside, every expat misses something at some point in time.

The main problem at this point was how to get there. With only a couple months' notice, flights were expensive, and I had six or seven suitcases. Add that on to the cost of a flight, and you're looking at well over 1200 dollars. And, well, flying! I started researching and thought, *I wonder if it's even slightly possible to take a ship? No, no way is that affordable.* But I was bored one night with no guests, and remembered that my father had taken Cunard to England back in 1971, and I remembered all his stories of the "white-glove liner." Hitting its website, I held my breath as I searched . . . and found they were having a winter transatlantic special. It was probably the cheapest time to take that route because no one in their right mind sails willingly during January across the northern Atlantic. No decision was even necessary as I saw the price was 1100 dollars and that included every single one of my suitcases ("if it fits in your cabin, it's free"). No airports, no flight hassle. And cruising for seven days on the luxurious Queen Victoria in true Cunard style; I couldn't have been happier to have found that.

It was settled. I booked and would leave on the second of January, arriving on the ninth to New York, where Kim would drive from Virginia to pick me up. In a way, it was kind of full circle. My Sicilian ancestors sailed across the ocean and came in to Ellis Island. Seeing the Statue of Liberty, they knew their lives would change. My circumstances were entirely different, though, and I couldn't have known just how much my life would change and what the future would have in store for me.

Oh, I forgot to mention something here. Remember how I fell in love in Sicily, and decided to give that love up to keep fulfilling my dreams? How I put it up on a shelf somewhere in my heart? Well, Kim's house was about six miles from his. I would be those few miles from him for a year and a half. But it had been four years since we'd said goodbye. I knew I'd have to think long and hard, and make the right decision there.

Time to Say Goodbye

London. What an amazing and exciting city! You did the job you were supposed to, for a weary heart and soul. I will miss your light, your pride, your architecture, your history. I will forever remember your strength, determination and resilience. Even with all the stresses of the hotel management job, the 12-, 13- and sometimes even 14-hour graveyard shifts, seven days a week (yes, seven, until the last six or so months when I insisted on a day off); the living in the small storeroom-cum-bedroom outside the kitchen under the street; being woken up two and three times with questions or asking for my help; even with it all, it never dimmed my love of this amazing city. I will miss it so much!

Yes, this place holds a special place in my heart, even with the stresses of yet-another fire-breathing employer that I won't go into, as it's not necessary to the story really. He was a good man at his core, proud of his Moroccan heritage, strong in his Muslim faith; but he had a ridiculously hot temper with the shortest fuse I've ever seen. He had given me the storeroom that he'd made into a bedroom for my use, allowing me to not have to pay for lodging anywhere. The problem was there was a lot of mold and mildew as it was under the street, and London is not exactly a dry city! Could I have changed my circumstances? As I mentioned before, the city is expensive. Crazy-expensive. There wasn't what you'd call a ton of available jobs for someone in her late 40s, and with my shift schedule, being three feet from the office seemed okay. I didn't know the problems all of it together would cause me in the future.

Back to London! Okay, so I guess one of the advantages of no time off is that you get to save a little bit of money, giving just a bit of a cushion. I had no idea at the time how much I'd need it, but once I knew I'd be going back to the States for a year and a half, I was so glad I had it. While I was at the hotel, I found I had a knack for that type of work; while similar to what I did in Sicily, it was of course a bit more involved and much more varied. All those times I'd planned and coordinated the dinners and cultural aspects in Sicily, I transferred that over there. Sitting with various guests and helping them plan their time best; where the most delicious food was from various countries; plotting out walking routes on the map; getting them tickets; basically being a concierge. I loved it. I really don't think I'll ever forget so many of the people who came through—from Italy, repeat customers from Tampere, Finland who became like family, just so many. Oh, Tampere looked like a really nice place.

Because this field seemed to suit me, I decided to use those long, boring hours after about midnight or 1:00 a.m. by taking some online courses in hotel management. I researched and looked and looked, and found one, coupled side-by-side with one on European Hospitality Management. The courses were fully accredited and affordable, so I signed up. After a couple weeks, I decided to add on a TEFL course—Teaching English as a Foreign Language. Smartest move I ever made!

Over the next three months, I took many walks around London, to all the places I knew I wanted to see; walked the paths along the Thames; gazed at the lights. I took it all in, tucking it away inside me as I visited the Peace Pagoda a few times, searching for peace in the decision I had made to leave Europe's shores to return to a place I swore I'd never return to.

It wasn't easy to do. Yes, my best bud needed me, and I couldn't wait to see her and my furry loves again! But leaving was so hard, filling me with an angst that was overtaking me. On the other hand . . . on the other hand there were seven days of glorious ocean-gazing ahead of me on the Cunard Queen Victoria.

Somewhere in the Middle of the North Atlantic
4 January 2009

As I watched the European shoreline fade away and felt the gentle sway of the ocean liner on the still-smooth waves, it hit me—this is really happening. I'm leaving. I had found a comfortable chair and stared out as the shore got further and further away. It wasn't long before the tears began and my heart felt like someone had taken hold of it and squeezed, squeezing the life out of me. As I wasn't wailing and wracked with sobs like they show in movies, no one came near me and I was left alone. It was what I needed, though; to get the emotions out, think about the changes going on, and force myself to realize that it wasn't going to be for long. It was just going to be a short break in my plans, a new little adventure, and I'd be home soon.

And besides, the purr monsters and Kim—I so couldn't wait to see them all. Three years is such a long time to not give your best bud a hug. Just too long. This would all be okay; I believed it would.

So I decided to just shake the shit off, wipe those tears, and set off to enjoy being on the ocean for seven days. And it was amazing. The Queen Victoria is a beautiful ship, no question. You become special, treated like royalty, in true Cunard style. Food was plentiful and delicious; service was attentive and outstanding. I don't really recall seeing any kids. Nevertheless, the beginning of January in the north Atlantic is not for the faint-hearted, with the ship's massive rocking and swaying and dipping as it cuts through the water. Somewhere around the 6th and 7th, as we were I believe somewhere east of Nova Scotia, even I was feeling it just a little bit. I didn't get sick though; it seems that no matter how bad it gets, I just love being on the water so much that I've never gotten sick. But ship personnel were kept busy keeping the sick-bag containers topped up. Most of the time, I bundled up really well and stood out on deck as far as I could go without slipping or falling—I didn't go and stand at the railing, as I'm not completely nuts.

    I met some wonderful people on the voyage, and have remained friends with a few over the years. We would just sit and relax, enjoying the trip, sharing stories of travels. That's the thing about slow travel, something I've always tried to opt for; the time you have to make acquaintances, spending time with new friends, talking and sharing tales of life. Nothing beats that.

Chapter 16

Buddy Hugs, Kitty Kisses, and Fear

My beautiful ocean voyage came to end on the morning of 9 January, a day that dawned crisp with a gorgeous, cloudless, blue sky. As we slowly sailed past the Statue of Liberty, I felt the pull of my ancestors who had made this same trip (with a couple differences such as a not so luxurious a ship, and the departure port, and they didn't deal with the far north Atlantic leaving from Sicily); gazing at the statue as they dreamed of their new lives away from the strife in their land. My grandmother, pregnant with my father, joining her husband who had sailed ahead a few months earlier. I have her name, and I felt her with me.

Because I'm a dual citizen, entry to the US had to be made using my US passport, of course. That meant I sauntered past all those people, seemingly half the ship, sitting there in groups, waiting for passport control and customs. As I walked off the ship with no more hassle than scanning my key in the box and dropping it in (I could've been just getting off a bus), my suitcases were already there in a special dedicated corner, and I loaded them on to the porter's cart. As I saw the entry control, I stopped, suddenly frozen in fear, panicked. "What have I done?" I'd been gone for just about seven years. I think the porter saw something in my face, and he quietly chatted with me as we walked—that should be as I duck-walked, trying to get my land-legs back—to passport control, asking who was meeting me, little things like that. I asked him if he thought the control officer would say "Welcome home" to me like they did in the movies. He gave a little smile and said, "Of course he will. But if he doesn't, welcome home."

Control was easy, no one was in front of me, and after having my passport scanned, the officer looked up with a smile, and welcomed me home. Entry complete!

Directly in front of control was a long passageway leading to the final guards and the crowd standing behind the barricades. The porter asked if I saw her at the barrier, and as I scanned, standing there at the very front, our eyes met and we both broke into huge grins, yelling out "BUUUUUDDYYYYYYY!" Yes, we actually yelled. Like, really loudly.

A word of advice: when you still have one final guard to pass, never ever skirt around the barricades and go running to someone, arms high and waving. As we took off running down the corridor (seriously, I waddled; you simply cannot run on land when you've been on the ocean for seven days), one of the loudest voices I've ever heard yelled out "STOP!" Kim's sneakers absolutely squeaked as she stopped, being the good military-trained girl she is, retreating back behind the nearest barricade as instructed ("Get BACK behind that line!"), jumping up and down with excitement. I stopped immediately as well, grabbing on to the porter's cart. He laughed and said, "She didn't mean you."

As I passed the guard, I glanced at her. She looked at both of us and our grins, laughed and said, "Go." That's all we needed to hear as we ran, arms wide, among a lot of laughter from others around us and even a few tears to match ours, as finally—finally—two best friends got to hug again, gaining strength from each other. Yin and yang.

I was home, there with my buddy. Whether there, or Europe, or Timbuktu; I was home.

Re-Entry and Reverse Culture Shock
Virginia; 9 January 2009

Being back in the States was surreal to me, especially knowing that I was going to be there for a year and a half. It didn't feel right to me, but what did feel right was being with Kim until she had to go, and also being with the rescued cats. We didn't know how long until she got her orders, so it was basically a daily waiting game. So we made sure to take advantage of the time we had.

During the ride from New York to Norfolk, we had tons of time to talk; in that time she asked what the first thing I wanted was. I think she knew I already had a list. What popped into my head was *Dunkin' Donuts* because that has always been my favorite brand, and I had never found them outside the US; she said there was one just a mile or so from the house. First thing the next morning, off we went! In we went and got our coffee and my donut, okay two, and I enjoyed every second of them! I always liked just the simple, lighter-feel of the regular glazed or chocolate glazed donut, nothing fancy or cake-like. As I bit into it after those three years, it was like a sigh. I absolutely love Mediterranean food, good, clean, pure. But occasionally a small missed indulgence pops up. I truly never had found a donut like it anywhere. The two donuts I had were enough to satisfy the craving for the rest of the trip, which is usually all it takes. Just a bite of memory.

Getting up to leave and go shopping, I had my to-go cup and walked across the short space, giving a side-glance to the *caution, wet floor* sign—and then promptly slipping and falling hard on the floor, smacking my knee in the process. As the guy came running, I looked up to see Kim just looking at me and I busted out laughing, saying: "That didn't just happen, did it? Not even 24 hours here!" She said, "Yep, of course it did, it's you." I kept telling the guy I was fine, he kept asking if he should call an ambulance and I repeated, "Geez, no, seriously I'm fine."

But I will take a free coffee and another donut to make up for it, thank ya' kindly!

A couple weeks passed and we basically just were living. Kim was getting things packed in readiness to go at a moment's notice. About two weeks later, I woke in the middle of the night after feeling a "boom" and "thump" in my heart; it started racing and then slowed, then raced, it was beating really strangely. Being stubborn as I am, I chalked it up to all the recent stress of the work schedule in London plus going back to the States, along with the emotions of it. Over the next two and a half months, the strange heartbeat never evened out, but as I had no insurance and no money, I never said anything (I didn't want to ask Kim for money) and never went to a doctor or hospital. Every few days I began to get more and more tired, my heartbeat was racing, my skin was getting pale, I couldn't sleep for the noise it was making in my ears—I was a mess.

After just about three months, I called Kim one morning at work, told her I was struggling for breath, there was a rattle to my exhales, and that I was scared to death. She came home, took one look at me, and said, "I had no idea it was this bad, why didn't you say something?" She rushed me to the hospital and, immediately upon walking into the emergency room, I collapsed on the floor, struggling for air, tears streaming down my face. They rushed me to triage, put an oxygen thing in my nose, took all my vitals and after they asked how long it had been going on.

"Three months," I said.

Their response was: "So you're sitting here with a heart rate of 185, it's been beating this fast for three months and you never came into the hospital?"

"I have no insurance and no money," was all I could think to say.

The next part scared me even more, as they put me on a gurney and wheeled me into the back, but the kind nurse said, "In just a minute you are going to have at least 10 people around you doing 10 different things to you—stay calm, don't be afraid, you're okay now."

And I was. They increased the oxygen, pumping me full of stuff in an IV; I could breathe more easily, and they let Kim into the treatment room where I could see her. I locked eyes with her because I needed the comfort of a loved one there. I had never before had anything like this happen, and the only other time I'd been rushed to an emergency room was when I'd had my face ripped to shreds by a pit bull (172 stitches outside and inside and a hair's width from my eye, I still carry the physical scars) and that was 20 years earlier. They were doing a hundred things and machines were beeping but I kept hearing "The heart rate is coming down." Both the nurses and Kim were doing a countdown.

After being stabilized, they all left me except for a nurse or two; about 30 minutes later a cardiologist came in, explaining everything that had happened to me since arriving in the ER, and explaining a previously unknown term to me: atrial fibrillation, or afib for short. He started drawing a heart and electrical nodes and lightning bolts, making sure I understood everything. He said they were going to admit me for probably about a week and hook me up to a 24/7 heart monitor, etc. I began to panic again about insurance and money and no job. They said the hospital had a charity fund, and that I needed to calm down about it. The next morning, a different cardiologist (who would become my cardiologist for the next year) came to me after doing tests and gave me the news. I'd been in afib for three months, my lungs were full of fluid and my heart was working at 10% capacity. But that I would be okay with medications to even out the beat. We talked of the future: he'd watch it closely and if we got my blood thinned enough and the medications didn't get me back to a normal rhythm, he'd do a cardioversion to accomplish that.

Nothing like being told you're going to be strapped down, sedated, and paddles put on your chest—*clear!* Of course it's not like that, but you couldn't convince me of that. But thankfully we have the Internet and I watched a few cardioversions and said, "Well, I can handle that."

A few months passed and I slowly got better. Kim still hadn't gotten her orders yet. The cardiologist and I talked medical, life and work history, trying to find out why this had happened out of the blue. He said my thyroid was basically not working either, but had no idea what had caused any of it. A couple months later, the cardioversion was done and I felt like a new person! The heartbeat immediately went to normal sinus rhythm, I could breathe without problems, I could walk and do things again.

Excellent timing, as a week or so later, Kim got her orders. She insisted she'd be fine on deployment and I was to not worry and throw my heart into another freak-out. I promised I would.

The next year would find me in a world of hurt financially—unemployment in Portsmouth, Virginia, was sky-high and I couldn't find work anywhere. Bus transportation was extremely bad, and I ended up working in the deli of the supermarket a couple miles away. Two management diplomas, a teaching certification, two languages, doling out fried chicken and slicing deli meat and cheese; we do what's necessary.

It was an emotionally trying time for me, and my ego took a tremendous hit. I sliced up my fingers really badly a couple times, getting yelled at and spoken down to by the much-younger-than-me "supervisor" who could barely speak passable English, even though born and raised there. As my ego began to take a huge hit making five dollars an hour, standing on my feet ten hours being spoken to rudely by people declaring I didn't give them exactly x-ounces of their bologna, I started going into a deep depression, and all I wanted was to go home.

Kim was finally due to come home the end of September, 2010. She arranged for a friend to feed the cats every day for the rest of the short time, and told me to get on a plane. She loved me enough to know that if I stayed, I was at serious health risk, and she had that back-up.

The day before my birthday, after hours of tremendous kitty hugs and nose-bopping kisses, long talks over Skype with Kim, and a heavy heart (I felt like I was letting my best buddy down), I boarded a plane back to Europe. To the land where I felt most comfortable; the attitudes and cultures I knew and could relate to. I would stay in London and work at the same hotel for a few months while I figured out my next move.

◈ ◈ ◈

Are you wondering whether I ever traveled those few miles to see John, or stopped into his studio to simply see him again? To see if time had completely changed us both, and to see whether we had merely been each other's safe harbor in a storm?

I didn't. Was it because I didn't want to? No. I had made the decision back then; I knew that while this was where he was happiest, most comfortable, and where his life was—it was not mine. Living the kind of life I do means that sometimes hard decisions have to be made. But I've always thought that I usually end up making the right decision for myself.

Who knows what the future holds? But that particular future wasn't mine. He and I were not meant to be.

Chapter 17

My World Falls Apart As Death Pounds on My Door

A Not-So-Whirlwind Tour of Italy
Sicily; January 2011

After a brief three months back in the work and life situation at the hotel in London, I decided to go back to Italy. It took a lot of hard thought and long conversations with Lynda, trying to work through my love-hate relationship with Italy. Going back was not an easy decision. At the same time, I knew I needed to give it another shot. It had been my dream once, long ago, and though two people had made it horrible, I couldn't let that turn me against an entire country.

Kim was stationed back in Sicily again, and I was in a kind of not-so-great living situation in Rome. It was with a lot of trepidation on both sides that we decided to do the housemate thing again, so that I could be there to help with the cats again as she would be needing to return to the States for much-needed and long-awaited surgery.

As I arrived at her house in Lavinaio, situated (again!) on the side of an active volcano, we sat, opened a bottle of wine, and had a long talk about everything that had been going on in our lives over the past months. Over a second bottle of wine, the Kim-and-Maria Show began again. Two best friends who realized just how important a friendship like this is, and what was truly important in life.

September 2011

In my eternal search for work, I came across someone on an expat board living and working for herself in Castelvetrano, Sicily. As it was in tourism, it was right up my alley. She was offering a room in the building, plus pay, for work in writing, revamping her website, using my hotel background as she rented vacation homes and had culinary tours. So I went. One of the best parts about it? Her father owned a small, award-winning olive oil company. After arriving and getting settled in, I toured the facility, watched the organic extraction and pressing, and helped with the bottling. I learned so much about olive oil, about the care of the trees and groves, and about what to look for on the olive itself to know when it's time to harvest. I learned what to do and not to do. And oh, the tasting! It was those few months there that started my desire to learn even more about it as the years went on.

I left in January, going back to Kim's house for a couple months to help out as she had just returned from having had her back surgery. She had only been sent back for about a year, so things changed again shortly for her.

And me? It was time to find my way back to a semblance of earning a living—something that just wasn't happening in that small town in Sicily. So I put out the call on some expat boards on Facebook, plus on a mailing list, looking for apartments in Rome. I chose Rome because it was a big city, a city I knew, and Lynda lived there to help ease me back in.

Rome; May 2012

Lynda introduced me to one of the account managers at a language school where she had previously done some teaching, and we arranged an interview meeting. Thus began my at-the-time main career of teaching English as a foreign language, specializing in business English because of my long history, to Italian mid- and upper-level company managers. What it also started was two years of crazy working hours, traveling all day to and from companies scattered throughout the city and even into the suburbs. I began developing and instituting some new ideas and methods, and seemed to be in high demand. I was making a professional name for myself with the language school and the businesses.

Financially, that was nice—but physically it began to take its toll. There never seemed to be time to eat anything except something "street food-ish" on the run from one place to the next, dealing with transportation strikes, walking (or so many times practically running) from one company to the next with only a few minutes' break between classes.

With still no health insurance because of continued issues with the system, I had long run out of the medication the American cardiologist and endocrinologist had given me. Without the prescriptions, the pharmacies wouldn't release the meds to me. I had neither time nor money to get to a private doctor; it began to take its toll.

I landed in the emergency room a couple times with increasingly high blood pressure, and no pills to stabilize it. Each time, I heard what became a medical mantra for the next three years: "You're fat, that's your entire problem. You need to diet and exercise." Once I remember being told, "You're fat and American. That's your problem. There's nothing wrong with you except that. I don't know why you're in my emergency room.

That's the only thing wrong with you." I have to admit that this was a far-cry from the amazing triage work at the Virginia hospital; being whisked away and placed on beeping machines, doctors and nurses surrounding me there, compared with being given a diaper in the emergency room when stating I had to pee desperately after being given a diuretic to bring down the blood pressure, being told to put it on myself with everyone (staff and patients alike) watching. My physical well-being seemed to be going downhill, along with my health. I was getting so physically tired. My work schedule wasn't changing, so my rushed eating habits never changed either. So I did what many did in my situation.

I ignored it. I really didn't know what to do about it, to be honest. I knew something was going on, but had no ideas. I finally stopped into a doctor's office by my apartment. While she gave me no blood pressure meds (eat right, I was admonished), she asked if I remembered the thyroid medication dosage. I told her what I thought it had been, and she gave me a prescription for it.

So off I went, continuing my crazy life and feeling sicker and sicker. I decided it was time for a change. I spoke to some colleagues in a city further north, and heard great things about it. Since the language center I presently worked with had no courses there, I got in touch with another center that had actually started out in the new area less than a year prior.

Reggio nell'Emilia; April 2014

Now, let me tell you something. The land of parmigiano reggiano is a gorgeous place. Very flat in the town and surrounding areas itself, so really cold in the winter and crazy hot in the summer.

But parmigiano reggiano! Beautiful, creamy, tangy; the tantalizing aroma as you enter the small villages of Reggio Emilia, producers of the highest-rated parmigiano in the world.

And with the land of Parma prosciutto a half hour away to the south—ahhh, what could be finer!

It was during this time that I got in touch with the *comune* (that governmental paperwork-from-hell office) and went in and talked with a woman about all the issues with still not having a health insurance card, even though I was paying full taxes. She took a look at my identification card and then looked me up in the computer. "Why is your middle name not on your card?" she said.

I told her the story of having gotten the card through regular channels in Rome, and was floored at her next comment.

"You've been paying into an account that isn't registering anything because your card was issued with no middle name. Therefore it technically isn't you." And then, after just a moment's hesitation, she said, "But don't worry—it's an easy fix. I'll call them, and you come back here tomorrow."

Tomorrow? Did I leave Italy and its famous bureaucracy? I left her office thinking how different things were done in the north. While it's not exactly the finest, superbly oiled machinery, it's still pretty well-oiled!

When I went back the next day and sat down, she produced a form. That was already filled out by her and needed only my signature. Did I mention well-oiled? Five minutes later, she said she'd call me when my new identity card was ready with my new, correct tax identification number merged with my old account. And I could then go directly to the health insurance offices and get my medical card. Two days later I had my identity and tax card in my hands, and the next day I went to the insurance office.

Unbelievably, the card was issued and ready for pick-up two days later. My next-door neighbor at the apartment building was a cardiologist. However, he was in high demand as a "family cardiologist", but for some reason things were going my way. The health office saw that I was number nine on the list, but somehow he became my main doctor. And that's how it works there.

I began some great classes, getting in with a couple very large companies, which let me keep busy and make a decent amount of money to live on. The doctor was trying to figure out what could be wrong, and put me on a regimen of blood-pressure meds to try to stabilize my issues. It was all so sudden, and basically the doctors were just throwing pills at the problem, rather than looking for something possibly underlying. I got in with an endocrinologist who was trying to stabilize my thyroid. That one was easiest to do! Unfortunately, nothing we did was stabilizing the blood pressure, and I ended up on three meds. I began to eat extremely well, drinking only water, watching everything and cooking everything from scratch, doing everything I was supposed to and walking everywhere. And gaining weight the entire time. My glucose level was rising and I was two minutes away from full-blown diabetes. No one could figure it out. So the general consensus was: "It's genetic."

☙ ☙ ☙

Off the medical stuff—let me tell you about this beautiful city. I really liked Reggio nell'Emilia. In the center of town were some amazing cafés with the best *aperitivi* I've ever had! For one or two glasses of wine, you could eat plate after plate after plate of various appetizers that even included pastas. *Aperitivo* that was basically dinner.

The land around Reggio Emilia (the province) is gorgeous. Though the town itself and the surrounding towns are very flat, as I mentioned, it is next to the Apennine Mountains. In those mountains is Cascina, a small village where consistent international first-place award-winning parmigiano is produced. Those areas get absolutely inundated with snow in the winter.

Even though I liked the town, I wasn't getting any better physically, and was getting worse. Not knowing what to do, I decided to go elsewhere. Somewhere even further north—was I subconsciously "making a run for the border"? I think part of me was trying to find a solution, find a way to get better. I was doing everything I was supposed to, yet I kept hearing that mantra from every doctor. Maybe up north were more modern hospitals. I didn't know and was grasping at straws.

I had colleagues throughout Italy, and a few lived in Lecco, a beautiful town on Lake Como. The language center had clients there, rents were affordable, so I decided to take a final chance. After all, I couldn't get much further north! Of course I could in reality, but it didn't seem like it in my mind and it was more fun to think like that.

Lecco; July 2015

What a beautiful small city! Lecco lies in a little bowl, completely surrounded by high mountains, and sits along the northeastern shores of Lake Como. Compared to many other places further south, Lecco is clean (relatively speaking), fresh, young, growing and evolving. A little further north is home to Sassella and Grumello, among a couple others, wines. Beautifully peppery and spicy, deeply burgundy and just oh-so amazing. The lands are perfect for steppe planting of vines. The cheeses produced here are incredible also.

It has a really nice walkable center where some festivals and markets are held, and even a couple huge national supermarkets and a mall have been allowed to get built. I lived just a little bit outside of the center, about a 15-minute walk into town, but was right near about 10 kilometers of path along the lake. I lived two blocks from the lake. Between classes, I was able to walk every day and indulge my love of water, the peaceful soothing nature to my soul I needed. The language center had begun a new type of course that involved telephone calls. It was perfect for those who desperately needed to practice their skills at listening over the phone in preparation for multi-country conference calls. It was also the perfect type of schedule, as I didn't need to physically go anywhere, running from company to company. Things were looking up!

Because I was near the border, I was able to take a wonderful trip to Switzerland to visit an old school friend, Oliver. It was an easy train ride to Milan and then up to Neuchatel via Bern. It was such a wonderful week spent up there. Tasting some great Swiss foods, lazing by the beautiful lake, and spending time with a friend. I so love Switzerland, and Neuchatel is an incredible city, edging on a beautiful forest with long walking trails.

So while things were definitely looking up work-wise and personally, it certainly wasn't the case physically. Two more doctors, and the mantra continued. I was barely eating at this point, but when I did, it was healthy. I was walking one and two hours every day along the lake. And still gaining weight. I was exhausted, not sleeping, on three blood-pressure medicines and still landing in the emergency room three times in the span of a month and a half. Doctors looked at my medical history and could only come up with the old mantra and "It must be hereditary." "You must be lying about what you're eating—it's obvious you're eating McDonald's and hotdogs and baskets of French fries and sitting down all day." I fell into a deep, dark depression, cutting people off.

I felt like I was dying, and I didn't much care.

I had had blood tests taken, and one of my students, fortuitously, worked in a lab. As practice, I sent her the results. She said, "Though I'm not a doctor, I think you should ask for a cortisol test." She told me about high levels of cortisol in the blood and what it could do. It could cause heart problems, blood pressure issues, high glucose levels and diabetes . . . and weight gain.

I asked the family doctor for the test, and he agreed while saying, "You don't need this." The endocrinologist looked at the blood test result and said, "It's a little high—here, raise your thyroid milligram pill and come back in six months." He then ordered a thyroid ultrasound—the first available appointment was one and a half years away.

One day a few weeks later, I was talking via Skype to an old friend, Juan, with whom I'd gone to both middle and high school in Rome. He lived in Paris and I wanted to ask him about France, thinking maybe everything I'd heard about their good health care was true. As we talked and talked, he mentioned Hungary, asking if I'd ever been to Budapest. I hadn't, but decided to do some research. "It's so cheap," he said. As I began research, on one of the websites was a link to a medical university with a brand-new hospital and cardiology wing attached. It was in southwestern Hungary, in a large town named Pécs. I started looking at prices and apartments, and couldn't believe how inexpensive it was! Especially compared to Budapest, which was more expensive than Lecco and was on par with Rome. It happens to pretty much any city that starts gaining lots of expats and students. My research continued on the medical school and hospital. On the university staff was a professor of endocrinology who had done some ground-breaking research into various endocrine and thyroid issues.

I figured I had nothing to lose at this point. My eyes and skin and hair were dull, I had weird stretchmarks on my body of a red and purple color, I could barely walk without wanting to cry. I had no energy. My brain seemed to be always in a fog, and I couldn't control my emotions—one minute I was empathetic, the next crying, the next berating someone for being too slow at the supermarket. I couldn't control what came out of my mouth. I always felt so horrid afterwards. No one could figure out what was wrong with me and I was at the end of my rope. It was try one more time, or die.

Or give up and end it myself.

I emailed the university endocrinology professor, gave my history, and asked if she took private patients. She emailed back, making me an appointment for two weeks after my arrival.

Leaving Italy for Hungary—
April 29, 2016

20 hours and it's the final voyage out. I loved and adored you once, with everything in me and with a full, overflowing and joyous heart. You were all I wanted, the only thing. You were once a beautiful and amazing dream. I am sad in a way, believe it or not, to say goodbye. But as a song goes, although it hurts to say goodbye, it's time for me to fly. I'm tired of holding on to a feeling I know is gone, I do believe that I've had enough. I think I waited too long to leave, perhaps it would've been better when I only started feeling that something was gone—rather than waiting until all I want is the view from the proverbial rearview mirror. I suppose there will always be a place in my heart for you, albeit small, because you once occupied all of it. That will never change. Thank you for what once was.

Chapter 18

Answers Come and a New Passion is Born

Hungary
Pécs; 1 May 2016

Okay, I knew the minute the old, rickety, slow-chugging, hard-bench-seated rail car stopped at this small station, that this would be interesting to say the least. As I rode in the taxi to my hotel, all I heard in my head was: "So this is what Eastern Europe is like; ridiculously cute little towns." The architecture was amazing; the buildings incredible to look at. I actually got the feeling of alpine architecture in a way. The Hungarian language is crazy hard and I never found myself in the mood to knuckle down to learn it. That's not to say I didn't learn some words, enough to be polite and try to assimilate a bit. Maybe somewhere inside me I knew it wouldn't be for a long time?

But what was really cool was that the day after I arrived (even while still staying in a hotel while finding an apartment), there was a wine festival beginning.

A wine festival. In Hungary. Hungarian wine. What? The very

next day began a love of not only Hungarian wine, but a greater passion for wine itself, especially the unknown producers and lands, like Hungary. I began to think about creating a website focused on wine, olive oil, gastronomy, complete with chef interviews, and travel, aptly named Pouring the World. Shall I plug the site? Okay . . . it's at *pouringtheworld.xyz*.

With a tired and heavy heart, I took my aching body to the festival. The first wines I tasted at that festival are still, to this day, my favorite Hungarian wines. They are lovingly produced by Joszef Schunk, of Schunk Pince (*pince* meaning 'winery'). I made friends with them and even went to the vineyard for tastings and an interview a few months later. It was my first winery interview that I put on my website. He is even now winning award after award. And he deserves every single one.

Answers

The next two weeks passed, and my medical appointment came up. As I walked into the doctor's office, ragged and beaten down, she asked me to turn around a couple times, felt my neck, and got my history again. Little did I know that with six simple words, what had started long ago with an ankle rash would change my life forever.

"Have you ever heard of Cushing's?" she asked. One, two, three, four, five, six. Such simple words.

She then explained what it was, and what the symptoms were: a rounded "moon shaped" face, a hump (like a lump) of fatty tissue on the back of the neck, the unexplained and unresolved sudden onset of high blood pressure, sudden heart issues, weight gain while eating healthily and exercising, diabetes, muscle and bone aches and pains, and not sleeping. While I wasn't diabetic, blood tests showed I was well on my way in a very short period of time with extremely high glucose. As she rattled off all these symptoms and signs, while many people might start getting anxious and fearful, I was the opposite—I felt my heart rate slow as I took a few deep breaths. Could the answer have been found? Finally? She ordered another baseline set of blood tests of cortisol and ACTH—which came back with very high cortisol and very low ACTH (from the pituitary). She said, "It is a classic case of Cushing's Syndrome, all the signs are there in your blood and your body and history, and we simply need to see where the tumor is." And then she added words that let me, finally, exhale once again: "Cushing's is fatal if left untreated—but it is completely treatable. But, had you waited two more months, you would most likely be dead."

I admit I was still freaking a bit at the word tumor, but I focused on what she was saying, that it was almost always benign, but a tumor, nonetheless. It would be attached to either an adrenal gland (called Cushing's Syndrome) or pituitary gland (called Cushing's Disease), or, depending on the numbers on the blood tests, could be in a lung. One immediate abdominal CT scan a few days later, and there was a picture of a large tumor attached to my left adrenal gland. The cause of all of my medical problems over those past eight years. After talks with one of the cardiology professors who did an extensive ultrasound examination, he determined that the ankle rash was a probable first sign that something was wrong, and that the onset of the atrial fibrillation a short time later was the first 'casualty' of the tumor as it seeded, took hold, and began to grow. And grow. And grow. Wreaking havoc with everything in my body.

She scheduled surgery for removal of the adenoma and left adrenal gland for a few short weeks later. Long talks followed about recovery and what it would be like, along with the necessity of taking cortisol replacement pills until my right adrenal "woke up." This happens because the other one is over-producing on a ridiculous scale (think 24 hours, 7 days a week, of constant, non-stop "fight or flight" hormonal responses). The non-tumor gland stopped working. With the removal of the other one, the replacement is needed until the body begins to produce what is needed, as cortisol is necessary for life and the function of all other glands.

Just not so damn much of it!

I was essentially alone in a foreign country where I didn't speak the language. I knew no one. And Italy and Hungary were fighting about who should pay. Italy wanted me to either change my residency and claim retirement to start paying taxes in Hungary, or to go back to Italy for all new tests and 'possible surgery if necessary.' A kind woman at the Hungarian tax office said I could change my residency, start paying the health tax as a resident without having to change my work status, and I would be covered for surgery. As I knew now that Cushing's is fatal if untreated, if I waited and redid all tests over the span of weeks and months in Italy, then I would in fact die.

During those two months pre-surgery, I had discovered what would become my home away from home. A small wine bar called *Eleven*. I absolutely adored Petra (owner) and Ricsi (sommelier, pronounced Ricky, from Richàrd). They both spoke English, and I would spend two or three evenings a week doing five or six 'flights' (a line-up of wines, usually of the same region, style or depth, and usually containing anywhere from three to six 'tastes', learning all about the wines of Hungary. It was absolutely fantastic. I also wrote about them on my website.

So I paid the first installment of taxes (a whole thirty euros or something), and surgery was performed three days before my 58th birthday. I came through surgery with no problems and when the doctor showed me the photo he had taken of the adrenal gland and tumor, I nearly passed out. That was in my body? Wide and long, it looked almost kidney shaped, growing on a baby-pea-sized gland. The adenoma itself had started out the size of the adrenal gland, and grew to 6mm over time. I had a couple blood pressure issues while in the hospital, which was perfectly normal as my body had a complete loss of normally produced cortisol, but they gave me the replacements I needed. As I had no clue what was going on the entire time I was in the hospital, because not one single nurse on that floor spoke English, I spent my days there basically terrified. Normally you can leave after this surgery (amazing, considering it's life-saving) in a couple days, but because of a few issues and last-minute screw-ups with the Italian embassy in Budapest, I stayed in four days. On the morning of my birthday, Petra picked me up from the hospital and took me home, promising to come back that evening and take me to the wine bar for a birthday drink. If I could handle it! I didn't know if I could or not, or how it would act with the cortisol replacement, but wine! And my birthday. And a toast to being alive!

Over the next four months, recovery was hard. I knew it would most likely take one to two years until I felt right again, especially being alone. I lived on the second floor, so it was up to me to get myself up and down those stairs a couple times a day after a laparoscopic thing had been cutting and slicing and dicing on my left side, walking to the grocery store and walking the two kilometers back carrying bags—normally not an issue, but this was days after major surgery and removal of an organ. If it was totally necessary, I took a taxi, such as when I went up to the clinic for check-ups. But you know what? I wouldn't trade a minute of it—my right adrenal woke up six weeks later (which doesn't happen often, as some people are still waiting one and two years later); one month later my glucose level went down to just below the mid-level range, meaning I was now cured of any diabetes; two months later my blood pressure stabilized and I was taken off the last of the medication about three months later. A heart ultrasound showed normal function.

And 35 kilos came off in the next six months with no real effort at all.

The endocrinologist pronounced me cured. I was given my life back.

Was I angry with the medical community in Italy? I would be lying if I said no. While Cushing's is rare, as more and more doctors are understanding it and not just blowing it off with "the mantra" it is getting less rare. It strikes adults, but also children and teens. So next time you see unexplained weight gain, a face getting rounder, get a cortisol blood test followed by cortisol urinalysis and midnight saliva test. Insist on it to the doctor who says, "No, it's too rare, you don't have that, you just need to diet and exercise." Get the test.

So! Want to hear about beautiful Hungary now? I spent the next six months still going to the wine bar constantly, learning more and more, and realizing that I was developing a passion for the wine world. Petra had some olive oils from Portugal and Spain, and I began to get interested in those also. I wanted to continue my website, and expand it, talking about wines and oils and small gastronomic gems from little-known places (like Pécs).

This ancient little city, approximately 2,000 years old, is situated just about a 30-minute drive from the Croatian border. It has a lot to see and I'd suggest a day or two wandering around (with at least one night spent in the fabulous wine shop called *Eleven*) as its architecture is eye-catching. Among its cobble-stoned streets are such wonders as an early (fourth century)

Christian necropolis with frescoed tombs, evidence of it having been part of the Roman Empire long ago (a UNESCO heritage site). Its crowning glory is the beautiful domed Mosque of Pasha Gazi Kasim—built in the 16th century by the Turks during the Ottoman occupation, it's now a Catholic church. The cool thing about it is that the crescent moon was never removed, but simply merged with the Catholic cross; inside the walls remain the same as when it was built, but again the stations and icons have been merged. Two religions alongside each other, even if services are only Catholic, is still pretty special.

There are a few nice museums; pretty walks around town; the Mecsek hills surrounding Pécs are quite pretty; there are many restaurants, some cultural but many with an overall westernized American menu such as burgers and fries, chicken wings, fried this-and-that smothered in sour cream that were a bit hard to understand.

Tourism seems to be geared strictly towards those who have taken one of the Danube river cruises and stop in the city for a few hours and then get back on the bus to go to a hotel an hour away, close to the river. Unfortunately, tourism is neither sophisticated nor far-reaching outside of Budapest itself. They could do so much more that would entice people to come and stay for a night, especially as it was one of the 2010 European Capitals of Culture. While I absolutely didn't find it a city I would've wanted to settle down in, many do—but more of them settle outside of this city, up in any of the expensive towns dotting the full coast of Lake Balaton, a gorgeous area of land (with amazing wines).

Pécs is most famous for its decorative porcelain arts from Zsolnay, and the factory founded in 1853 is worth a visit. The tiles produced are quite beautiful and are found adorning buildings all over Hungary. The city is a mix of elderly and young, and the cultural attitudes are striking. Many of the elderly still think and conduct their lives as if still under a Communist regime, even though they've been free of it for over 25 years; the younger generation is the complete opposite. It's actually interesting to see the differences.

Pécs, and Hungary itself, just didn't seem to be the place for me, though. While its medical community and knowledge did indeed save my life, I really think that was its purpose for me—well, that and the intense wine education I received and the fire it ignited in me.

Teaching online (still with the same language center, and those same companies wanting the high-level conversational phone lessons), doing Italian-to-English translations, editing and proofreading, I was able to make enough to live on cheaply. I started looking for another cheap country, and knew I wanted to cover Spain and Portugal for my website. Those two countries, as we all know, have just far too many enticing and glorious wines and olive oils to discover.

You know what my next line is, don't you? I started doing research.

Chapter 19

Can you say Jamón? How about Flamenco, baby!

Spain
June 2017

So after all those tastings of beautiful Spanish wines and olive oil at Petra's wine bar, I decided to do some research into Spain. I knew that it was an expat haven and was a bit concerned about that aspect, but the language wasn't an issue—I had my Italian and, while Mexican Spanish is very different, I still had a lot of the words and nuances from having grown up in southern Arizona and being surrounded by the language as a child. I spent time asking a hundred questions on Facebook groups in/about Spain, asking specifically about where there were small, family-type producers of wines and oils.

A short year and a half post-surgery, still in the midst of recovery, and I found myself doing the planes, trains and automobiles thing again. Well, not planes, but trains, automobiles and buses. And a boat. By myself, with my two large suitcases. I had gotten my life down to these two suitcases, after yet another purge of "stuff". Having arranged a ride from Pécs to Ljubljana with friends who were happy to have me pay gas so that they could have a weekend away, I didn't have to deal with the suitcases and long waits and three trains getting from Pécs to Ljubljana. It worked for me, especially as it took one quarter of the time—the Hungarian transportation infrastructure is pretty bleak.

After getting dropped off at the bus station, an hour later I boarded the bus for Trieste, where I boarded yet another bus for Genova. Sounds almost like the way I got to Hungary in the first place. I had decided to take advantage of the fruits of a bit of deeper travel research. I found that I could get from Genova to Barcelona on a small ship for less than the cost of the same route on a train. And it was overnight and in a cabin—and, well, ship! You know I chose that route. I was picked up at the bus station in Genova by the brother and sister-in-law of a dear Italian friend and colleague, and they helped me with the suitcases to get on the ship. Though it had been a year and a half, the "Cushing's body" can take up to five years to show no further signs of the issues, and slight abdominal problems remained for a long time from all the sawing that took place inside. Not to mention the muscle weakness and bone aches. Care also always has to be exercised in most situations, as I only had one adrenal gland to give my body whatever cortisol it needed in any situation—whether a flight-or-fight circumstance, an infection, a fever, or any injury of any kind.

The following morning, I arrived in Barcelona, rested and ready to take on my new world and new life.

Tortosa

What had come up in my research was a small city called Tortosa, in Catalonia, about a two-hour ride south from Barcelona. I started searching for apartments, talking to people, and the decision was made. My first stop in Spain would be there. I'd been offered a ride from Barcelona (paying gas and tolls, which I thought was a fair exchange) and a place to stay for a week or two until I found an apartment. Plus these people had land with olive groves and produced oil!

It was perfect, and a great introduction to the country. There were very few, maybe a handful, of expats in the town, and with my Italian, I was able to get by with no real issues.

Unfortunately, because I was in a hurry to find an apartment, I chose unwisely. Fortunately, I was able to get only a six-month contract. I had insisted on negotiating a shorter lease because something in me knew this wasn't the right town to stay in. It didn't have that *feel* to it for me. Nothing about it called to me, once I was there. As I would wander the old center, I would look at the buildings, the architecture, and it wouldn't move me. So I stayed six months, discovered a couple wines and oils from there—and began the Spain section of my site with these discoveries. I do have to admit, though, that I became lax about inserting wines and oils on my website and still to this day of writing this, have a huge stack of pages to insert.

About Tortosa itself, this isn't a tourist town, though there are a few interesting architectural aspects to it, along with a pretty cathedral. It's situated in an area that offers tons of walking to the small villages surrounding it stretching into and among hill areas. With the paths, I was able to take an easy 5-10 kilometer walk every day to begin the arduous task of attempting to regain muscle strength and stamina, and take off more weight. I started with one or two kilometers and then just put the headphones on a great track and took off until I got tired, sat for a little bit and then started again. On really pretty days, there were usually quite a lot of people on those paths, walkers and bike riders, so I was constantly finding a new turn here or there.

The city has an old town and a newer, more modern one, each on the opposite side of the river. The culture was more of a bar/café one, with no particularly interesting restaurants. I found a nice wine shop though.

Because the town just didn't feel right to me, I decided that I wanted to continue discovering what Spain had to offer, so talked to more people and was told about the Cádiz area, on the furthest southern coast. I had heard so much about Rota, not only from an old friend of mine, but from nearly every sailor who ever came through Sigonella in Sicily throughout the time I was there. They all loved it and swore they would move there in a heartbeat.

Being right on the ocean, it sounded like it would be great, but I was a bit concerned about whether it would be "little America", with the huge US Naval base there. I was assured by a friend who had an apartment there (living four to six months a year there), that it wasn't. He swore up and down it wasn't.

Rota

As I wandered the streets of Rota, I was hard-pressed to hear Spanish spoken. It seemed that all the grocery stores and small markets carried American grocery items. Hell, I was even able to satisfy my Reese's peanut butter cup cravings whenever I wanted by walking a couple blocks to the supermarket.

I can't complain about the apartment and where it was. I was, literally, a five-minute walk from the ocean beach. Five minutes! I was in friggin' heaven about that aspect of this city. Every day I walked there, wandering five and more kilometers up and down the beach, my shoes off, my feet in the water. I was thrilled and my heart sang!

If only it were somewhere else, though, as all I kept hearing was English spoken. Yes, of course there was Spanish spoken, but damn, it seemed everywhere I turned there were American-style bars, hamburger joints. It was not what I had come to Spain for. I was also having issues finding wines and oils from the region. It seemed that Cádiz itself (just a 30-minute ferry ride across the bay) had a few local wines, but really no olive oils. So I couldn't find local items to write about. I discovered by talking to people that this was not an area for either product, so I kind of made a mistake in choosing Rota when it came to that.

But the ocean! The five-minute walk! What was inevitable was a really, supremely difficult decision for me. More research, more thought; should I continue to another area in Spain? Maybe Portugal instead? Portuguese wines and olive oils are killers, absolutely stunning, delicious and mind-blowing flavor bombs!

Unfortunately, I wasn't in a financial space to be able to afford Portugal. It's also not always easy to find areas that are super-easily accessible without a car, and where one doesn't need a car to go to town, restaurants, etc. I would've needed to be in either of the two large cities, Porto or Lisbon, and they were both out of my reach financially.

Back to the drawing board—or, as Kim calls it, my dart board. Every single time, without fail, when I call her and say, "What about here? What about there? What about . . . ?", she replies to me: "Oh, just put a map on the wall and throw a dart, because you're making me crazy." She knows me best, and that I'll also make myself crazy going back and forth. Maybe one of these days I'll take her suggestion and do just that.

Monte Lope Álvarez

Through more posting on message boards, I was offered room and board in a house in a small—like really small, we're talking two streets out in the country—village from a British ex-chef expat named Phil. It was typically Spanish with one very small market, three bars, two bread shops, one bank with a sometimes-functioning cash machine, a tiny post office, and about five or six expats, though only a few were year-round. It was a village called Monte Lope Álvarez, and was in the middle of Baena and Martos, bordered by Córdoba and Jaén. Yes, Jaén of olive oil glory!

After many emails, messages, a few phone calls, and some research on Phil through many channels and people, I said yes and took off on a train, then bus. It was a great situation in a nice house with a person my age, actually a little bit older. The incredible smallness of the village was enough to kill me, but it was right in the middle of thousands of olive trees. Path after path winding around and through kilometer after kilometer of olive trees. Imagine the aroma as you wander the paths as the olives are waking up and growing during the summer.

The olives, the trees, the leaves, the pruned branches being used for outdoor cooking. I would walk and walk, with no headphones on for music because the silence among those trees was intoxicating. Peaceful. Absolutely enchanting. I would stop and sit on the ground in the middle of all those trees and just close my eyes, my face to the sun, and breathe.

But the village was two streets, with no transportation. It was a wonderful place to relax, recoup, and think. It was the summer of 2018, and in a couple months I would hit my 60th birthday, one I hadn't been sure I would ever reach. During my peace-out sit-downs under those trees, walking those dirt paths, I would think about everything I'd gone through in the past nine years, how close I came to losing it all, and how I regained my very life.

Though this small village was frustrating the hell out of

me with its lack of anything to do except walk the groves, no transportation to go anywhere, no restaurants, it served the best purpose. It gave me the time I needed to think about everything that had happened—yet also afforded the opportunity for me to clear my mind about what I wanted. Sixty is a pretty big milestone, and I knew there was more.

I knew I wanted more.

So I decided to take a much-needed vacation, designed to see if my 45-year-old memories were real, or twisted by time. I had always wanted to see Greece again but had never had the chance. Since I was researching where my next move would be, I decided to take a trip and see how much had changed and what that grand city of Athens held. It was only an inkling of a possibility for a move, but I needed a getaway anyway. Over a week-long period, the trip served its purpose, rekindling memories of a land I'd last seen at 14 years old, and one that I have always loved. I discovered many new things about its people, food, and most of all gloriously delicious wines. I knew it was my next destination. It would take a little research to figure out what part of the country, though, as there was so much to choose from!

CHAPTER 20

I Thought It Might Be Glue, But Velcro Reigns Again

02 March, 2019

When I look at that date, the significance of it couldn't be more clear. What would make me, unknowingly, choose this date to take the flight? Ahh, I know . . . happy birthday, Mommy!

OPA!

Touchdown and it was off to the new adventure! I decided to treat myself and put in a (seriously low-ball, we're talking the gauge needle didn't even register, it was so low) bid on the upgrade challenge from Aegean Airlines. Four days before the flight, I did a happy dance when I received an email: *Congratulations! Your bid has been accepted, you've been upgraded!* Yay!

When I take a vacation, I normally go the easiest and cheapest route—however, when I'm moving, I like to pamper myself a little bit. Besides, stressful moving with suitcases, etc., is still a bit harder than it used to be. I wouldn't have gone more than the lowest possible bid, but being able to use the VIP Lounge at Barcelona airport, where the pampering buffet spread was crazily overflowing, was so cool—I had refused to pay the five euros the hotel wanted for breakfast, which consisted of coffee and toast, and so the free stuff was an awesome way to begin this move. Or maybe it was the middle of the move, since I still had another hotel and one more four-hour bus ride transfer after arriving in Athens to get to my new home.

I discovered a little trick to help when I fly, which I still use—I make a point of meeting one or both of the pilots and speak to them for a few minutes, explaining my fear and that I was always told to ask to meet the pilot; that way you know there's a real human up there with your life in his/her hands. It works!

My two stewards in business class, Dionisia (Denise) and Konstantina, were wonderful. Thought not a top-notch business class, it was a short-haul Aegean Airlines flight with only three rows up front and the seats, while great, were mostly just a matter of being a bit larger and more comfortable than economy. But I loved it. The food was really nice and, if it hadn't been for my already upset belly from the bad food the previous night at the only place nearby to eat (a dirty little bar/café), I'd have taken advantage of the Greek wine offerings more.

Greece . . .

. . . land of gods and goddesses, philosophers and storytellers, a hundred islands, fiery people, and just as fiery wine and olive oil.

This aspect of wine was a total surprise to me, as back in the '70s when I visited, the only drinks on the table were ouzo and really horrid retsina. Over the years, when I'd thought about going to Greece to live, and most especially when I started writing about wine and oil, it entered my mind that this might not be the place to come.

Boy, was I wrong. So very wrong! In Hungary, there had been

a tasting titled *Balkan Borders* and one of the 10 wines from Balkan countries was a beautiful white from Santorini in Greece. I loved it and was so surprised. I started doing some research, and befriended a young, award-winning super-sommelier from Athens, co-owner of Oinoscent (and winner of *Sommelier of the Year* a couple times, along with a few other high-caliber awards in the wine world), a wonderful little wine bar in the city. What I found out was that Greece has been making some serious inroads into the wine world, producing some delicious, serious, award-winning wines.

As for olive oil—well, that's a whole other story. We all know about the Mediterranean diet that is still prevalent in Greece and to which the citizens have stayed true to their origins— much more so than some other countries that tout this way of eating. I think more people are familiar with Cretan wines and, of course, Kalamata olives, but there is so much more. Within a couple months of being there, I'd been fortunate to try two oils from Crete and two from the Peloponnese, and one from northwestern Greece.

Until September of that year, when I made my 60th birthday trip to Athens, I mentioned that I hadn't been in Greece since 1974, with the exception of a few-hours stop on the cruise ship. I remembered such quaint things, the beauty of a few temples we saw, the silly amount of ouzo we drank, even though we were "supervised" by teachers, and much of that trip remains basically an ouzo-fueled blur. To my credit and in an effort to be completely transparent, I was 14; it was the first trip without parents or siblings (brothers) to guard me and report everything back to the parents. That's all I remembered until I finally made the trip in 2018.

And I was enamored. I'm not sure if I mentioned this earlier, but in high school in Rome, one of my English teachers offered a few Greek Mythology classes, and I was able to take quite a few of them, every one that I possibly could. I have always loved Greek mythology, and the philosophers and teachers and storytellers. I think those classes were about the only ones I got good grades in. I had spent an evening during the vacation a couple months previous at Oinoscent with a guided tasting from Aris and the wines he chose to introduce me to the world of Greek wines were enough to seal the deal.

A couple days after arriving in Athens, I got on a bus and went the four hours to the south-central portion of the Peloponnese to the small town of . . .

. . . Gytheio

I really don't know if the spelling is right, but it doesn't matter—it's amazingly beautiful, all the same. For a short time, I chose the village of Selinitsa, which is really basically just a cluster of about 10 houses, about 3–4km from the main street in Gytheio, and a couple kilometers from a famous shipwreck named the *Dimitrios* (the rusted hull of the old ship stuck forever in the sand of the beach).

I was super-happy with the choice of Greece, and looked forward to tasting more wines and olive oils from small producers, as always, probably concentrating on the Peloponnese area first. I already had an idea what was next, stoked to discover the products that were being produced on the lands where the gods and goddesses once walked.

As an aside: unlike Hungary, which is only beginning to figure out a way to get its wines out to the world, so many, even the smaller, producers in Greece are beginning to understand the power of Internet marketing, e-shops, and international shipping. These wines and oils are worth the effort to find and get.

Selinitsa sits up the hill and across the bay from Gytheio, a small fishing town really. Both places are where people live; not a tourist town, but you get a feel of life in a small Greek town. A couple restaurants, none fancy, and many cafés. Smoking absolutely everywhere outside and inside, which was a really tough thing for me—I had smoked for 40 years but quit during the worst of the Cushing's, in December of 2015. It's an entirely quaint town and, though a bit too quiet for me, was a wonderful place to spend a few months. A short walk down the hill and over a couple small streets was the sea, with a rocky and sandy beach. A wonderful place to walk to as often as possible. In Gytheio there are a couple nice little archeological sites (it's Greece, of course there are!) to wander around.

Again there was an issue with transportation, and the only way to actually get to Gytheio was to either bother someone for a ride, or walk down the hill and walk the rest of the way—and that included if I needed to go grocery shopping. That's a long damn walk when you're carrying bags up the slight hill of the first kilometers, and then a really steep hill for the remainder to the area where the houses are. So you're basically relegated to taking a taxi each time. Doable and relatively affordable, but not exactly convenient.

I so enjoyed my time there and getting to know the owner of the house, sharing stories and coffee, and taking long walks up in the hills looking for wild greens. But it was soon time for something more.

❧ ❧ ❧

What a thrill take-off is. It holds the promise of new adventures, new places, new people. As you gaze out the window, what goes through your mind? What do you see? In that endless sky, maybe clouds; do your eyes focus on that, or are you seeing what is to come? Perhaps a kiss at the airport, long-awaited and only dreamed about for so long. A university child home for the holidays. Or your long-anticipated holiday. What will you see, do, eat, experience? Will you plan, or take it as it comes?

Or maybe you're moving homes again. Like me. Again! I can't seem to stop, you know. I have this insatiable appetite. I'm so afraid of missing something out there—hidden away behind and among those clouds. Some say to me, "Do you have to drink ALL the wine in the world? Pour every single olive oil over salads?" Why yes; yes, I do!

Rhodes

What can I possibly say about this crazy-beautiful, albeit overly touristy, island? That it's a Greek island deeply steeped in rich history? At the northern end is Rhodes City (also known as Rodos and Rhodes, and not to be confused with Rhodes Island). In the middle of this city is the old town, where everyone who has ever been to Rhodes stays, eats, takes day-ferry rides to other islands, and enjoys its outstanding, amazing seas of impossible shades of jaw-dropping blues. On one side calm and barely moving, the other has rolling crashing waves that will have you falling over constantly from their force, laughing hysterically as you try in vain to stand up to somehow get back up to the sand!

As in many places like this, there are an abundance of expats; some live in the old town (I'm not sure how with those prices— it absolutely reflects what happens when a place gets overrun with tourists and expats), or in the outlying areas and in various other cities on the island. Bus transportation is iffy at best, both in town and to get to the other places on the island. Most of the towns are smaller and a car is necessary. Near the airport are three-, four- and five-star hotels and resorts, generally open only in the tourist months. It's a very windy island for a lot of the time, too, which is great fun when you're flying in along the coast!

Where I lived, about two or three kilometers from the old town, I was a couple kilometers from a wonderful beach area that was more like a bay with its calmness. But once the weather got warm enough, I was there every day for at least an hour or so hanging out in the water. I've never been one to lie out on a beach as I get bored far too easily and just want to be in the water. I'd take a couple hours out of my work schedule (at that point I was still teaching online, but doing more editing and proofreading and translating) each day. I found a wonderful endocrinologist near the apartment who was well-versed in Cushing's and its after-effects, which was very helpful as every post-Cushing's survivor needs a specialist for strange things that invariably happen, and in case anything happens that necessitates someone knowledgeable to say, "Give her cortisol now!" Interestingly, it seems that every doctor and nurse in every town and city of Greece (even the very small clinic in Gytheio) knows all about Cushing's—it's quite prevalent there, as are endocrine/thyroid issues. My doctor told me they seem to have pinpointed it to after-effects of the radiation and chemical clouds from Chernobyl. Interesting. Many doctors chalk it up to extreme and long-term stress, others radiation, while others just simply admit that no one knows yet what its actual cause is and full effects, including long-term and lifelong after-effects. The great thing, though, is there is a research foundation with so much information, including a list of doctors and surgeons verified as experts on the disease: Cushing's Support and Research Foundation.

Right near where I lived was a huge twice-weekly outdoor market, with stand after stand after stand of beautiful fresh vegetables and fruits that went on and on, and the studio apartment was sandwiched between a butcher and a chicken shop. I could get fresh meat, and fresh chicken and eggs from her farm at any time. And I was near a wine shop. Priorities! Unfortunately, this studio apartment was also next to the huge fan and generator of the butcher—which of course ran 24/7 at an extremely loud volume and would cut off with this weird noise, and start back up with a bang two minutes later. It necessitated wearing earplugs every night and after a few months became more than I could take.

Because this was Rhodes City, everything was truly out of my budget. I had been fortunate to find this one-room studio at a low price, offered by an expat couple who had assured me the noise was low and "more like white noise". I think, as time went on, the generator started failing and got worse.

I've mentioned it before, but living this kind of life and not having "steady" good income means living as cheaply as possible, and kind of renting month-by-month so that you can leave quickly if something happens, so you don't get something with a contract (which necessitates two and three months' rent upfront, etc.). Of course, with that type of apartment offering, they aren't going to be the best. My first apartment in Rhodes City was like that, hence the move to the second one.

Anyway, after checking all over the city, I couldn't find anything, and knew it was time for a decision.

∽ ∽ ∽

I began looking into other Greek cities, as I knew there was so much more there to explore, but the problem was that it was just too damn hard to choose. Many places were too expensive, and I couldn't for the life of me figure out where I wanted to go.

I went through a hundred decisions while looking at the entire map of Greece and its islands, Athens, Thessaloniki, Patras, Piraeus, numerous cities up north and in the Peloponnese, various islands. I fell in love with all of them and it seriously got to be too much and too difficult.

While living in Rhodes, my second-older brother and I re-connected and re-established our relationship. We talked a lot, stayed in touch, and when he decided to try his hand at moving back to Italy, I was thrilled beyond belief I would have him—family—just a couple-hour plane ride away. I wouldn't be living alone over here in the EU anymore.

Two Grounding Trips, One Dream Trip
To Cross Off the #1 Bucket List Item,
Two Reconnections and Let's Throw In A Decision Too

At this point, Kim and I hadn't seen each other since 2010, yet always stayed firmly in touch through any number of social media video/call avenues. One day shortly after connecting with my brother, she called me, starting with a simple: "Hey Tes, how's it going?"

As nothing much was happening then, I replied: "Meh nothing new. What's up there?"

I really had no idea where this conversation was going as she slyly said, "It's been six years since we've seen each other."

I agreed. "Yeah, I know, it sucks. Miss you crazy much!" I began to suspect there was a method to her madness.

"So, like, aren't tickets about 300-500ish in late May, early June?" she said.

"Yeah generally speaking, though once you hit mid-June, they're nuts. Why, are you coming over here?" I nearly lost it as she said, "Do some research, find one, send me the info,

I'm paying for your ticket to come here to Virginia. I need to see you!"

In a panic, since my US passport had expired about seven or eight years prior and I couldn't enter the US on my Italian one (which I had also let expire since I generally always traveled in the EU and needed only my Italian *carta d'identita*, identity card), after a couple urgent passport-renewal snafus with the US Embassy in Athens later, I had my shiny new blue passport in hand, ready to go finally give my best bud a hug again after so long. It was a bit of a longer process than normal on the renewal because it couldn't be done by mail, and going to Athens meant a flight or overnight ferry trip.

From Rhodes to Athens to Frankfurt to Dulles to Norfolk I went. After four flights and 15 or so hours (which isn't the easiest thing for someone afraid of flying), I was nearly running through the Norfolk airport at 11:55 p.m., and there she was! With a run and a yelling BUUUUUDDDDDYYYYY, we were together again. All was right with my world again. The 15 days were filled with laughter, buddy-time, walks and talks and just being. I had the greatest time being with her and getting crazy amounts of kitty-kisses and purrs from the remaining old cats. I had missed this whole group so badly. I had a little list of about five items I had to eat (silly things I'd missed, like waffles and maple syrup, tacos, a couple other things). We visited *New Kent Winery* and another one, and had a great time wine tasting, over-indulging, and laughing our heads off. The Kim-and-Maria show really has no borders and no time constraints.

On the day I left, there were plenty of hugs, deep breaths, and a pact made that no way in hell would it *ever* be six years again. No way in hell. So with a final hug and kiss, I boarded my plane to Dulles, where I got on the flight to Rome. For a ridiculously long-awaited reunion.

BIG BRO!

When I walked through the exit doors at Fiumicino and scanned the crowd, I literally just dropped my suitcases (one full of goodies) and ran to my brother. I couldn't stop crying as I hugged him after 25 long years. 25 years! We couldn't stop talking for hours, as we tried to fit in everything in those hours. Even though we had two weeks. He introduced me to "his restaurant" and "his bar" by his house, and it was just a wonderful time. His apartment was in a very residential neighborhood to the west of Vatican City. Not the right place for any sightseeing or walking the streets of your youth, but it was nice.

The next morning found us at 7:00 a.m. getting on a train to Savona, where he was to pick up his car that he had shipped over. At the pickup place, we got in his little, 20-year-old BMW, took down the top and zoomed our way onto the highway back to Rome, with a quick stop in Pisa and an overnight in Florence on the way back to Rome. The shippers had stolen the radio out of his car, so it was a relatively quiet trip back—with the top down. Since my brother is a former pilot who has a need for speed ("Bro, stop! This isn't a helicopter!"), it was impossible to talk anyway.

I joked that I should leave him to take his turn and dip his toes into the pool of famous Italian bureaucracy alone. He needed to get his residency paperwork and sort out his Italian citizenship from so long ago. However, he figured that, since I'd dealt with the Italian bureaucracy for so long myself, I was the perfect person to go with him and walk him through it. I did, we did, and all was well.

Back to the airport I went when the vacation was over, and after promises to yet another person to never, ever let it go so long like that, I boarded my plane back to Rhodes via Athens.

I wasn't back more than two days, when I received an email, where two short lines had been written. "Hey lil' sis, how you doing, safe and sound after your 8 flights? So I'm sending you a link to something I found on the Internet. Check it out and tell me what you think." I clicked on the link to a travel agency website showing small river-sailboats from Luxor, Egypt to Aswan, with an overnight stay in Cairo. I hopped on WhatsApp and sent a message to him, "Holy hell, I wish! Egypt has been number one on my bucket list since the first time I saw a pyramid in a book." Ding. "Good, me too. We'll choose one and go." Click. "Um. As I said, it's been a dream. It's not something I can afford to do. Not now." Ding. "Oh for goodness sake, I know that—I didn't mean that. Your birthday is in a month, and it's my gift to you."

I think I dropped the phone. Or sat there and simply stared at the screen. And then started cheering! And probably screaming while filling the message line with screaming emojis. Never, ever had I thought I'd actually get to Egypt, and here my brother was treating me to the trip of a lifetime to fulfill my dream.

I love my brother. Yes, I would love him if he wasn't buying tickets for us on an awesomely cool river-sailboat.

A short three weeks after the phone call, we boarded our respective flights and met at the Cairo airport to begin the trip, spending two days in Cairo. He hired a guide named Mina—a wonderful woman, super-knowledgeable, an Egyptologist (they spend four years in a special school to learn Egyptology, and leave knowing how to read hieroglyphics). As we walked through the sand to gaze upon the very first pyramid ever built, I approached and placed my hand on the rocks—closing my eyes and breathing in the spirit and energy of every bit of blood, sweat and tears that built it, forever changed my life. I will never forget the feeling it gave me, along with the first "perfect" pyramid built that became the blueprint for every other one. The very first was actually not "exact" and was incorrect, being off by something like four centimeters (or something like that). To touch these stones is to touch history.

Leaving Cairo, we took an early morning flight to Luxor, staying two nights and a day at the Luxor Winter Pavilion Hotel. It was a really nice hotel, gorgeous pool, nice buffet outdoors, and wonderful personnel. My brother hired another guide, who took us all over the wonders of Luxor: Hatshepsut's Tomb, the Valley of the Kings, Karnak, Luxor Temple. I was immersed in seeing with my own eyes all the things I had always read about. I'd always been fascinated with Egypt (even more so than Greece) and the old culture, and there really are no words for what I saw and felt as I wandered the land and sights. I was touching the most incredible, awe-inspiring history.

The day of the Nile boat trip arrived. We were picked up in a van at some silly time like 7:00 a.m., along with the other cruisers who were staying at the hotel next door, by the boat company and our guide for the next five days.

Leave it to me to have come down with the Pharoah's Revenge during the night. I was miserable all night and the following morning. I explained to the guide that I might have to stop, since it was about an hour and a half to the boat. There was a short tour scheduled for the town where the boat was docked and I tried. I really did. But about one minute into walking, I had to turn around and get taken to the boat and the cabin's privacy. It was explained to the crew in a phone call what had happened, and they took such amazing care of me, getting me tea and something to help the lingering cramping.

But this too shall pass! And it did.

Upon everyone's return, the real trip began. The *El Nour* sailboat slowly, softly glided through the water as we sailed down the Nile, stopping at places the big cruiseboats and large riverboats couldn't. At the small islands, someone jumped off the ship with a long metal stake, a rope was tossed to him, and he pounded the stake into the ground and wrapped the rope around it. The gangplank was lowered, and we walked off and jumped into the Nile to swim.

We swam in the Nile! It's relatively clean and refreshing, and you can just feel the history of all those who had swum in it before. The Queens and Kings. Oh, the history! So many think the Nile is full of crocodiles and is disgustingly dirty and disease-filled. I can't stress enough that it truly isn't. We were able to dock and go walking way off where tombs had been discovered.

On the boat I was treated as a queen, maybe because it was my birthday. The boat crew brought a cake and instruments and we were treated to a night of amazing Egyptian music and dancing. They can really dance! I think we all looked like little kids shaking our butts in comparison. But it was amazing to think, "Here we are, dancing on a sailboat when it's 105 degrees at night!" But who cared?

The cabins were a good size, and the beds so very comfortable. I could touch the water if I wanted to by just putting my hand outside the cabin window. I slept a deep sleep every night and woke up refreshed and relaxed.

It was truly a trip of a lifetime. If you ever get to take a Nile cruise, make sure to check out *Nour El Nil* with three boats to choose from, for a trip filled with amazing experiences, an incredibly knowledgeable Egyptologist who can read hieroglyphics as your guide, and a wonderful crew who will spoil you with music and dancing and food that will widen your eyes with its aromas and taste. And they have Egyptian wine, so you know I was thrilled with that little discovery. The top deck is open but covered, so you are fully and completely immersed in the views and land. And you stop and dive off the decks of the boat into the Nile.

Do it, do it, do it. But don't take one of the ones with lots of cabins and closed windows and that make the trip in two days. Choose the river sailboats. You will not be sorry.

❧ ❧ ❧

When I got back to Rhodes, I knew it was time to go. I was itching again, and Egypt had pulled at me; its smiling and laughing people in the face of poverty; children in the tiny villages, dirt-poor with nothing but t-shirts and underwear on, but laughing as they played soccer or chased each other around. It was cheap in Luxor, and there was a certain pull to it. Something about it, and being immersed in such incredible and rich history.

So off I went on my quest for information to groups and pages and all-things-Egypt. And finally, with all that information in me and tons of "here, there, maybe there, okay there," I made the decision.

CHAPTER 21

IS IT POSSIBLE I'VE LEARNED TO BE STILL?

THE THRILL OF MOROCCO
November 2019

Never in my wildest dreams of traveling around the EU in search of wine and olive oil, did I envision myself packing up and moving to Morocco. One, it's outside of the EU, meaning I had to think about visas for long-term stay, extensions of said visa, or a residency card, and whether I wanted to go through that whole process again like I had in Hungary. I had no idea if the process was difficult, what it would entail, what life was like in a mostly Muslim country, nothing. I had never needed to consider anything remotely like visas for the last 20 years. But all I can say is—oh my, the thrill of Morocco!

A land full of contrasts, whether talking about its land or people. When making the decision about where to land, I took various things into consideration, as always. Size of city, whether there were expats around, ease of travel. This was especially true this time as I was outside of the EU and, to be honest, a bit outside of my personal comfort zone as this was all new to me. I ended up choosing a place named El Jadida, forgoing all the popular, crowded and invariably expensive places such as Marrakesh, Fes, Tangier, Casablanca. Not that they'd lost their authenticity, but I figured that if I was going to a place completely outside my little EU comfort zone, then I was going to go all the way.

In El Jadida, I chose an Airbnb for the first month in *Cité Portugaise*, the *old medina*, the old Portuguese fortified citadel. At the end of the month, I moved into an apartment in the *cite* still. It's hard to describe whether this section of the city should have its own designation. It's like living in an old fort village, surrounded by towering walls that give an amazing view (and combat vantage point) of the coastline and the Atlantic Ocean. Now old and rusty and plugged, the numerous cannons are strategically placed in advantageous intervals along the walkways of the fortified walls, directed out to sea to discourage any thoughts of attack. Walking along the length of the walls surrounding that part of town makes you begin to understand what it may have been like back then. I seriously can't imagine anyone getting past the eyes of this citadel and its watchers.

෴ ෴ ෴

The people in the maze of tiny alleys were born and raised here, and many have small tourist shops that line the "main street" that leads to the wall entrance, or one of the four small hotels/riads, or the café or one of the three bakeries (each a big fire pit in the walls, which is the coolest thing—I call them "the fire people"). I think they're all related in some fashion. So much of the daily food is taken there to be baked. Who needs an oven?

The feeling was one of "home," and I seemed to be everyone's sister. When I first arrived, I was constantly being sold to, and it took only a few days for them to realize I was not a tourist in the real sense of the word, but was staying in an apartment and moving to a new apartment for the long term. It took only one person knowing it before the village grapevine took over and the rest began to say to me: "I heard you're taking XYZ's apartment and staying—Okay, I won't try to sell to you anymore!" At least they were honest about it.

And that was pretty much all it took for the whispers of, "Come . . . I've found the perfect husband for you!" It didn't matter how many times I said that I was so very much not interested in that; that I was far too old to settle down; and, besides that, that there was still so much more of the world to see.

But you know what? I couldn't remember when I had had so much fun in a small village like it. When confronted with one or two local "crazies," I was immediately surrounded, watched, and fully protected. I had no fears walking these small alleys, no matter when, as I was soon considered family.

The culture in Morocco goes hand-in-hand with the contrasts between village, town, city, and the internal mountainous areas, where the cultures of Berbers and others reign (and where they still live everyday lives according to age-old customs and traditions). Though times are indeed changing outside of the tiny villages, there are those places that have not. In the cities of this country are modern buildings and offices, financial and otherwise, that help to slowly increase the country's wealth and international stature.

In my village, I've come to be known as the crazy foreign woman: the one who refuses to get married, and dances in the street with the neighborhood children or just dance-walks down the street and up on the fortress wall walkways, laughing and giggling and flirting with the adorable men, as if there were no age-old traditions to ignore. Whether I'm sitting and drinking a glass of freshly made mint tea, or writing or working at a table here in the café, one or two of my brothers will come over to me, break off a piece of their bread or cookie or snack and hand it to me, as if the most natural thing in the world.

And I think it is.

CHAPTER 22

OF PANDEMICS, LOCKDOWNS, AND ANIMAL RESCUE

2 January 2021

I promised you at the beginning to always be honest in this story; the good and the bad. Here we go. So much has happened in the last year here in Morocco. Because I was no longer in the EU and needing to deal with visas, my choice was to go through the long, involved process of getting residency for a year (when I wasn't even sure how long I'd be staying), or to do what so very many living here do—the border hop every 90 days. While technically illegal, all parties involved basically just turn their heads, under the guise of "all tourists must be given a 90-day tourist visa upon entry". Yes, I went ahead and calculated the correct timing of when I needed to cross, and did the research online. What I found was the terminology of both 90 days and three months. So I faithfully counted 28 October to 28 November, to 28 December and on to 28 January, subsequently purchasing my ferry ticket to Spain for 27 January, just to be safe. Off I went to Tangier, approached the border control, handed my passport and saw him scan it. As he did so, he looked at me, then over to his co-controller, and back to me. "Is there a problem?" I asked. "Your visa has expired," he responded. "But that's impossible, I counted three months..." As my heart began to pound and fear took over, he said, "The visa is for 90 days, not three months." Having heard countless stories from tourists and expats who have been sent over the border with a stern lecture to not go over their time, I asked what to do. He directed me to the chief of the border police's office and I stepped into his office to plead and beg.

The chief was very nice, looking me up in the computer and saying, "Yes, it's just one day. You need to go to the tourist office at the police station and talk to him there. Tell him I sent you there, and he will give you the code we need to unblock you. They do it all the time."

I guess said guy was in a super-bad mood that day and had no desire to deal with someone saying the border chief sent me there, thinking I wanted special treatment; he said I had to go back to El Jadida and talk to the tourist office there, get the code, and, "It won't take long at all; you'll be able to get back up here for the last ferry." It was 2:00 p.m., the train took four hours one way, I still needed to get the police station, and the last ferry was 8:00 p.m.

Off I went to get the next train out, which was at 4:00 p.m. Calling my *khoya*, my super-brother, Mostafa, who always took care of me and translated, I told him what had happened. He made some calls (dude knows everyone in this city, I swear) and reported back that the police chief said there was no way to do it that day and he would pick me up at the train station. The next day we went, made the "report," got into the court a couple hours later, and waited. And waited. While all the people in jail had their turn. Finally at about 4:00 p.m. they called my name and, with my trusty translator, I stepped up. He asked only a few questions, one of them being how long I'd been there.

When I said I'd arrived three months prior and was going to go to Spain for a month or so and come back, he asked why I went one day over. "Your honor, it's because I'd read sometimes 90 days and sometimes three months, and in my head that was the same thing. I was wrong." He also asked if I had another ticket, and I told him I did, for two days because that's how long I was told that process would take. I was told by everyone to simply tell the truth and they'd probably let me off without the fine. We were told to go and wait for the written decision.

An hour later my name was called again and Mostafa read the decision. "Oh," he said. "Oh? What does that mean?" I began panicking. "Do you have 110 euros on you, or do we need to go the bank? It says here that 'due to your age, you got confused between 90 days and three months', but they still hit you with the full fine." I don't think there has been even one person in all the subsequent days who wasn't completely surprised. Even one of his judge friends said: "You're kidding!"

I paid my fine, went home, and went to Spain for two days. Coming back on the 4th of February with a brand new stamp in my passport, good for another 90 days (yes, I'd learned my lesson, and I think five people had 88 days from then circled on their calendars) and one week later I began to get sick. Really sick. Like I'd never been before. Coughing, aches, pain, fever of 102 for four or five days that then went down to 100 and 101 for a few more days. Not really sure how to navigate the medical system here, and having heard some horror stories of the state of hospitals in this city, I nursed myself back to health, using pharmacy services or having Mostafa call any of his doctor friends to ask questions.

Three weeks later the world heard of Covid-19 and Spain closed its borders due to a severe outbreak, along with others. As our borders in Morocco closed, I began wondering . . .could it have been? I stayed locked in my apartment while I was sick, and masks became mandated and El Jadida went into major lockdown. You could only go out with special governmental permission, which I didn't have. Mostafa did, so he was my lifeline for groceries and anything I needed. Nearly every other day, he brought me some delicious Moroccan dish (or cookies) that his wife, Rachida (my *chkika*, sister) made.

After I felt better, I began thinking of how to take advantage of the lockdown. Stray animals are a huge problem in this country, mostly because sterilization is seen as "haram," a sin and wrong. So even in little Cité Portugaise there were so very many stray cats and tiny kittens running around. Because we were in a "walled" city, it was okay to go within a one-mile radius of your home. I had Mostafa buy me a 20kg bag of cat food, a smaller one of kitten food, and every morning I would walk throughout the streets, putting out food and water. When I would have my bowls stolen, I would replace them and when word got around who I was "friends" with (Mostafa, his brothers, and his family are very well-known and respected), that gradually stopped. I began working with a local vet, who also works with another group of people who do this same thing in the next city over, and I began a funding drive online for contributions to my little venture. We concentrated on feeding, caring (veterinary), education and most of all, TNR (trap, neuter, release) to try to stop the endless cycle. The streets in the neighborhood are small, and cars fly through; when it's dark . . . well, you can imagine.

As the days went on and I received a couple hundred in donations, I began looking at giving the stray kittens some safety as they grew, until they could be sterilized and make their lives in the medina. I looked at the 'catio' that Kim had made for hers, and Mostafa started talking to construction people he knew.

Before long, the Angels of Cité Portugaise had a physical shelter in a quiet little alcove next to the oldest bakery in the cite. Though times were (and still are) hard for people all over the world, it wasn't surprising that donations dried up; so I began working harder to get small editing or writing jobs, and put aside half my social security check each month to expand the shelter to three separate rooms, one of which is a quarantine area. I do it with love. Mostafa helps immensely (I seriously could not do it without his help), and we have a fantastic vet, Salwa, who does everything she can and treats our kittens like her own.

It hasn't always been easy at the shelter; we were vandalized once and had to replace all of the fencing and walls, and one of the kittens was killed. Not long after, we were hit by a four-day torrential downpour storm, and had a roof collapse on the final day, drowning four of the kittens and three more later died. But we now have nine gorgeous survivors; one of which is a beautiful all-white, blind girl who doesn't let that stop her from running around chasing a ball, and one is now recovering from having to have one of her legs amputated after being hit by a car (which is why she was in the shelter). We are known in the cite; the children come by and watch us, learning as we talk to them about caring for animals, especially the kittens who are so vulnerable. The police know about us also, and this has helped with things such as vandalism.

As for me . . . I write the final chapter of this story while going to the shelter each day to feed, clean, give medicines of all sorts, and make sure all is well. I'm grateful that my "brother" Mostafa has not only helped me get the shelter going, but takes a morning and night "shift" to help.

Oh! I forgot to mention, as you must be wondering how all this time went by and I was on a tourist visa. With the borders closed, governmental offices were working, and no applications for residency were being accepted. I knew that I wanted to stay for a while because of the shelter, so that I could get it to a place where I could leave and the cité would be able to use it. About a week before the borders opened for Moroccans and residents to come in and tourists to leave, we went to the visa office and asked for the list of documents I would need. She informed me that I had only until the specific border opening date, or I would have to pay a fine for overstaying. As I wasn't going to do that again, I immediately got on the phone and had all of my paperwork in my hands in one week. At a very pretty price for rush, overnight deliveries! I guess sometimes it really pays to know people, because on the day the border opened, I gave her my papers and got my receipt. Two weeks later I heard I was approved, and I now have my official residency permit card.

And all for those kittens. All the beauties hang out on Facebook, posting videos of themselves, too. Especially our all-white, blind girl; she's so proud of herself for chasing a little ball around as if she had sight. Crazy little kids.

❦ ❦ ❦

Well. It seems I've come to the end of this story. It's very strange to me, in a way. Something that started with a dream, a desire, a longing for home—or was it merely a place to call home, somewhere that felt like home—almost twenty years ago. I can't say I've come full circle, because this country is new to me.

After all these years of traveling and moving around, I made a decision to leave my comfort zone, the EU and her visa-free borders. All I knew of Morocco was what Ahmed in London had told me and the photos he'd shown me of his hometown, Nador. Well, and the food his wife made! Say the name Casablanca, and it conjures up smoky visions of a movie.

A friend said to me once: "Maybe one day you'll find somewhere that . . . sticks. A place to call home; somewhere you feel at peace." Is this it? Have I found glue?

Or is it velcro . . .

Epilogue

I would love to be able to describe just what these past 20 years have taught me, but I'm not sure I can. I'll try.

If you'd asked me way back then whether I could pick up and just leave, ending up moving around to various countries sight unseen, knowing nothing about them nor even their language of most, I'd have said you were nuts. I knew I didn't have that courage—especially to do it alone! At that age? No way.

Even now, as I think about whether I'll stay here or move on to a new country, I look at the fact that I am now 62, not in the best physical shape, and can't run around like I did back then. My body has been through hell, but made it out to the other side, albeit with a lot of aches and pains that will never go away. My hair is gray and I don't wear makeup anymore.

But that doesn't stop me from putting on those sneakers and jeans, sticking a cap on my head, throwing stuff out or donating to get the suitcases down to a manageable one large and one small, plus a backpack (I have to put the laptop somewhere), and pulling out a map and a dart.

I've learned I can. There is nothing holding me back from fulfilling my dreams. Doing it alone is scary. Really, seriously scary. But the alternative is to always wish you had. To hear someone describe placing their hand on the stones of the first pyramid ever built and swimming in the Nile, all while thinking, "I've always wanted to see the pyramids."

So I say to you . . . do it. Go. Live it. Live your life and love every single moment of it. You CAN do it.

I truly hope you do, and that one day we'll cross paths in some foreign land. And we'll high-five to conquering the fear.

∽ ∽ ∽

Where I will travel next is a mystery still.
Stay tuned for further adventures!

About the Author

Maria is basically a dreamer who wouldn't be able to sit still even if you duct-taped her to a chair. She believes the world is there for all of us to see; to taste all its wines; to eat all its foods; to interact with and learn as many other cultures as you can because it's the only way to truly experience the world and all the amazing things it holds.

Originally born in New Jersey to a Sicilian father and West Virginian Mom, her parents couldn't seem to sit still either, and moved their brood of four (Maria and her three brothers, Fred, Arthur, and Anthony) often. Being the youngest, and the only girl, she learned very early how to be strong and stand up for herself. She took that strength with her on each step she has taken throughout her life.

Writing and travel have always been her two main passions (of course we can't forget wine and olive oil!), though she's been a legal secretary, legal assistant, hotel manager, hospitality manager, EFL teacher, translator, editor, proofreader, and content writer. She has a crazy fear of flying even though she flies very often, and has a brother and a couple good friends who are pilots; but insists that if she ever won the lottery, she would buy a small boat and live on it forever. If she can get to her intended destination by ship, she will, though she thinks high-speed trains are great fun too.

When asked if the last chapter has been written, she said: "Well, my best friend, Kim, is due to join me in the next year or so, and we plan to travel all over the world. We're not sure of our final destination yet, but I know we'll enjoy the journey."

Maria would love to hear from you—please share your comments or questions about the book. She enjoys talking about travel and can't wait to hear your own stories!

You can connect with Maria on Facebook. Her personal page is www.facebook.com/maria.vano.96. She also has a page for her animal shelter in Morocco, www.facebook.com/citeangels, where she welcomes donations. Part of her book sale proceeds will go to funding and operating the shelter.